SUSAN HAYWARD
in Paramount Pictures

THE FILMS OF
SUSAN
HAYWARD

by

EDUARDO MORENO

CITADEL PRESS   Secaucus, New Jersey

To the memory of
My mother Ofelia, who gave
me a taste for the movies
and
Susan Hayward, who gave me
countless hours of delight
from the silver screen.

ACKNOWLEDGMENTS

To my friend Orlando Roig, who planted the first seed for this book in my mind, my deepest gratitude.

My thanks to every friend—and stranger—who contributed in different ways to put this book together: Andrew Anthos, Dawn Andon, Peter Bitlisian, Thomas G. Blass, John Cocchi, Elsa and Domingo Gomez, Needham Russell, Richard Warman, Margaret Terrana, Gene Andrewski and Rilda Ramirez of M.C.A.; to Ronnie Warman and Glenn Newman of Pro-Photo, and to the staff of the Library at Lincoln Center for the Performing Arts.

For lending me some valuable photographs, my deep appreciation to Howard Frank of Personality Photos, Inc., to Doug McClelland, Eric Benson, Frank Driggs, Leonard Maltin, Christopher Young, and most especially to Carmine Capp, who gave me not only interesting new photos, but also valuable information.

Special thanks to Lou Valentino for his all-round collaboration, and to Carmen and Dolores Malvido for correcting and typing the manuscript.

And last but not least, thanks to Lester Glassner for his masterful design of this book.

Library of Congress Cataloging in Publication Data

Moreno, Eduardo, 1936-
The films of Susan Hayward.

1. Hayward, Susan.   2. Moving-picture actors and actresses—United States—Biography. I. Title.
PN2287.H378M67   791.43'028'0924   [B]   79-17937
ISBN 0-8065-0682-2

Contents

What makes a person stand out among the millions of human beings in this world? Is is talent, looks, intelligence, luck, determination, wealth? Not any one of these qualities alone, but a "magic" combination of them is what makes a person leave a mark.

Susan Hayward started out with looks, intelligence, a certain amount of talent . . . and a steadfast determination to be "somebody."

The way to the top was not an easy one and along the way she was called everything from "stinker" to "great," lambasted by her peers, and praised to the skies. But it was impossible to ignore her. And, in the end, she was the most underrated of the superstars.

Her story is an inspiring one. She really went from rags to riches, though hers was not a Cinderella story. Her deserved triumph was all the more deserved because she had to claw her way step by step to attain her place in movie history.

She was accused of being "cold as a polar bear's foot," aloof, selfish, ruthless, and temperamental, a loner who didn't want to mix her business and social life. It was said that she owed her success almost exclusively to her own efforts, but she remained grateful to those who helped her and treasured their friendship.

She was nurtured and developed during the last stages of the star system. She wasn't a product of the system itself, but of real talent and very hard work. She was no Turner or Lamarr, who were made superstars almost overnight, protected by a powerful studio and backed by major movie moguls. She was a bit player in her early movies, and for a long time she was cast as the perennial "other woman."

She was always, in those early roles, the bride who lost the groom to the leading lady at the brink of the altar, or the one who stole him away from her. Either way, not a happy role. By the mid-forties, she was wondering if she was ever going to make it.

At first her career was poorly publicized, which could help account for her not achieving earlier stardom. The forties were tough years for the starlets (hundreds of them never got anywhere) as the "big sellers" were the established stars of the thirties and early forties: Gable, Crawford, Grant, Cooper, Davis, to name a few.

Susan Hayward managed to acquire her own fans and followers and graced the covers of many magazines, but she couldn't be considered the most popular of cover girls. When, after a long struggle, she got to the top, she had to work hard to stay there because suddenly the movie industry was threatened not only by European movies, but by the latest electronic invention, television, and movie moguls were looking for new faces which, together with new techniques, would help them keep at least part of the audience.

Susan's career, which started in the late 1930s, spanned the forties, fifties, sixties, and early seventies. Her film days could be divided into five stages: (1) early Paramount days, when she called herself "God's gift to the lower part of the double bill"; (2) stardom days at Universal, under Walter Wanger's

The Hayward figure at its best

tutelage, her first real opportunity; (3) major starring roles at Fox (if the star system had not begun to deteriorate, along with her domestic life, she might had been the first lady of the screen for years to come); (4) consolidation period, when she found both happiness in her personal life and recognition as an actress, and (5) ascent to the "movie star Olympus," when she became a legend in her own time.

Wanger called her "a redheaded Bette Davis." Magazines referred to her as a "bargain basement Davis." Always Davis. But there was only one Hayward, who didn't play second fiddle to anybody, not even the great Davis. They were unique and individual, as all great actresses have been.

Her mannerisms were countless: the way she walked, straight, almost stiff, yet with a bouncy step; the way she lit a cigarette; the way she extended a hand to greet someone; the way she crossed her arms, at waist height, and then pulled them down as if she were going to start some kind of breast exercises (which she didn't need); the defiant way she put her hands on her hips; the way she thrust out her lower lip in disdain; the way her eyes blazed in anger. These mannerisms could be called "Haywardisms."

She was accused of being a "mechanical actress," but the sum of her mannerisms created Susan Hayward. Every major movie personality has been characterized by unique mannerisms—take Davis, Crawford, Cooper, or Hepburn. One thing she *never* displayed was "a nostril flaring" when under distress, as a magazine once stated. This mannerism belonged exclusively to Vivien Leigh, with whom she was often compared. Hayward's ability to ad lib was widely known around the studios.

Her face was changeable, and she could run the gamut of look-alikes with unusual credibility: from early photographs where she looked strangely Garboesque to more recent ones where she sometimes resembled Shirley Temple or Ida Lupino or Gloria Grahame, or even Mitzi Gaynor. There were other actresses who resembled *her* in some fashion: Piper Laurie, Elaine Stewart, and Marla English, who was considered a combination of Hayward, Lamarr, and Leigh. Yet the Hayward face was as distinctive as her rebellious spirit. She didn't need Women's Lib. She had been a free soul since her birth.

Her many hobbies included horseback riding, bicycling, fishing, swimming, painting, knitting, collecting records, photography, and . . . eating.

Her many superstititions she blamed on her Irish blood, which was also blamed for her temperamental outbursts. She was a redhead all the way, inside and out.

Her fears included the dentist's drill and stray cows ("you don't know what they are going to do next when they look at you with those sad, big, stupid eyes"), darkness ("I'm terrified of the dark; I keep the lights on all the time"), and acrophobia (fear of high places), but when her friends suggested that she try psychology she would retort, "Phobias, shmobias . . . as long as I stay healthy."

She never made the list of the ten best-dressed women,

Looking a bit like Gloria Grahame, one of many look-alikes

although her taste improved through the years. There was a time when she believed that looking like a movie star meant wearing everything she had in her wardrobe (as stated in *Photoplay* magazine). Her thriftiness must have played an important role here; she wasn't clothes-crazy and was known to wear the same outfit on several important occasions. She even managed to keep gowns and dresses from movies before the Ross Hunter era!

Susan's charisma has been explained in many different ways. Her cinematographic appeal can be found in a series of sharp contrasts: the childish, piquant beauty and the violence that exuded from her performances; the ultrafeminine self and the almost masculine intensity she projected. Anyhow, she had enough appeal to appear—at least for two consecutive years—in that seventh heaven of the nation's top ten box office stars.

Her name was up for many roles which eluded her, and the list of films she didn't make is almost as long as the list of the films she did make.

Not getting *Gone With the Wind* was a disappointment. She seemed a natural for the role of Scarlett O'Hara, but she was considered too "green" at the time.

Dark Waters was a heartbreaking loss.

What might she have done with the Mitzi Gaynor role in *South Pacific* and what about *Can-Can*? Yes, her name was up for both.

She developed a taste for strong drama, and her movie ventures were so abundant in personal misfortunes that she was called "Hollywood's best sparring partner" and "the first female masochist of the screen," sharing the honors with her male counterpart, Kirk Douglas.

Her cinematic mishaps include the following:

- drowning in a sinking ship in *Reap the Wild Wind*
- escaping from fire with Paulette Goddard in *The Forest Rangers*
- wounded by Japanese bullets in *The Fighting Seabees*
- manhandled by William Bendix in *The Hairy Ape*
- burned and disfigured by fire and having her first bout with chronic alcoholism in *Smash-Up*
- escaping from fire again and suffering from schizophrenia in *The Lost Moment*
- burned to death in an auto crash in *They Won't Believe Me*
- taking a crippling fall from a horse in *Tap Roots*
- escaping again from fire in *Tulsa*
- slapped and pushed around by Richard Conte in *House of Strangers*
- stricken with a serious disease in *I'd Climb the Highest Mountain*
- struggling with Tyrone Power and almost raped by hoodlums in *Rawhide*
- almost stoned to death for adultery in *David and Bathsheba*
- crippled by an airplane crash in *With a Song in My Heart*
- harassed by a hyena in *Snows of Kilimanjaro*
- mobbed in *The President's Lady*

- persecuted by savages and a deadly tarantula in *White Witch Doctor*
- almost strangled by Jay Robinson in *Demetrius and the Gladiators*
- knocked out by Gary Cooper in *Garden of Evil*
- brutally beaten by Richard Egan and hit by tropical storms in *Utamed*
- having her second bout with chronic alcoholism and delirium tremens in *I'll Cry Tomorrow*
- maltreated by Genghis (John Wayne) Khan in *The Conqueror*
- falling in a pool, fully clothed and drunk, in *Top Secret Affair*
- executed in the gas chamber in *I Want to Live*
- having a miscarriage in *Woman Obsessed*
- escaping from fire and Indians in *Thunder in the Sun*
- blackmailed in *Ada*
- convicted of euthanasia in *I Thank a Fool*
- dying of a brain tumor in *Stolen Hours*
- committing suicide in *Where Love Has Gone*
- poisoned by Rex Harrison in *The Honey Pot*
- dewigged by Patty Duke in *Valley of the Dolls*

John Wayne helps Hayward cut her birthday cake, during filming of *The Conqueror* in 1954; Dick Powell is on the left and Susan's twins are at her side

Spicy roles, indeed! Can any other movie star match this list?

Although Susan was a very private person, many photographs show her in animated conversation with co-workers on movie sets. Many referred to her as "pure business" and she once made this comment: "When you're on top they're all your friends. When you're in trouble, then where are they?" But others, like John Gavin, Rory Calhoun, and Wayne, seemed to enjoy her company; and still others considered her one of the screen's finest actresses—among them, Robert Fuller, Jason Miller, Debbie Reynolds, and even Garbo.

As a movie star, Hayward was the epitome of glamour and sex appeal in a Hollywood which aimed at making people dream of better things—escapism, they called it.

No beauty by traditional standards, Susan had luminous eyes, beautiful hair ("sexiest hair" in the movies), and a warm, delightful smile. Her profile was best described by Hedda Hopper: "her perfect profile goes clear down to her ankles!" Her face was one of the most photogenic ever—in stills and in movies. Whenever artists with overheated minds tried to create "the perfect face," they would choose the eyes of Maureen O'Hara or Sophia Loren; the mouth of Ava Gardner or Marilyn Monroe; the nose of Hedy Lamarr or Elizabeth Taylor; but the "perfect" hair was invariably Susan Hayward's crowning glory!

Susan was so proud of her long, lustrous hair that for many years all of her contracts included a clause to the effect that her hair could not be cut, no matter what role she played.

She always looked better from the waist up (her bust was one of her main assets). Unfortunately, the beauty mark on her right shoulder was usually removed from her studio stills by retouchers who thought it was a spot in the photograph.

There was a slight disproportion between the upper and lower half of her body: very slim hips and derrière, thin thighs and legs, with slightly prominent knees and very slim ankles, which made her feet look larger than they really were. Sometimes her abundant red hair also made her head seem slightly larger.

With husband Eaton Chalkley, around 1961

Her roles covered the whole spectrum of human relationships—she played daughter, sister, sweetheart, lover, wife, mother. She never played a grandmother because she looked too young, although she did become one later on in real life. She was

- daughter to Maude Eburne, Katherine Alexander, Ward Bond, Jessie Royce Landis, Robert Keith, Jo Van Fleet, Bette Davis
- sister to Barbara Britton, Julie London, Richard Long, Virginia Grey, Diane Baker
- cousin to Judy Canova, Paulette Goddard, Eve Arden
- niece to Elizabeth Risdon, Hedda Hopper, Beulah Bondi, Agnes Moorehead
- sweetheart to Ray Milland, Fredric March, Dennis O'Keefe, Brian Donlevy
- wife to Michael O'Shea, Lee Bowman, Kent Smith, Arthur Kennedy, Gene Barry, Don Taylor, Eddie Albert
- mother to Gigi Perreau, Dennis Holmes, Joey Heatherton
- in-law to Warner Baxter, Richard Denning, Margaret Wycherly, Blanche Yurka
- lover to Robert Young, Victor Mature, John Gavin, William Holden
- widow to Kieron Moore, John Justin, Carl Esmond, Arthur Franz
- rival to Paulette Goddard, Veronica Lake, Marsha Hunt, Jane Greer, Ava Gardner, Julie Newmar
- "other woman" to Loretta Young, Rita Johnson, Vera Miles, Debra Paget

Her leading men were the cream of the crop. The list looks like a "Who's Who" of male actors in Hollywood: Clark Gable, "Duke" Wayne, Gary Cooper, Charlton Heston, Tyrone Power, Gregory Peck, Jeff Chandler, William Holden, Peter Finch, Dean Martin, Ray Milland, Robert Preston, Van Heflin, James Mason, Kirk Douglas, Robert Mitchum, John Gavin, Dana Andrews, Robert Cummings, John Payne, Rory Calhoun, William Lundigan, Dennis O'Keefe, Michael O'Shea, Richard Conte, Dan Dailey, George Sanders, Victor Mature, Robert Young, Stephen Boyd, Fredric March, Richard Egan, William Bendix, Michael Connors, and others!

Her first marriage ended in a turbulent court case that harmed her screen image (those were the pre-Farrow, pre-Streisand, pre-Duke times, when even the great suffered from the reigning mores). By the mid-fifties, she was still hot copy for magazines like *Confidential*. She went from headline to headline, at a time when Hollywood was Hays Code oriented. Looking back, using today's moral standards, what she did could almost be filmed for a kids' matinee show.

Then her second marriage brought the blessed years of her life, though they were short lived. She said about them, "When you are truly happy, nine years could be like a moment."

Susan Hayward was a vibrant, fiery personality; she was one of Hollywood's best actresses, adored by millions of fans the world over, and recognized even by the occasional moviegoer. She was a hard-working actress with a drive for perfection and strong convictions for which she never hesitated to fight.

HAYWARD

29

EXIT BROOKLYN, Enter Hollywood

"Brooklyn is a great place to have been born in, and is as well a great place to leave from." These words, spoken by Susan Hayward after she was well established in Hollywood, can give you an idea of her feeling toward the "asphalt jungle" she struggled through for her first nineteen years.

The saga of Edythe Marrener, who became the controversial star Susan Hayward, could easily be taken for the story line of one of her own movies. Rags to riches the hard way; no Cinderella story hers.

The Marreners, Walter and Ellen, could be described as average working people. They already had two children, Florence and frail little Walter, but even with their meager income they decided to have another child. Red-headed Edythe was born on June 30, 1918, in a tenement in the Flatbush section of Brooklyn (Church Avenue and East 35th Street). (Biographers have given her a variety of birth dates, going from 1917 to 1923, but 1918 is the year most often cited.) A Cancerian by birth, and star ridden in more ways than one, she was not the prototype of persons born under that sign, though she was later known for her bluntness, directness, and dedication.

Little Edythe was the cutest of the Marrener kids: with pale rosy freckled skin, big hazel eyes, small upturned nose, and beautiful mane of red hair, which was to become her most famous trademark, this and the hazel eyes a gift inherited from her father.

Walter Marrener, of Irish and French descent, was a Coney Island barker who moved up to be a subway guard. Ellen, said to have been a very temperamental woman, was of Swedish descent. Edythe's grandmother on her father's side was an actress, and a famous one, in County Cork: Kate Harrigan.

Edythe's parents were poor. The little girl knew that five pennies were a fortune and she seldom had even one to spend. Her favorite playground was Prospect Park, where it didn't cost anything to play and dream. She loved to go horseback riding and spent hours riding the ponies whenever she could afford it. But she learned, too, that there was a much better world than hers; a world she started dreaming about at a tender age, when most children are happy and carefree, interested in little else but playing. But Edythe was not like most children. Whenever she could go to the movies she would sit in the darkened theatre, wide-eyed, awed at the marvels displayed on the screen. What kind of wonderful and mysterious world was this, so different from the grim realities of her Flatbush surroundings? How she yearned, even as a child, to become a part of that world!

She and her sister Florence shared almost everything from the time she was born, not only because they loved each other but out of sheer necessity. Florence, six years older, considered herself Edythe's guardian.

Grim, however, can get grimmer; one day Edythe got three cents from her mother and ran out to the corner candy store. She bought a paper plane, which flew at the end of a string. She was running in the streets, looking back over her shoulder to admire her new toy, when suddenly a car hurtled around the corner and ran over her. When the ambulance came, the intern

Edythe was only a few weeks old when she posed here with her proud mama

Susan, two and a half years old

31

Susan, four years old

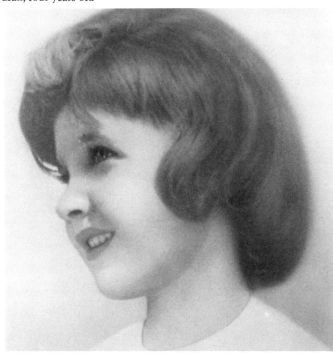

Susan Hayward at eight years

told her family that her legs were probably fractured. They rushed to the hospital and were dismayed to learn that it was far more serious: she had a hip fracture and the probability of her walking again was very slim.

The neighbors were desolate when they heard what had happened. They knew Mrs. Marrener was saving money to pay for her daughter's dancing lessons, and what would become now of Edythe's dreams of a dancing career?

The outlook would have been gloomy for any kid but this bouncy young Marrener. She fooled the doctors by walking again six months after the accident. Even so, she had to spend a whole year at home—in bed most of the time or using crutches, which she hated, to move around—but she knew that this was the only way to find her way back to normal walking. And she was determined to walk perfectly once again. Being out of school (P.S. 181) wasn't that hard to take—not with all the gifts from her classmates. Every day her mother woke her up with a new present from her school chums or from the neighbors. One thing was sure: her family had a worse time than she did! But she recovered very nicely, and after a year she was able to resume her school life again.

Her father was a reasonably intelligent man, tender and understanding toward her. She always felt close to him, following him around the house, asking questions about everything she couldn't figure out herself. Her father (who fondly called her Edie) would say, "You have to learn to behave like a rubber ball: the harder they hit you, the higher you bounce." At first this meant getting up when one of the neighborhood boys socked her. Much later, she learned the real meaning of her father's saying, in the ups and downs of her life as the Susan Hayward the world knew. Because, indeed, she learned by living. But Edythe had a long way to go.

Pride was something she couldn't afford at the time, and she had to swallow hard when she went to the bakery for left-over bread, the only kind her family could afford. And she suffered when she saw the new icebox and, later, the new stove, go because they couldn't keep up the payments.

One of her few "semipleasures" was going to the public pool in the summertime, and yet she would smell in disgust the "fragrance" of the grayish towels she was handed. She dreamed of someday having a closetful of snow-white, thick, fluffy towels. And she longed to have clean clothes (the dirt was imbedded in her dresses from so many fights) to go to the movies, which she managed to do quite often. Hollywood was booming in the late twenties with Garbo, Novarro, Gilbert, Gaynor, and Farrell, and in the "shadow palaces" she made believe that she too was part of that fabulous world so alluring and full of glitter (the mental "manna" of the escapists of those times). This dream became more of a premonition than a dream.

The Depression did not hit the Marreners too hard. For them it was more of the same because they never had much; life went on as before.

At school, Edythe became less popular as she grew up. Apparently, she was building an invisible barrier of self-pro-

High school days

Susan at sixteen (rare photo)

tection even then. She had one close friend who shared her secret ambition. His name was Ira Grossel and he, too, would achieve film glory along with Edythe Marrener, when the world would know them as Jeff Chandler and Susan Hayward. However, their friendship did not develop into anything deeper.

Edythe's family moved to 2568 Bedford Avenue, and she got herself a paper route delivering the *Brooklyn Daily Eagle,* the first girl hired by that newspaper as a carrier. She had to fight to keep up with the boy carriers; they didn't like a girl taking jobs away from them. Sometimes she borrowed a bicycle to deliver the paper, but mostly she walked. When she wore out her shoes, she stuffed old newspapers inside to cover the holes.

Edythe had no time for beaus when she started studying at Girls Commercial School, where she managed to get into the school plays. She wasn't interested in being the heroine or the "ingenue." She wanted meaty parts she could sink her teeth in, and she got them. She portrayed older women, witchy women, "heavies."

She was determined to be an actress, to be noticed, to be somebody. She wanted very much to be loved, but her self-protective barrier would scare people. It was a mental way of barking without biting, of driving people away before they were able to hurt her. This aggressiveness resulted in unpopularity, preventing her from becoming a member of the Arista League, even though she was scholastically eligible. Her aloofness and acid tongue ruled her out.

Her English teacher, Eleanor O'Grady, believed in Edythe, and encouraged her ambitions. She helped her at rehearsals and told her, "I believe you have real talent, Edythe, maybe more than you really realize, and I'll try to help you as much as I can to get you on your way." She made Edythe join the dramatic club; soon the young redhead was playing leads.

Edythe got another lucky break at school. She won a seventy-five-dollar prize in art by sheer accident. She had just finished her painting—a watercolor—and accidentally dropped a glass of water on it! The colors were still fresh and, naturally, they rapidly became a messy rainbow, to Edythe's dismay. But then she realized that the water had not ruined her work, but made it more interesting. She mixed the already mixed colors and came up with a first-prize winner. She was so excited that she decided to pursue a career in the field of textile designing.

By then her sister Florence was working as a chorus girl on Broadway, and although Edythe had blossomed into a petite beauty, everybody thought that the one destined for success was the elder Marrener sister. The family and friends had occasionally watched Edythe's performances in school plays but, after all, that was kid stuff. There was already an actress in the family and Edythe, after graduation, started working as a designer.

In early 1936, Edythe was making designs for a handkerchief factory. She was getting restless doing the same thing day after day. The "factory feeling" was unsatisfactory. She

With Walter Thornton, her boss at the modeling agency, 1937

was considered an "artist" by everyone but herself. She wanted to be noticed.

Florence was dancing in Broadway shows. Some days Edythe went to pick her up, wishing she could meet "somebody." She managed to get inside the theatres and watch all the backstage byplay. She was fascinated by it.

"Want to meet Eleanor Powell?" her sister asked. She didn't hesitate: "Yes, I want to." That very night she was shaking hands with the graceful lady of the tap dance. "You are a beautiful girl," Miss Powell said. Edythe was delighted to meet Eleanor. "She is so glamorous," she sighed, eyes glowing. Going back home, in the subway, she said to herself, *I have to be a real actress someday*. Finally, one day when she came to pick Florence up, she informed her surprised sister, "I just quit my job; it was too boring for me; I couldn't take it anymore. I'm going to get a theatrical job."

She took a course at Manhattan's Feagan Drama School, and started storming the theatrical agencies around Manhattan. When asked about experience, she didn't have anything to say, but they didn't really have to ask. Nobody with a theatrical background would go without makeup, or dress or behave the way she did. Disappointed, she persisted in making the rounds, until another idea hit her. In a coffeeshop she heard a group of girls talking about modeling, saying that if you were a natural redhead you were "in," particularly with the tremendous new popularity of color photography.

Without hesitation, she decided to pursue a modeling career. By then she was a beautiful redhead with a shapely figure, and she got a job at the Walter Thornton Agency. She posed for advertisements of beauty creams, girdles, gasoline, foods, teas, bathing suits.

Her vital statistics from the Thornton Agency

RITZ GOES TO A PICNIC

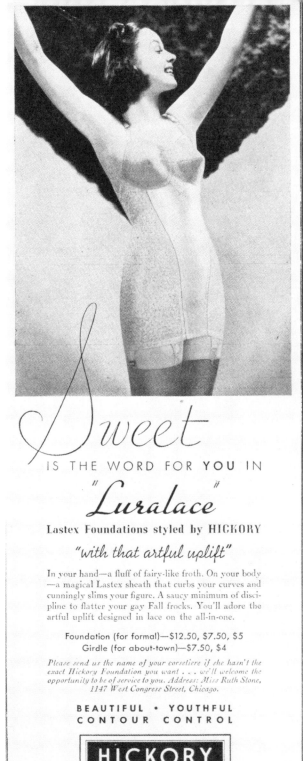
As a model she faced movie cameras for the first time in a 1936 Vitaphone short, but her real break was just around the corner. In mid-1937, she was selected by Thornton to pose for an article about New York models. They wrote about her: "Edythe Marrener, a Brooklyn girl, today is one of the country's most successful models and her flaming red hair has contributed largely to making her popularity . . . a flaming mop of red hair was not to be dismissed without a second or third thought. Color photography had produced a loud chorus of calls for redheads and more redheads." This article, entitled "The Merchant of Venus," which appeared in the *Saturday*

Evening Post, fully illustrated with eight beautiful color shots of her by photographer Ivan Dmitri, brought her to George Cukor's attention, not a magazine cover, as has been stated. (The only time she appeared on the cover of this magazine was in 1939, and by then she was known as Susan Hayward. Another story with less credibility is that she was discovered by Irene Mayer Selznick at a millinery show.) The magazine had fallen into Cukor's hands during the 1937–38 search for Scarlett O'Hara. Susan's beautiful face struck him and he wasted no time. He took it to David O. Selznick and hours later she received a wire from the Selznick office, offering her a test for

the O'Hara role and a two-way ticket to California.

That Edythe was deliriously happy with the offer is an understatement, but her parents were not. Her mother finally agreed to the journey only if Florence would accompany her. Her father, whom she worshipped, surprised her by saying, "I hope you don't get the part of Scarlett O'Hara." "Why?" she asked in bewilderment. "Some day," he replied, "you'll be able to play a part like that, but right now you don't have any experience, and it's very difficult to start at the top. I only hope you won't feel too hurt because, if you suffer, I'll suffer too." She departed, confused by her father's words, which she couldn't quite understand then, and saddened by the fact that his health was not improving (he had been in and out of hospitals for some time).

Before going to Hollywood, she gave Walter Thornton a signed contract giving him 10 percent of her earnings—a hasty action she was to regret later—and a photograph of herself on which she inscribed: "For whatever success I may be fortunate to gain." (Her vital statistics at that time, given by the Thornton Agency, were: dress size, 12–13; height, 5'3" [5'6" with heels]; weight, 114; shoes, 6½AA.)

THE MERCHANT OF VENUS

By WALTER THORNTON

Natural-Color Photos Taken for THE SATURDAY EVENING POST by Ivan Dmitri

I MARKET beauty. I sell beauty to the famous painters who illustrate your magazine stories for you, to art photographers and to the agencies which handle most of the country's advertising. My customers, I think, are the most exacting connoisseurs of beauty in this modern or any other world. They are more. They actually create what the public comes to accept as perfection in the woman beautiful.

Beauty still lies in the eye of the beholder. Ziegfeld, who had what I consider some rather extraordinary fetishes, saw perfection in the long, luscious and large-featured show-girl type. Through energetic and ingenious promotion, he made this type the popular ideal of Beautitia Americana. I am certain that if he had seen perfect beauty in another type of girl, this other type would have achieved the same position in the popular mind. Motion-picture and stage producers, artists and photographers create standards of beauty through visual ideas peculiar to them. Their eyes conceive an ideal of beauty, and they demand flesh-and-blood beauties who will fit the pictures of their dreams. That is where I come in.

I see thousands of beauties each year in my search for those whom I, as an agent, can supply to the painters, photographers and advertising-agency art directors. And I must see each one through a thousand eyes. Because in each there may be something that may appeal to a certain individualistic demand of one of my clients. For example, Henry Raleigh and John La Gatta demand tall, sophisticated girls when they need models for their paintings and illustrations. Rolf Armstrong wants languid, exotic types. Arthur William Brown's skill glorifies the sweet young thing. Leading photographers today are hungry for vivacious, wholesome juveniles. And specialized clients ask nothing more than that the models have beautiful eyes, or legs, or hands, or hair, or teeth.

Of course, in my business of supplying models on demand, I do not develop and market the modeling talents of beautiful women alone. There are demands for other varieties of models. But about 70 per cent of all the calls I receive are for beautiful women between the ages of eighteen and thirty-five; which is to say, for the simple beauty of youth or the smart beauty of maturity. The verdict of art editor and advertising art director alike seems to be that a beautiful woman has more appeal than lovely landscapes, or sweet old ladies, or jolly oldsters, or British-looking gentlemen with hairbrush mustaches and smoky-blue eyes, or Gothic cathedral arches, or even babies.

To put it another way, beauty today is the world's champion salesman, or rather saleswoman, no matter whether a striking short story or a box of talcum powder is the thing to be sold by an illustration. Beauty does the hardest job in the intricate ritual of processes called selling. It arrests and stops the traveling eye, it lays imperious hold on the attention. It performs the task that a battery of high-pressure salesmen cannot perform. The words which follow beauty's lead do the rest, whether they are words on the printed page, or words spoken by a traveling salesman.

I must qualify this immediately by saying that simply a beautiful woman in the flesh does not constitute a beautiful model. The most beautiful woman of all the thousands who have come to my offices during the last eight years proved to be a colossal flop. I was simply in seventh heaven when she walked in, because, to this day, she remains the only perfect, flawless beauty I ever have seen. I thought I had the find of a century. The girl passed every test to which I submitted her.

But the next day my find of a century came back to the office in the wake of a rather blistering report

from ___ client. The cli___ reported that she sim___ could not register anything exc___ the placid classicism with which Na___ had endowed her. I was amazed, because in ___ office I had established that my discovery c___ register emotions, and very well too. Besides, ___ was definitely an emotional type. I went to w___ directing her—screaming at her, growing furi___ laughing with her, putting her through the ga___ required of models. She reacted successfully. ___ the very next job proved another flop. The ___ could register well enough in my office, but the s___ of a camera or paintbrush invariably despoiled ___ of all ability to react to order.

My find was worthless. Today, beauty can___ afford to be only skin-deep. If a beautiful girl ho___ to model today, she must be able to register rap___ or pain, anxiety or expectation, love or hate, irr___ tion or blissful content, even illness or health. A___ she must be able to cry to order. The developmen___ photography has made this ability a necess___ requisite of any successful model.

However, I cannot afford to dismiss a girl me___ because I suspect that she will not be able to regi___ what clients may require of her. Sometimes a p___ pect fools you. If I did not painstakingly work ___ developing the emotional reactions of prospec___ models, I should have lost Ruth Starrett, for ___

This is the article seen by George Cukor in the *Saturday Evening Post* (Susan was Edythe Marrener at the time)

Crowned Queen of the Titianettes of America, in Hollywood, July 12, 1939, by Elfreida Skaggs

II FROM NOTHINGNESS TO ALMOST NOTHING
The Double Bill Syndrome

She arrived in Hollywood, with sister Florence, in the fall of 1937, and there are innumerable stories about her encounter with the movie capital.

There are many contradictions about her first steps in Hollywood. It is uncertain as to the date on which she made her *Gone With the Wind* test. It is not known either if she was tested first, and got her Warner Brothers contract later, or vice-versa.

In any event, she made the test under George Cukor's direction, with Alan Marshall playing the part later played by Leslie Howard in the movie. That she didn't know her feet from her head at this point was obvious, and Cukor had to let her know where the camera was located. Her indomitable spirit, however, was evident from the beginning. When Cukor tried to give her a few tips, she answered in typical Hayward fashion: "Who is playing this part, you or me?" In the end, she didn't. (In 1969 her test was part of the TV documentary "Hollywood: The Selznick Years." Her portrayal was a gem to watch, especially her spontaneous hilarity after they yelled "Cut!")

Not getting the part of Scarlett was a blow, but she remembered her father's words, which were to be a guiding light throughout her life, and wired home about the failure. "Your wish came true, Daddy, but the higher I'll bounce." The message came too late; her father had died hours before.

Heartbroken, she started planning for her future. Selznick tried to give the inexperienced girl some advice: "Go back to Brooklyn and learn how to act." She answered, "I like California and the orange trees; I think I'll stay." "Well, in that case," said Selznick, "you should give back the return ticket." "I'm sorry; I cashed it already to eat."

Anyway, Susan apparently didn't wait for the results of her test but hired an agent, Benny Medford, who showed the test to Warner Brothers and got her a contract. They signed her for six months at a starlet salary. It was said that she met Medford when, bicycling around Hollywood, she fell on his lawn.

There was another story claiming that one day she was informed by her landlady that there was a phone call from Warner Brothers to report at four p.m., but when she got there nobody knew about the call. Just as she was about to leave, a producer from a movie they were shooting came out looking for someone to play a cigarette girl and, as soon as he saw her, he said, "Stand up! Lift your skirt! Never mind, c'mon!" and she was on camera. The next day she found out what had really happened: she got a postcard from Werner Photographic Studios asking her to make a new appointment for casting stills. Her landlady had mistaken Werners for Warners!

She did appear in a few films for Warners as an extra or bit player. It seems that the first time she appeared in a movie she showed her back! She was listed in the 1938 Bette Davis opus *The Sisters* as a telephone operator. In one scene, several operators are seated at a switchboard in the background; one can identify them only by the backs of their necks.

Her next movie was Busby Berkeley's *Comet Over Broadway,* starring Warner Brothers' "down-on-her-luck" ex–movie

Two rare shots of her famous test for *Gone With the Wind*

queen Kay Francis. Here Susan had a better bit part: one could see her face, and she had one line of dialogue! She was also supposed to have a bit part in Edward G. Robinson's *The Amazing Dr. Clitterhouse,* but this role did not materialize.

It is doubtful if she had any other acting chores. She could, perhaps, be found in other Warners movies, since this company was grinding out films at a fast clip and kept all contractees busy. Warners changed her name to Susan Hayward (she wanted to take her grandmother's name, Katie Harrigan, but was told the name sounded like that of a burlesque queen), and finally gave her credit in *Girls on Probation*, in which she made a not-so-promising "debut" (*Probation* was thought to be her official debut until recently). Probably her tiny role in *The Sisters* was her real debut in Hollywood—if a part as an extra can be counted.

She dated Ronald Reagan, the star of *Probation*, a few times, perhaps at the studio's instance, and began to be seen publicly around Hollywood. She also made a short for Warners, *Campus Cinderella*, directed by Noel Smith, with a number of studio hopefuls, among them Johnny Davis, Penny Singleton (later, the "Blondie" of the series), and Peggy Moran (a Hayward look-alike who seemed destined for better things at Universal, but retired early when she married director Henry Koster), but her part was small She was announced for films she never made: *Golddiggers in Paris* and *Three Broadway Girls*.

For the rest of her contract, she did what she was doing before going to Hollywood: posing for studio photographers. She was furious. After all, she didn't go to Hollywood to model.

The Golden Circle of Paramount (1939): Patricia Morison, Joseph Allen, Judith Barrett, John Hartley, Janice Logan, Robert Preston, Susan Hayward, William Henry, Ellen Drew

The Hayward legend, about being difficult, strong willed, and calculating, started growing during those times. Talent executive Maxwell Arnold said about her, "She had a wonderful mind, but no heart. It took a long time to teach her to cry."

There are still a few puzzling questions about her Warner Brothers period:

- Was her contract kept a secret because of her test for "Scarlett O'Hara"?
- Was she really a stand-in for "Scarlett," having failed her own test? This is doubtful: Hayward, second fiddle?
- Why was her Warners sojourn ignored in favor of her next contract with Paramount?

Hayward's bit parts are not included in most lists of her films, even in recent books. The titles of the films in which she had a bit role came to light only a few years ago. Many questions remain unanswered about her first months in Hollwood.

When her option was up, Warners dropped it. Her agent took her to Republic, one of the cheapest companies, and when she was tested for a western the director said, "She stinks. She won't get any place with that bump at the end of her nose." She was told to get rid of her Brooklyn accent. "She sounds like Ebbets Field." (Later, her diction was referred to as pseudo–Bryn Mawr!) She went to see Colman's *The Prisoner of Zenda* something like a hundred times till her accent was smoothed out.

She and Florence managed to survive on shredded wheat and beans for weeks, and there was no money to pay her drama coach Frank Beckwith, who had such faith in her that he gave her lessons anyway.

Artie Jacobson, who was Susan's friend, was promoted to a top executive position at Paramount, so she visited him to ask for a loan. Before she could explain why she was there, he offered her a two-hundred-dollar-a-week contract. She phoned her mother. She was to appear in *Beau Geste* with Gary Cooper and Ray Milland. (Her mother and brother came to California to live with the girls.)

For years, Susan's biographers erroneously cited this 1939 "all-male" movie directed by William Wellman as her official debut in Hollywood. There were only two other women in the movie: Heather Thatcher, as her aunt, and little Ann Gillis, who played Hayward as a girl. All were marginal roles, and Susan had only a few scenes in the opening and closing sequences.

When *Beau Geste* was released, she was seen at her first Hollywood première with John Conti as escort. Then, when she went to New York for the first showing of the movie, her name made the headlines for the first time.

Thornton, of the Walter Thornton Agency, was suing her for $100,000, charging breach of contract. He had never believed she could become a movie star. Now, he was holding the contract she had signed for him against her. As they shook hands in farewell, Susan said, "It is a fight," and he replied that he was sorry about it. He later said, "But it was the only

thing I could do. I made her famous. When she left for Hollywood on a contract I got her with Selznick, she kissed us all goodbye at the train—and cried—and then proceeded to forget all about us."

Susan's only comment was that he was "a nasty man."

The Thornton Agency lawsuit was only the first of many battles to come, in and out of court, and she was called "an actress going through life with her fists up and a chip on her shoulder."

Hayward was in two other movies in 1939: the Bob Burns vehicle, *Our Leading Citizen,* and the Joe E. Brown–Martha Raye vehicle, *$1,000 a Touchdown.* She and Joseph Allen and John Hartley, her leading men in the movies, were selected for the "Golden Circle" of Paramount hopefuls. She made it, along with such future stars as William Holden, Ellen Drew, Robert Preston, and Evelyn Keyes.

Hayward was very shy when she first came to Hollywood. Her shyness was mistaken for aloofness, and most people stayed away from her. She was hard-working, punctual, and studious. She tried to follow directions, but would argue a point, if she had to. (Yet only once did she walk away from a set after an argument with a director, and she came back when he apologized.)

Being a natural redhead, proud owner of "the sexiest hair" in movies, she never endorsed a hair color dye because she "didn't want people to believe there was anything phony about me, least of all my hair color." She was once offered $5,000 to endorse a hair dye to be called "Susan Hayward Red," at a time when she needed the money, but said, "No, I am a natural redhead."

She took part in Louella Parsons' Flying Stars, making a promotional tour around the principal cities in the United States. The success of the Flying Stars was outstanding, sparked by the talent of Jane Wyman, Ronald Reagan, Arleen Whelan, June Preisser, and Joy Hodges. Susan would start her act by howling, "Is there anybody here from Brooklyn?" Her lifelong friendship with Louella Parsons started at this time; Louella was one of the few lady journalists whom she really liked.

Susan was getting tired of touring; she wanted to appear in films. By mid-1940 she had not made another movie, although she was announced for a role in *Mystery Sea Rider* (the part went to Carole Landis). At an annual convention at Paramount she met salesmen and exhibitors who asked, "Why don't we see more of you in pictures?" Each of the new Paramount players was supposed to appear on the platform, say a few nice words, and make way for the next one. When Susan appeared, she turned to Frank Freeman, her boss, and said sweetly, "These gentlemen have asked me why I'm not seen more often in movies. I know you can answer them, will you?"

She was loaned out to Columbia for what was to be the best role she had to date, the home wrecker in Ingrid Bergman's *Adam Had Four Sons.* Hayward and Bergman got along beautifully and Susan commented, "She worked as hard for my closeups as for her own." (Years later, when Susan was asked about her favorite actress, she said, "Ingrid Bergman.") She also got along well with the director, Gregory Ratoff, who was one of the first to believe in her as an actress. When something went wrong he would say, "Susan, you are the most ste-e-enk-ing actress I've ever seen," and she would laugh. But when she did as he wanted, he would beam, "Ah, you are mar-r-ve-lous, wonder-r-r-ful!" She later named one of her twins after him.

Adam Had Four Sons was released early in 1941 and became a very popular film. In this movie Hayward had to enact her first drunk scene. She got good notices and in an interview said, "Someday I'm going to win an Oscar." The statement raised a few eyebrows. As promotion for the movie she was named president of the "Perfect Legs Institute of America," by illustrator Joseph St. Amand.

In New York Susan and sister Florence shared a suite at the Waldorf-Astoria. They quarreled and parted company. Susan rejoined her mother and brother in California, and Florence remained in New York.

After *Adam*, Susan was on loan out to Republic to pester Judy Canova in *Sis Hopkins*, in which she "sang" the first of many dubbed songs; her partner was Bob Crosby, whose stiff acting made everybody else look like a real pro. (Susan repeated her role for the new CBS "Hollywood Premiers" radio show, hosted by her friend Louella Parsons. Judy Canova and Jerry Colonna were also on hand.)

Since Paramount was blind to her acting powers, Susan lost a good role in Olivia de Havilland's *Hold Back the Dawn*; the part went to Paulette Goddard, soon to become a star at the studio. Susan did play the part on radio, with Charles Boyer, who was also the male lead in the movie. Susan's throaty, sexy voice was an asset for radio shows, which she played intermittently through her Hollywood years.

Always money-conscious, Hayward became part owner of an ice cream parlor, at Santa Monica Boulevard in Beverly Hills, in 1941.

By the end of the year she had another good role, back at the home lot: the money-mad Millie Pickens in *Among the Living,* a "B" picture that could have been popular if the main characters were big names. Albert Dekker, Maude Eburne, and Hayward made the most of their parts in this deserving thriller. Frances Farmer, as Dekker's wife, was wasted in one of her last Hollywood roles.

Hayward put her best foot forward when it was needed. Together with Irene Dunne, Hedy Lamarr, Linda Darnell, Ann Rutherford, Lew Ayres, Charlotte Greenwood, Jane Wyman, Claire Trevor, Joe E. Brown, Hobart Bosworth, and others, she visited the Orthopaedic Hospital, All Nations Foundation, Salvation Army, Children's Hospital, California Babies Hospital, Home for the Aged, Los Angeles Orphanage, etc. She never forgot where she came from, and helped the poor and needy every time she had a chance. When the war broke, she immediately "enlisted" as a voluntary helper. She

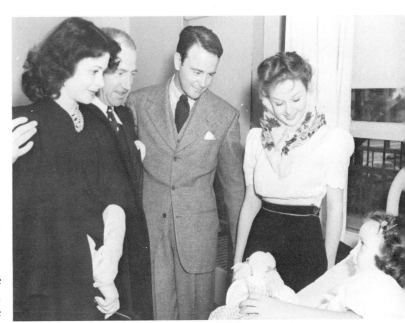

With Hedy Lamarr, Carey Wilson and Lew Ayres at The Los Angeles Orthopedic Hospital, 1941

With Lew Ayres in an early CBS "Lux Radio Theater"

posed for Bradshaw Crandell (of *Cosmopolitan* magazine cover fame). In army uniform and cap, she graced the cover of *Cosmopolitan* in October 1942. (Only three other actresses posed for Crandell, for a *Cosmopolitan* cover, in 1942: Rosemary Lane and Lana Turner before, and Joan Bennett after, Susan.)

Finally, in 1942, she had an opportunity to be noticed in a major movie production: Cecil B. DeMille's *Reap the Wild Wind*. It was the first time she was photographed in "glorious Technicolor" (à la Natalie Kalmus). And it was her first costume period movie.

Her role wasn't too long and she was billed seventh, way under Ray Milland, John Wayne, and Paulette Goddard. Her death scene at the end made a deep impression with audiences, her first death in the long chain of cinematic calamities to befall her. *Reap the Wild Wind* was tremendously popular, one of the biggest Paramount money makers. It drew a special mention from *Screen Guide* magazine as winner of the "Picture of Merit" award.

After *Reap* she got third lead and star billing in *The Forest Rangers*, her second Technicolor film, sharing the billing with Fred MacMurray and Paulette Goddard. During the filming, she had a scene where she was supposed to do some log rolling. She jumped short of a log and fell in the water amid the huge tree trunks. She had a badly peeled leg, but was ready to continue filming the next day; her accidents never interrupted the shooting of any of her movies. (Poor eyesight caused some of her accidents. She was very nearsighted. She wore glasses to read, but would remove them as soon as she spotted a photographer. Her faulty vision could have been the reason for her indifferent behavior toward fellow actors and actresses: she was always afraid to mistake someone for someone else.)

Rangers got another "Picture of Merit" award from *Screen Guide* magazine, helped by Hayward's volatile performance. (This movie introduced the 1942 hit tune "Jingle, Jangle, Jingle.")

Paramount apparently was not impressed. They took away her star billing in all the rest of the pictures she made for them throughout the term of her contract.

Susan made a war propaganda short, called *A Letter from Bataan*, directed by William H. Pine, with Richard Arlen, Janet Beecher, and Will Wright; next, she had another "other woman" role in Fredric March–Veronica Lake's *I Married a Witch*. She was billed fourth, under Robert Benchley, and her scenes were few in this excellent comedy directed by Rene Clair. Paramount sold this movie, along with *Young and Willing*, to United Artists when they were short on production (the latter was not released until 1943), and must have been surprised when *Life* magazine chose *Witch* as "Movie of the Week" in their weekly feature: "United Artists' *I Married a Witch* is another of those fancifully funny movies extracted from a novel by the late Thorne Smith whose Topper series tested the ingenuity of Hollywood's 'special effects' men to the limit. Here you get smoky incarnations, invisible voices, unnat-

ural apparitions, Rene Clair's able direction—and Veronica Lake playing comedy." (The movie is considered a classic today.)

Susan was dating the RAF's American Spitfire pilot Carroll McCalpin, and playwright William Saroyan, who was said to be as "wacky" as she was. She also dated artist Jon Whitcomb, a good friend all her life. (In 1956 Whitcomb painted her for a cover of *Cosmopolitan* magazine.)

Susan was tested for the part of Maria in *For Whom the Bell Tolls*, but Ingrid Bergman won it. Susan made the test with Phillip Terry, Joan Crawford's husband at the time. Would she have let them cut her hair in a short crew cut for the part, had she gotten it?

Later, she was featured in a special radio broadcast for NBC with two strong personalities: Mary Martin and Bing Crosby. This was one of the rare occasions when she was photographed wearing glasses, which she needed to read her lines. (In later years she made life easier for the photographers by wearing contact lenses.)

At the end of the year she was seen briefly as herself in the all-star *Star Spangled Rhythm*. She had a sketch with Ernest Truex.

Susan's hair, a prime asset thanks to the fluffy hairdos of the forties, caught the eye of photographer George Hurrell, famous for models reclining on sofas, beds, or rugs with their long hair spread out. Hayward was a natural for him.

One of Hayward's photos by Hurrell graced a whole page of *Esquire* magazine, with her disarranged hair (in color) gloriously falling like a turbulent waterfall. The magazine and Hurrell's photos were popular with the servicemen during World War II, and Hayward became a pinup girl. She also did "cheesecake" during the war, posing in bathing suits.

Young and Willing, released in 1943, looked like a showcase for young talent at Paramount (although it was distributed under the United Artists banner), including William Holden (in his last wartime movie), Eddie Bracken, Barbara Britton, Martha O'Driscoll, and James Brown. The picture also featured Robert Benchley and Florence MacMichael, the latter from the original New York show *Out of the Frying Pan*, by Francis Swann.

Susan lost a role in the film *No Time for Comedy* to Claudette Colbert. Next she was on loan out again, to Republic, for one of the "Hit Parade" series (1943 version). In this big musical she played a music writer who was "ghosting" songs for publisher John Carroll, and got to "sing" (dubbed again) a few songs. Although considered a good musical by almost all the critics, Hayward and her leading man Carroll received bad reviews from Wanda Hale of the *Daily News*: "Seldom, if ever, has one picture had two such performances as amateurish as are John Carroll's and Susan Hayward's." But *Silver Screen* commented: "Susan continues to perform outstandingly . . . Why, then, isn't she worthy of stardom?"

Susan dated her co-star John Carroll. This became a serious romance for a time. By midyear she was living alone in a

Posing for Bradshaw Crandall, for *Cosmopolitan* magazine, '42

When Lieutenant Commander William McManus presented her with a scepter making her Queen Bee of the SeaBees, in 1943, during filming of *The Fighting Seabees*

At the "Hollywood Canteen," 1943

Wedding photo, 1944

"bachelorette" apartment. She moved out from her mother's house when Florence came back from the East, divorced and with a baby. She dated actor Robert Lowery, artist friend Jon Whitcomb, Captain Robert Benjamin, Bob Ritchie (Jeanette MacDonald's ex-manager), Lieutenant David Heyers, and others. In an interview for *Silver Screen* magazine, she discussed her "dream man." She said she had refused about eight recent proposals because "some of them were from actors, just acting."

She was busy at the Hollywood Canteen, entertaining troops, serving food, dancing with the soldiers, when in November 1943 she met Jess Barker, a promising young actor from South Carolina with a Broadway background. At first she hesitated about going out with him because of his reputation as a "ladies' man." Barker said, "I bet you won't go out with me tonight," and Susan answered, "I bet I won't either," so they started going out. It is said that she slapped him on their first date when he tried to kiss her, and that he was surprised. He managed to get her telephone number and a stormy courtship followed. They had known each other only two weeks when they decided to get married. But then they had an argument and called the whole thing off. A few days later, they made up and were again discussing marriage. And so it went.

Susan had another cruel disappointment, losing to Merle Oberon the lead in *Dark Waters.* She thought she had the part when she read in the newspaper that they had already signed Oberon. Susan ran to her boss, Buddy De Sylva, almost crying, to find out that he had okayed the last-minute cancellation "to teach her a lesson." So she swallowed her pride, and waited for her opportunity.

Her next assignment looked more promising than it really was. In *Jack London,* on loanout to United Artists, she played Charmian Kittredge, who was Mrs. Jack London in real life and the author of *The Book of Jack London,* on which the movie was based. But *London* was a vehicle for its masculine star, Michael O'Shea, and it didn't fare too well. John Garfield, whom the studio sought unsuccessfully, would have been better as this adventurous man. Susan's role was relatively small; she appeared only in the second half of the movie. This was, however, her first movie during a year in which she appeared in four that were released.

Early in 1944, *Silver Screen* magazine published an article, "Why Can't They Win Stardom," about a few Hollywood personalities, among them Susan. They wondered if maybe her current releases, *Jack London* and *The Fighting Seabees,* would do it for her. (Others in the article were Geraldine Fitzgerald, Franchot Tone, Jane Wyman, Patricia Morison, Anita Louise, Francis Lederer, Robert Young, Anne Shirley, Gail Patrick, Jean Parker, and Allan Jones.)

Her next picture was her only war movie, another loanout to Republic, starring with John Wayne and Dennis O'Keefe in *The Fighting Seabees.* How did they manage to send Susan to the war front? As a war correspondent, of course. But she wasn't too noticeable in this one either. It was almost an all-male picture, a popular movie that started "Duke" on his way as one of the "ten top box office attractions." As part of the publicity for this film Susan was crowned "Queen Bee" of the real Seabees, at Camp Rousseau, in Port Hueneme, California. She got another beauty title, "Miss Pin-Up 1944," and an honorary membership from the International Boilermakers, and a steel cap inscribed with her name. Her publicity was paying off: she received honorary memberships from the New York Police Department and the Montana State Penitentiary. (Did they want to see her behind bars?)

She made a short for the U.S. Government Office of War Information, *Skirmish on the Home Front,* with William Bendix (her leading man in her next film). They shared this propaganda vehicle for war bonds with Betty Hutton and Alan Ladd. She also guested, together with Jack Carson, in a popular wartime radio show, "G.I. Journal."

Susan's next release, *The Hairy Ape,* based on Eugene O'Neill's 1922 play, gave her one of her best roles in the early forties. As Mildred Douglas, femme fatale, she was at her best, outshining William Bendix, who was the main character in the movie. Her portrayal of this soul-less temptress was best described by the critic who wrote, "She is Hollywood's ablest bitch player." But the movie, released under the United Artists banner in another loanout, wasn't popular.

After the release of this movie she starred in a much more important role: as real life bride to groom Jess Barker. They finally married on July 23, 1944, at St. Thomas Episcopal Church. Photographs of the wedding showed a radiant pair of lovebirds. The only witnesses present were her press agents Henry Rogers and Jean Pettebone.

Only two months after the wedding they had their first fight. Susan walked out of the house and was reluctant to go back to Barker, even after finding out she was pregnant. She confided to her old friend Louella Parsons, in a newspaper article, "Maybe it was the psychological effect of his never having a job since we married." Louella asked her, "Don't you think you will make up? Isn't this just a lover's quarrel?" Susan shook her head vigorously, but a few weeks later they were reconciled. "I love him. I guess that is the only important explanation I can give. . . . I think you, Louella, know better than anyone, except my mother, how deeply and sincerely I have wanted to make a success of marriage. It is too deep and too serious to let a quarrel come between us just because we are too proud to say we made a mistake." A few months later, Susan, coming out of the X-ray room, broke the news to the stunned father-to-be: the baby was going to be twins!

By the end of the year, she had her last Paramount release, which turned out to be a very popular soap opera, *And Now Tomorrow,* based on Rachel Field's novel about society people in 1930s New England. She was billed third, under Loretta Young and Alan Ladd. The ads showed her as the vixen they thought people wanted her to be. This was her last Paramount picture under the old contract, and when they offered her a lot of money for a new one for another seven years, she told them what they could do with it.

At Paramount, she had been slated to play the part of Helen Walker in *Murder, He Says,* a popular comedy of the forties which would have paired her with Fred MacMurray again, and she was also scheduled for *Duffy's Tavern,* another all-star musical revue where she might have regained star billing. But she left the company before either of these movies was ready to roll.

With director Irving Pichel on the set of *And Now Tomorrow*

Campus Cinderella with Peggy Moran (second from left), Johnnie Davis (center), Dorothy Comingore (behind chair) Susan Hayward (far right)

SHORTS AND FEATURETTES

Pictorial Short

VITAPHONE, 1936
Susan was seen as model Edythe Marrener, of New York.

Campus Cinderella

WARNER BROS., 1938
Directed by Noel Smith

Cast

Johnnie Davis, Penny Singleton, Anthony Averill, Oscar O'Shea, Wright Kramer, Emmett Vogan, Joe Cunningham, Ferris Taylor, Stuart Holmes, Max Hoffman, Jr., Janet Shaw, Susan Hayward, Peggy Moran, Kay Winters, Sally Gage, Sidney Bracy, Jan Holm, Alice Connor, Rosella Towne.
Running time, 18 minutes

A Letter From Bataan with Janet Beecher and Will Wright

A Letter from Bataan

PARAMOUNT, 1942
Directed by William H. Pine

Cast

Richard Arlen, Susan Hayward, Janet Beecher, Jimmy Lydon, Joe Sawyer, Keith Richards, Esther Dale, Will Wright.
Running time, 15 minutes

Skirmish on the Home Front

PARAMOUNT, 1944
Distributed by the U.S. Government Office of War Information.

Cast

Alan Ladd, Betty Hutton, William Bendix, Susan Hayward.
Running time, 13 minutes

Think 20th

20TH CENTURY-FOX, 1967
Directed by Richard Fleischer
Narrated by Richard D. Zanuck

Cast

Julie Andrews, Richard Attenborough, Candice Bergen, Olinka Berova, Paul Burke, Michael Caine, Peter Cook, Richard Crenna, Bette Davis, Patty Duke, Judy Geeson, Rosemary Harris, Linda Harrison, Rex Harrison, Susan Hayward, Charlton Heston, Edward Judd, Deborah Kerr, Steve McQueen, Dudley Moore, Anthony Newley, David Niven, Barbara Parkins, Eric Portman, Giovanna Ralli, Joyce Redman, Beryl Reid, Rachel Roberts, Gena Rowlands, Tony Scotti, Frank Sinatra, Jill St. John, Sharon Tate, Raquel Welch.
Running time, 30 minutes.

Gloria confronts Connie with the "borrowed" dress, while Neil and Connie's boss watch (Susan Hayward, Ronald Reagan, Joseph Crehan, and Jane Bryan)

Girls on Probation

Warner Bros. 1938

CAST

Connie Heath, Jane Bryan; *Neil Dillon,* Ronald Reagan; *Tony Rand,* Anthony Averill; *Hilda Engstrom,* Sheila Bromley; *Judge,* Henry O'Neill; *Kate Heath,* Elisabeth Risdon; *Roger Heath,* Sig Rumann; *Jane Lennox,* Dorothy Peterson; *Mrs. Engstrom,* Esther Dale; *Gloria Adams,* Susan Hayward; *Terry Mason,* Larry Williams; *Mr. Engstrom,* Arthur Hoyt; *Ruth,* Peggy Shannon; *Marge,* Lenita Lane; *Prison Inmate,* Janet Shaw; *Dave Warren,* James Nolan; *Todd,* Joseph Crehan; *Prosecuting Attorney,* Pierre Watkin; *Public Defender Craven,* James Spottswood; *Head Matron,* Brenda Fowler; *Matron,* Kate Lawson; *Matron,* Maude Lambert.

CREDITS

Directed by William McGann. *Original screenplay by* Crane Wilbur. *Photography by* Arthur Todd, A.S.C. *Art Director,* Hugh Reticker. *Film Editor,* Frederick Richards. *Dialogue Director,* Harry Seymour. *Sound by* Leslie G. Hewitt. *Gowns by* Howard Shoup. *Running time, 63 minutes.*

THE STORY

Connie Heath (Jane Bryan) borrows a dress from a friend, Hilda Engstrom (Sheila Bromley) not knowing that it had been appropriated from a dry cleaning shop where both girls work. Connie wears the dress at a party, but the owner of the dress, Gloria Adams (Susan Hayward), is at the same party and recognizes her dress. Gloria has Connie arrested for grand larceny the following day.

Gloria changes her mind and drops the charge, but the insurance company, protecting the dry cleaning business, decides to prosecute and Connie is brought to court. A young attorney, Neil Dillon (Ronald Reagan), gets her off with a suspended sentence. However, the girl's father (Sig Rumann), a martinet, throws her out of the house. She finds employment in a distant city but runs into Hilda again—during a bank holdup by the latter and her boy friend, Tony Rand (Anthony Averill). In the getaway, Connie is pushed into the car and when the law catches up with the robbers she is convicted as an accomplice and put on probation for three years.

Going back home, she keeps her troubles a secret and gets a job as secretary to Neil Dillon who has been appointed assistant district attorney. They fall in love and become engaged.

Hilda reappears, threatening Connie with blackmail. Connie, to prove that she's on the side of the law, puts the police on the trail of the bank robber, Hilda's boy friend, who had escaped from jail. In a spectacular gun battle the bandit is shot to death after he has unwittingly slain his sweetheart, Hilda, and finally Connie can relax.

REVIEWS

NEW YORK WORLD TELEGRAM *William Boehnel*

"Even done well, it is doubtful if all this might have resulted in exciting and satisfactory entertainment. But when done as it is here—in a slipshod and slovenly manner—it is a decided disappointment."

BROOKLYN DAILY EAGLE *Herbert Cohn*

Girls on Probation is a conglomeration of three or four themes that have seen service before. Chief among them is the pathetic problem of a girl who hasn't the nerve to tell her boy friend that she is on probation. It was the idea for Sylvia Sidney's *You and Me* where it made a neat emotional plot. Here it is only one of several threads that are woven into a bulky fabric with a rough texture and a too familiar pattern."

VARIETY *Char*

"The cast does not include strong Warner Brothers marquee talent, but performances by the various members of the company are adequate. . . . The story, an original by Crane Wilbur, is routine. . . . Wilbur's dialog generally does not rise above the average."

NOTES

In this programmer, Hayward was billed tenth, and her part as the socialite Miss Adams, played with a thick Brooklynese accent, was unnoticed by the reviewers. After this picture, she was advised to improve her diction and get rid of the accent.

This was her first Warner Brothers movie with any credit, but for years it was not listed in her filmography. Her whole Warner Brothers period was not mentioned, as opposed to her Paramount break in her next picture *Beau Geste,* and her tenure at the first studio is obscure and surrounded with confusion.

This insignificant movie was re-released in 1956, after Hayward's *I'll Cry Tomorrow* triumph, and the billing was changed so she was at the top. The ads were also misleading.

Nice kid today . . . jailbird tomorrow
SUSAN HAYWARD
(I'll Cry Tomorrow)
in her most daring role
GIRLS ON PROBATION

Worse still, the ads had a drawing of Hayward lighting a cigarette, looking like a gun moll.

Beau Geste

Paramount, 1939

Director William Wellman and Susan Hayward between scenes

CAST

Beau Geste, Gary Cooper; *John Geste,* Ray Milland; *Digby Geste,* Robert Preston; *Sergeant Markoff,* Brian Donlevy; *Isobel Rivers,* Susan Hayward; *Rasinoff,* J. Carrol Naish; *Schwartz,* Albert Dekker; *Hank Miller,* Broderick Crawford; *Buddy McMonigal,* Charles Barton; *Major Henri de Beaujolais,* James Stephenson; *Lady Patricia Brandon,* Heather Thatcher; *Augustus Brandon,* G. P. Huntley, Jr.; *Lieutenant Dufour,* James Burke; *Renouf,* Henry Brandon; *Renault,* Arthur Aylesworth; *Renoir,* Harry Woods; *Voisin,* Harold Huber; *Maris,* Stanley Andrews; *Beau at 12,* Donald O'Connor; *John at 10,* Billy Cook; *Digby at 12,* Martin Spellman; *Augustus at 12,* David Holt; *Isobel at 10,* Ann Gillis; *Lieutenant Martin,* Harvey Stephens; *Krenke,* Barry Macollum; *Bugler,* Ronnie Rondell; *Burdon, the Butler,* Frank Dawson; *Cordier,* George Chandler; *Glock,* Duke Green; *Colonel in Recruiting Office,* Thomas Jackson; *Sergeant-Major,* Jerome Storm; *Sergeant,* Joseph Whitehead; *Corporals,* Harry Worth, Nestor Paiva; *Arab Scouts,* George Regas, Francis McDonald; *Legionnaires,* Carl Voss, Jor Bernard, Robert Perry, Larry Lawson, Henry Sylvester, Joseph William Cody; *Trumpeter O. Leo,* Joe Colling; *Girl in Port Said Café,* Gladys Jean.

CREDITS

Directed by William A. Wellman. *Produced by* William A. Wellman. *Based on the novel by* Percival Christopher Wren. *Scenarist,* Robert Carson. *Photographers,* Theodor Sparkuhl and Archie Stout. *Art Directors,* Hans Dreier and Robert Odell. *Editor,* Thomas Scott. *Sound Recorders,* Hugo Grenzbach and Walter Oberst. *Technical Adviser,* Louis Van Der Ecker. *Musical Score,* Alfred Newman. *Orchestrator,* Edward Powell. *Running time, 114 minutes.*

THE STORY

A relief column of the French Foreign Legion has crossed the desert and reached Fort Zinderneuf. The fort seems strangely silent.

Major de Beaujolais (James Stephenson) halts the column and fires his pistol. A rifle bullet richochets on the sand in front of him and he rides toward the gates, only to find that every man at the embrasures is dead.

He sends his bugler to the fort, but when the man doesn't return, the major goes. He finds the bodies of a sergeant and a legionnaire. There is a note in the sergeant's hand—a confession that he stole a gem called "The Blue Water." The major orders his men inside but when he tries to show them the bodies, they are gone. Hearing shots, they retire to an oasis outside the fort just in time to escape from an explosion that sets the whole fort on fire.

Ray Milland and Susan Hayward

Lady Brandon shows "The Blue Water" sapphire to the Gestes and Isobel and Augustus (left to right: Robert Preston, Ray Milland, Susan Hayward, Heather Thatcher, J. G. Huntley, Jr., and Gary Cooper)

Isobel and John (Ray Milland and **Susan Hayward**) are
concerned about the disappearance of "The Blue Water"

Fifteen years before, the three young Geste brothers are
playing. They have staged a viking funeral for a "dead" toy
sailor, placing a toy dog at the sailor's feet and setting the ship
on fire. Beau, the oldest brother (Donald O'Connor), makes
his brothers John (Billy Cook) and Digby (Martin Spellman)
promise to give him a viking funeral when his time comes.

The boys are wards of Lady Brandon, and so is Isobel (Ann
Gillis). Lady Brandon (Heather Thatcher), wanting to give
the children a good education, sells a family heirloom, a
sapphire called "The Blue Water," replacing it with an imitation. Beau witnesses the transaction quite by accident, but
keeps it a secret.

Years later, Lord Brandon (G. P. Huntley), who comes
home only when he needs money, returns to sell the famous
sapphire. Beau (Gary Cooper), not wishing dear Lady Brandon to suffer the embarrassment of explaining that their sapphire is an imitation, steals the jewel. Then he leaves home to
join the French Foreign Legion, leaving a note for his brothers.

Digby (Robert Preston) and John (Ray Milland) join their
brother (for John it means leaving Isobel, played by Susan
Hayward, with whom he's in love).

The three brothers meet at the Legion's training post, where
Rasinoff (J. Carrol Naish), a thief, overhears them boasting
that each has the gem, and informs their sadistic sergeant,
Markoff (Brian Donlevy), who plans to steal the jewel and
decides to separate the brothers. Beau and John go with him to
Fort Zinderneuf and Digby is sent to Fort Tokotu.

At Fort Zinderneuf, Markoff takes over after the death of
the young lieutenant in command and turns the place into a
living hell. Finally, the men rebel, and he orders the Geste
brothers, who were not involved, to shoot the leaders of the
mutiny. When they refuse he threatens to kill them, but the
fort is attacked by a desert tribe and most of the men are
killed.

Beau is shot. John sees Markoff searching Beau's body and
Markoff tries to kill him, but Beau clutches his feet, giving
John the opportunity to kill Markoff with his bayonet. Beau
dies in John's arms after giving him two pieces of paper: a
note confessing to the theft of "The Blue Water," to be put
in Markoff's hand; and a letter to Lady Brandon explaining
his actions.

John remembers his promise and prepares to give his
brother a viking funeral. He places Markoff's body at Beau's
feet and sets fire to the fort.

Escaping the blazing fort, John is reunited with Digby, but
soon after Digby is killed by nomads.

Alone, John returns home to Isobel's waiting arms.

REVIEWS

NOTES

Susan had a lot of publicity for this movie, and hundreds of
stills, but her part was so small that one wonders why they
bothered to use so many of her photos to promote the film.

In her last scene she's at the piano when Milland returns,
but you can hardly see her face when she welcomes him back
with an embrace.

The reviewers who mentioned her wrote about a new, very
pretty red-headed starlet from Brooklyn.

Her part, played by Mary Brian in the silent Ronald Colman
version, was first announced for Patricia Morison.

Although the film suffered in comparison with the first one,
the second *Beau Geste* also stands as a classic today.

Brian Donlevy got the best reviews and a supporting actor
nomination for his sadistic Sergeant Markoff.

The film earned another nomination in the Art and Set
Direction category.

Our Leading Citizen

Paramount, 1939

CAST

Lem Schofield, Bob Burns; *Judith Schofield*, Susan Hayward; *Clay Clayton*, Joseph Allen, Jr.; *Aunt Tillie Clark*, Elizabeth Patterson; *J. T. Tapley*, Gene Lockhart; *Shep Muir*, Charles Bickford; *Mr. Stoney*, Otto Hoffman; *Jim Hanna*, Clarence Kolb; *Jerry Peters*, Paul Guilfoyle; *Tonia*, Fay Helm; *Mrs. Barker*, Kathleen Lockhart; *Druscilla*, Hattie Noel; *Miss Swan*, Kathryn Sheldon; *Frank*, Monte Blue; *Chief of Police*, Jim Kelso; *Director*, Harry C. Bradley; *Maid*, Frances Morris; *Frederick (first butler)*, Thomas Louden; *Charles (second butler)*, Olaf Hytten; *Janitor*, Phil Dunham; *Doctor*, Gus Glassmire.

CREDITS

Directed by Alfred Santell. *Produced by* George Arthur. *Screenplay by* John C. Moffit. *Based on a story by* Irvin S. Cobb. *Photography by* Victor Milner, A.S.C. *Art Directors,* Hans Dreier *and* Roland Anderson. *Film Editor,* Hugh Bennett. *Sound,* Earl Haymann. *Running time, 89 minutes.*

THE STORY

Lem Schofield (Bob Burns), lawyer-philosopher, welcomes Clay Clayton (Joseph Allen), son of his deceased partner, into the firm. Judy Schofield (Susan Hayward), Lem's daughter, is happy to see the young man back from New York, where he had been practicing law.

Clay suggests that he and Lem become counsels for J. T. Tapley (Gene Lockhart), local industrialist. Lem agrees after pointing out that Tapley has been cutting corners to gain greater profits. Tapley precipitates a strike of the workers by putting through a 10 percent pay cut at one of his mills. Lem resigns as Tapley's counselor but Clay remains and estranges himself from Judith.

Tapley calls in strikebreakers, led by Shep Muir (Charles Bickford). This causes the mill to be bombed, and one man is killed. The citizens call a protest meeting.

At the meeting Lem pleads to settle the trouble with no outside influences. Surprisingly, Tapley seconds him, rescinding the pay cut and proposing Clay for junior senator from the state. Lem points out to Clay that Tapley's move is a political one, but Clay doesn't believe it. Lem forces Tapley to agree that he won't nominate Clay to the Senate by threatening to reveal the fact that he stole valuable property from a mountain woman, Aunt Tillie Clark (Elizabeth Patterson). Lem makes Tapley sign an agreement to pay her and shows Clay the signed document.

Joseph Allen and Susan Hayward

He promises to nominate Clay himself. Next Lem runs the agitator out of town, and has a fight with him, but finally he brings Muir to justice.

Tapley nominates another candidate, and Clay nominates Lem to run at the state convention. Later in his office he is congratulated by Clay and Judith, who are reunited.

REVIEWS

NEW YORK TIMES *Frank S. Nugent*

"Irvin S. Cobb . . . as the author of the Paramount's remarkable social document, *Our Leading Citizen*, presents the appalling spectacle of a man who is not merely beyond his depth but insists on showing off as he goes down for the third time. Armed with a primer in economics, a well-thumbed copy of the Golden Rule and a deal of conceit, he has created his own straw men, has blown them away with gusty laughter and has pretended—with what sincerity we know not—that life is just that simple."

NEW YORK HERALD TRIBUNE *Howard Barnes*

"The whole problem of industrial unrest is settled with preposterous dispatch in *Our Leading Citizen*. Al! that is needed to keep the peace on the labor front, according to this Paramount film, is Bob Burns."

Lem gives his daughter some fatherly advice (Susan Hayward and Bob Burns)

TIME

"Hollywood version of Broadway's The American Way. Despite the skepticism of Hollywood leftists, cutters left intact most of its supposedly inflammatory scenes."

NOTES

In the Paramount press book, they wrote: "*Our Leading Citizen* is a picture destined to make film history in more ways than one. It is a picture with the courage to speak out for the American way of life—and it is a picture that shows the true measure of the ability of Bob Burns as a character actor." (The picture was a complete failure.)

They even invited twenty-one governors to the opening of this "B" film. The publicity campaign for Hayward consisted in making her a candidate for the "Oomph" girl title.

Susan's romance with Joseph Allen was secondary to the main character played by Burns. The latter, an actor from the radio era, was trying to become the next Will Rogers.

Most reviewers hated it.

Joseph Allen, Jr., Bob Burns, and Susan Hayward

Left to right: Joe E. Brown, Martha Raye, John Hartley, and Susan Hayward

$1,000 a Touchdown

Paramount, 1939

CAST

Marlowe Mansfield Booth, Joe E. Brown; *Martha Madison,* Martha Raye; *Henry,* Eric Blore; *Betty McGlen,* Susan Hayward; *Bill Anders,* John Hartley; *Bangs,* Syd Salyor; *Lorelei,* Joyce Mathews; *Mr. Fishbeck,* George McKay; *Popcorn Vendor,* Tom Dugan; *Brick Benson,* Matt McHugh; *King Richard,* Hugh Sothern; *Hamilton McGlen, Sr.,* Josef Swickard; *Two Ton Terry,* Adrian Morris; *Cab Driver,* Dewey Robinson; *Guard,* William Haade; *McGlen's First Son,* Jack Perrin; *McGlen's Second Son,* Phil Dunham; *Duke,* Constantine Romanoff; *Stage Manager,* Charles Middleton; *Hysterical Woman,* Dot Farley; *Coach,* Emmett Vogan; *McGlen's Sons' Wives,* Fritzie Brunnette, Gertrude Astor; *Buck,* John Hart; *Babe,* Wanda McKay; *Blondie,* Cheryl Walker; *Big Boy,* Wayne "Tiny" Whitt.

CREDITS

Directed by James Hogan. *Produced by* William C. Thomas. *Original and Screenplay by* Delmer Daves. *Photography by* William Mellor. *Art Director,* Hans Dreier. *Editor,* Chandler House. *Assistant Director,* Harry Scott. *Music,* Ralph Rainger and Leo Robin. *Running time, 71 minutes.*

THE STORY

Marlowe Mansfield Booth (Joe E. Brown) is unable to continue in the tradition of his illustrious stage family. He has stage fright and loses his voice when the audience is any larger than ten people.

When he meets Martha Madison (Martha Raye), who has also failed as an actress, they put to use an old, broken-down school that she has inherited. With the aid of a group of stranded stage people and money borrowed from stingy Mr. Fishbeck (George McKay), they manage to open the school, but students fail to appear.

Martha's ex-butler, Henry (Eric Blore), suggests that they get a football team, and with Marlowe's inducements and Betty McGlen's (Susan Hayward) romance course, they attract a host of football players from other schools, including Bill Anders (John Hartley), who falls for Betty. Then girls start to flock to the school, attracted by the football players.

With the aid of a book, *How to Coach Football,* Marlowe puts the team together, but they can't get any other school team to play against them, so Martha hires a professional football team for an exhibition game and wagers every penny on the outcome.

The school team is not doing well and Martha, in desperation, bets Mr. Fishbeck $1,000 that her team will score a touchdown. Then she promises the pros' captain the same amount for every touchdown her team scores. Mr. Fishbeck is forced to pay off, but when the boys keep scoring touchdowns, he quits. The pros then start to score again until finally Marlowe himself enters the game and, recovering his confidence, wins it, and Martha.

A couple of lovebirds taking a ride (John Hartley and Susan Hayward)

REVIEWS

NEW YORK POST   *Archer Winsten*

"With *$1,000 a Touchdown* new depths of the Hollywood collegiate legend are plumbed by those inveterate plumbers Joe E. Brown and Martha Raye.

"Frankly, this picture will disappoint even Joe E. Brown and Martha Raye fans, which is saying just about as much as can be said in a family newspaper."

VARIETY

"Par's *$1,000 a Touchdown* is a lightweight programmer that will carry adequately as a supporter in the duals. It's a hokey and innocuous comedy that secures laughs from elemental and obvious situations aimed at the family and juve trade. Picture teams Joe E. Brown and Martha Raye, giving it certain marquee strength in the secondary houses. Brown does his regular routines."

BROOKLYN DAILY EAGLE   *Herbert Cohn*

"With the football season just three days old, the movies obviously were losing no time when they sent *$1,000 a Touchdown,* the first of the year's inevitable gridiron films. But timeliness stops short right there, for *$1,000 a Touchdown* reaches back a season or two to the days of screwy comedies to find a pattern for its little story of Joe E. Brown, Martha Raye and the latter's family institution, Madison University."

NOTES

Delmer Daves, who scripted the movie, would direct Hayward fifteen years later in *Demetrius and the Gladiators*. The script wasted the talents of comedy stars Brown and Raye.

This movie, as the previous Hayward flick, did not have a very large distribution, especially in South American countries, where it was hardly shown at all. The only one in the cast who got a few good lines from the reviewers was Eric Blore, playing a butler.

Although Susan and John Hartley were the handsome young lovers, they didn't draw comment from the criticis, but the reviews were so bad that they were better off unmentioned

Susan Hayward and John Hartley

Adam believes Hester's lies, to Jack's horror (left to right: Warner Baxter, Susan Hayward, and Richard Denning)

Adam Had Four Sons

Columbia, 1941

CAST

Emilie Gallatin, Ingrid Bergman; *Adam Stoddard,* Warner Baxter; *Hester,* Susan Hayward; *Molly,* Fay Wray; Older Boys: *Jack,* Richard Denning; *David,* Johnny Downs; *Chris,* Robert Shaw; *Phillip,* Charles Lind; Younger Boys: *Jack,* Billy Ray; *David,* Steven Muller; *Chris,* Wallace Chadwell; *Phillip,* Bobby Walberg; *Cousin Phillippa,* Helen Westley; *Vance,* June Lockhart; *Otto,* Pietro Sosso; *Dr. Lane,* Gilbert Emery; *Photographer,* Renie Riano; *Sam,* Clarence Muse.

CREDITS

Directed by Gregory Ratoff. *Produced by* Robert Sherwood. *Screenplay by* William Hurlbutt *and* Michael Blankfort. *Based on the novel* Legacy *by* Charles Bonner. *Photography by* Peverell Marley. *Art Director,* Rudolph Sternad. *Film Editor,* Francis D. Lyon. *Associate Producer,* Gordon S. Griffith. *Running time, 81 minutes.*

THE STORY

Adam and Molly Stoddard (Warner Baxter and Fay Wray) acquire the services of a French governess, Emilie Gallatin (Ingrid Bergman), to take care of their four sons: Jack (Billy Ray), David (Steven Muller), Chris (Wallace Chadwell) and Phillip (Bobby Walberg). She gets attached to the boys, and soon finds herself admiring the father also.

Molly dies and the family has financial problems, so Emilie has to leave their employ and go back to France. Years later, however, the Stoddard family, finances straightened out, brings her back to the household.

The four sons, now young men, are delighted to have her back, and so is their father. Jack (Richard Denning), Chris (Robert Shaw), and Phillip (Charles Lind) are still bachelors, but David (Johnny Downs) marries young, pretty Hester (Susan Hayward), who is malicious and irresponsible.

Wasting no time, Hester insolently makes her position in the household clear: she is to have the last word in all matters.

Emilie gives innocent-appearing Hester a nasty look (Ingrid Bergman and Susan Hayward)

And she makes sure that the governess is put in her place: she is just another servant in the house. Hester's malevolence shocks old cousin Phillippa (Helen Westley), who comes to visit the Stoddards. Hester has been flirting with Jack and the situation is getting out of hand in spite of Jack's resistance to his sister-in-law.

Emilie, who is now sure that she is in love with Adam, although he treats her only as a dear friend, finds Hester in Jack's bedroom attempting to seduce him. Wanting to spare Adam the anguish of knowing what was going on, she manages to get Hester out but Adam finds her with Jack and gets upset.

Hester, faking innocence, fools Adam, but not for long. She is finally exposed and Adam realizes that he is in love with Emilie. They find that they have much more in common than love for "their" four sons.

REVIEWS

NEW YORK HERALD TRIBUNE   *Howard Barnes*

"A dull adaptation of a rambling family saga, the production betrays its literary origins in the worst way.

". . . the screen drama is a generally pedestrian and implausible reconstruction of human experience.

". . . Susan Hayward as the siren who almost disrupts the Adam household, is much too emphatic for comfort."

PHOTOPLAY

"Unusual is this beautifully enacted story dealing with a father's love for his four sons."

DALLAS MORNING NEWS   *F.N.*
"Little Susan Hayward, heretofore an also-ran at Paramount, gives it the works as the mischief-maker."

NEW YORK POST   *Archer Winsten*

"Hayward . . . is also excellent as the hard-drinking faithless little baggage who almost destroys the entire Stoddard family and its governess."

RICHMOND NEWS LEADER   *Elizabeth Copeland*

"Two unusually talented and charming women walk away with the entire picture. Ingrid Bergman, as the gentle, loyal, fiercely devoted governess who would stain even her own name to save the honor of Adam's sons, is contrasted with Susan Hayward as the predatory and treacherous wife of one of them. Miss Hayward is stunning in the latter role, making it quite as outstanding as Miss Berman's exemplary one."

NOTES

Hayward herself asked Ratoff for the part of Hester in the movie, but he laughed off the idea. Her image as the sweet young thing from past movies almost prevented her from

David loves Hester, but does she really care about him? (Johnny Downs and Susan Hayward)

Phillippa collapses from the shock of finding out about Hester (left to right: Helen Westley, Johnny Downs, and Susan Hayward)

being in this film. But Mrs. Ratoff, the former actress Eugenie Leontovich, persuaded him to let her have the role, which was Susan's favorite for quite a few years.

She enacted her first brawl, with Bergman, no less. Another memorable scene is when she fakes tears to a distraught Warner Baxter, and as he comforts her, a scheming smile comes over her face.

Character actress Helen Westley had one of her last roles, a brief one: she dies, in a sudden and absurd scene, when she finds out the truth about Hayward.

Fay Wray appeared early as Baxter's wife and mother of the four boys. She died peacefully without meeting Hayward.

This was the first Susan Hayward movie to be released at Radio City Music Hall.

Horace shows Jeff a newspaper while Carol looks on unhappily (left to right: Charles Butterworth, Bob Crosby, and Susan Hayward)

Sis Hopkins

REPUBLIC, 1941

CAST

Sis Hopkins, Judy Canova; *Jeff Farnsworth,* Bob Crosby; *Horace Hopkins,* Charles Butterworth; *Professor,* Jerry Colonna; *Carol Hopkins,* Susan Hayward; *Clara Hopkins,* Katherine Alexander; *Ripple,* Elvia Allman; *Cynthia,* Carol Adams; *Phyllis,* Lynn Merrick; *Vera de Vere,* Mary Ainslee; *Butler,* Charles Coleman; *Mayor,* Andrew Tombes; *Rollo,* Charles Lane; *Joe,* Byron Foulger; *Mrs. Farnsworth,* Betty Blythe: *Jud,* Frank Darien.

CREDITS

Directed by Joseph Santley. *Produced by* Robert North. *Screenplay by* Jack Townley, Milt Gross, *and* Ed Eliscu. *Based on the play by* F. McGrew Willis. *Photographed by* Jack Marta. *Art Director,* John Victor Mackay. *Editor,* Ernest Nims. *Music Director,* Cy Feuer. *Songs by* Frank Loesser *and* Jule Styne. *Running time, 99 minutes.*

THE STORY

Reading in a newspaper that her wealthy Uncle Horace (Charles Butterworth) is "jobless after thirty years," Sis Hopkins (Judy Canova), believing that he has lost his fortune, invites him to visit her at her farm. The newspaper item really referred to his retirement from an executive position in a plumbing business.

Horace accepts the invitation but, arriving at the farm, finds that the house has burned down. He decides to take his naive country niece home. He is tired of his wife Clara's (Katherine Alexander) social gatherings and his daughter Carol's (Susan Hayward) selfishness. Poor Sis is snubbed by all her relatives, but Horace is determined to help and enrolls his niece in the same college Carol attends—much to his daughter's annoyance.

When the wacky dramatic coach (Jerry Colonna) gets Sis to participate in a college play, she shows talent, so her part is expanded at the expense of Carol's. To make things worse, Jeff Farnsworth (Bob Crosby), Carol's boyfriend, agrees that Sis is excellent in the show and he and Carol fight over this.

Carol is not about to take all this quietly, so she tricks her cousin into appearing in a burlesque show, making Sis believe that it is all part of a sorority initiation. Carol arranges everything and, at a given moment, by pulling a thread in Sis' dress, makes it fall apart. She, of course, has informed the police and Sis barely escapes. However, she is expelled from college.

At the last moment, Carol has a change of heart. When Uncle Horace explains to the dean what really happened, Sis is accepted again and rejoins the play. Everyone roots for her, and she turns out to be the sensation of the show.

Cousin Sis moves her belongings to Carol's room and Carol is far from pleased with her new roommate (Judy Canova on the left, Susan Hayward and Elvia Allman on the right)

Carol gossips with her college pals Lynn Merrick and Carol Adams about her cousin Sis Hopkins (Susan Hayward, extreme right)

Jeff and Carol singing "Look at You, Look at Me" (Bob Crosby and Susan Hayward)

REVIEWS

NEW YORK JOURNAL AMERICAN *Rose Pelswick*

"Headlining Judy Canova of the twangy voice and the hill-billy routines, *Sis Hopkins* gives its exuberant star plenty of opportunity to sing, dance and clown. . . . It even permits her to sing an operatic aria straight, if something less than success-fully. . . .

"The cast also includes Jerry Colonna, as a dramatic coach, and Charles Butterworth whose chore is that of Sis Hopkins' kindly uncle who sides with his niece against his social-climbing wife (Katherine Alexander) and their snobbish daughter (Susan Hayward)."

VARIETY *Walt*

"Republic materially advances the starring progress of Judy Canova in this, her second film assignment. Tailor-made for maximum display of her backwoodsian style of delivery, and individualized vocal abilities, picture purveys sufficient comedy and music to make it a profitable attraction in the regular runs as billtopper or solo.

"Susan Hayward is good as the snobbish cousin."

CLEVELAND PRESS *Albert Prudence*

"There must be something wrong with anyone who can sit through *Sis Hopkins* and not get at least one or two hearty chuckles.

"Susan Hayward as the plumber's daughter is as pretty a co-lead with Judy Canova as probably could be found."

NOTES

This was Susan's first picture for "poverty row" Republic, but this time the company went overboard and paid $50,000 for the old Rose Melville Broadway production (previously filmed as a silent vehicle for Mabel Normand in 1919).

Hayward was given a nasty role, but she looked so pretty that even the reviewers forgave her treachery and praised her beauty. As Canova's snobbish cousin, she kept some of the bitchiness that made her noticeable in her previous effort; but this was a comedy, so she reformed at the end.

Susan did the mouthing of the song "Look at You, Look at Me" with Bob Crosby, who, of course, did his own singing.

The movie included notable radio personalities like Elvia Allman, in her second movie, and Jerry Colonna.

Jean Phillips, Frances Farmer, Albert Dekker, and Susan Hayward

Trouble between Paul and Bill (Susan Hayward, Albert Dekker, and Gordon Jones)

CAST

John Raden, Albert Dekker; *Paul Raden*, Albert Dekker; *Millie Pickens*, Susan Hayward; *Dr. Ben Saunders*, Harry Carey; *Elaine Raden*, Frances Farmer; *Bill Oakley*, Gordon Jones; *Peggy Nolan*, Jean Phillips; *Pompey*, Ernest Whitman; *Mrs. Pickens*, Maude Eburne; *Sheriff*, Frank M. Thomas; *Judge*, Harlan Briggs; *Tom Reilly*, Archie Twitchell; *Woman in Café*, Dorothy Sebastian; *Minister*, William Stack.

CREDITS

Directed by Stuart Heisler. *Produced by* Sol C. Siegel. *Screenplay by* Lester Cole *and* Garret Fort. *Based on a story by* Lester Cole *and* Brian Marlow. *Photography by* Theodor Sparkuhl. *Editor*, Everett Douglas. *Music*, Gerard Carbonara. *Running time, 67 minutes.*

THE STORY

Paul Raden (Albert Dekker), traumatized as a child by his mother's screams when his father beat her up, became a homicidal maniac and had been locked up in a room of the family mansion for twenty-five years. His family made everybody believe that he had died when he was ten years old. Dr. Ben Saunders (Harry Carey), the family doctor, had signed the false death certificate.

Paul's twin brother John (Albert Dekker) is married to Elaine (Frances Farmer), is a millionaire, and controls Radentown.

After strangling his guard, Paul escapes and flees to the home of his only friend, Dr. Saunders. However, he suddenly turns against the doctor too, escapes again, and starts a reign of terror in Radentown. He befriends a girl (Jean Phillips), but while chatting with her at a bar one night, he becomes agitated. He kills her, throwing the whole community into panic.

While the whole town hunts for him, he befriends another girl, Millie Pickens (Susan Hayward), daughter of the landlady (Maude Eburne) of the boardinghouse where he is staying. Millie is ambitious and, seeing that Paul has a roll of money, shows interest in him and manages to make him buy her a dress.

Unaware of Paul's identity, and hearing on the radio that there is a $5,000 reward for whoever captures the killer, she gets a gun and persuades Paul, who has forgotten the killings, to join her in the manhunt. On a hunch, she takes him to the rambling Radentown mansion where he had been a prisoner for so many years.

His mania returns and he tries to attack Millie. The hunting party's timely arrival saves her, but Paul escapes again.

Millie later identifies John Raden, Paul's twin brother, as her attacker and the mob howls for his death. Everything is straightened out when Paul is finally shot and killed at his mother's grave.

REVIEWS

NEW YORK POST   *Archer Winsten*

"Albert Dekker, one of the best Hollywood exemplars of the amok-running brigade, has got himself a good workout in *Among the Living*. . . .

"Miss Hayward is too young and luscious to die right away. Throw one of the fading movie queens to the strangler, but not Miss Hayward."

VARIETY

"Here is a good 'B' that will get honeyed comment. It's possible in fact, that *Among the Living* may even be a sleeper for fancy takings.

"Hayward is likewise a sociological study as the clothes-hungry, sexy daughter of a rooming-house keeper who nearly gets herself strangled by the unsuspected killer.

"The acting is generally excellent. Besides Dekker, Susan Hayward is plenty sharp."

NEW YORK HERALD TRIBUNE   *Howard Barnes*

"*Among the Living* is head and shoulders above most of the filler shows which are ground out by Hollywood to perpetuate the double-feature system.

"Susan Hayward is especially good as a predatory tramp who is completely taken in by the murderer during his lucid moments."

NOTES

This movie finally gave Susan a role she could sink her teeth into at Paramount. Susan managed to make the greedy, amoral girl Millie a sympathetic character.

It was her second movie with Albert Dekker, although she had no scenes with him in the first one, *Beau Geste*. It provided Dekker with one of the rare opportunities he had to play a leading man during the forties. He was a splendid actor, but usually a victim of type casting.

This was the first of three hit movies that Susan made with director Stuart Heisler over the years. (*Smash-Up* and *Tulsa* were the other two.)

The script was (in part) by Lester Cole, who later became one of the "Hollywood Ten."

Arriving at the old mansion, Millie
is not aware of the sudden change in
Paul's expression (Susan Hayward
and Albert Dekker)

Albert Dekker and Susan Hayward

Loxi and Drusilla meet Stephen Tolliver at a party in Charleston (Martha O'Driscoll, Susan Hayward, Paulette Goddard, Janet Beecher, and Ray Milland)

Reap the Wild Wind

PARAMOUNT, 1942

CAST

Stephen Tolliver, Ray Milland; *Captain Jack Stuart,* John Wayne; *Loxi Claiborne,* Paulette Goddard; *King Cutler,* Raymond Massey; *Dan Cutler,* Robert Preston; *Drusilla Alston,* Susan Hayward; *Captain Phillip Philpott,* Lynne Overman; *Mate of the* Tyfib, Charles Bickford; *Commodore Devereaux,* Walter Hampden; *Maum Maria,* Louise Beavers; *Mrs. Claiborne,* Elisabeth Risdon; *Mrs. Mottram,* Janet Beecher; *Aunt Henrietta Beresford,* Hedda Hopper; *Ivy Devereaux,* Martha O'Driscoll; *Widgeon,* Victor Kilian; *Salt Meat,* Oscar Polk; *Chinkapin,* Ben Carter; *The Lamb,* William Davis; *Sam,* Lane Chandler; *Judge Marvin,* Davidson Clark; *Captain of the* Pelican, Lou Merrill; *Doctor Jepson,* Frank M. Thomas; *Captain Carruthers,* Keith Richards; *Lubbock,* Victor Varconi; *Port Captain,* J. Farrell Macdonald; *Mace,* Harry Woods; *Master Shipwright,* Raymond Hatton; *Lieutenant Farragut,* Milburn Stone; *"Claiborne" Lookout,* Dave Wengren; *Cadge,* Tony Paton; *Charleston Ladies,* Barbara Britton, Julia Faye, Ameda Lambert; *Charleston Beaux,* D'Arcy Miller, Bruce Warren.

CREDITS

Directed and produced by Cecil B. DeMille. *Associate Producer,* William H. Pine. *Associate Director,* Arthur Rosson. *Screenplay by* Alan LeMay, Charles Bennett, *and* Jesse Lasky, Jr. *Based on a story by* Thelma Strabel. *Photography by* Victor Milner, A.S.C., *and* William V. Skall, A.S.C. *Underwater Photography by* Dewey Wrigley, A.S.C. *Art Directors,* Hans Dreier *and* Roland Anderson. *Editor,* Anne Bauchens. *Sound Recorders,* Harry Lindgren *and* John Corps. *Special Effects,* Gordon Jennings, A.S.C., W. L. Pereira, *and* Farciot Edouart, A.S.C. *Musical Score,* Victor Young. *Color by Technicolor. Running time, 124 minutes.*

Drusilla hides in a basket aboard the doomed ship
(Susan Hayward)

THE STORY

Loxi Claiborne (Paulette Goddard), owner, and Philpott (Lynne Overman), captain, put a Key West salvage schooner to sea in a hurricane to aid a ship wrecked nearby. But when they arrive, King Cutler (Raymond Massey), his brother Dan (Robert Preston), and their salvage crew are already there, and the captain of the wrecked ship, Jack Stuart (John Wayne), is lashed to the mast.

Captain Stuart tells Loxi, who has nursed him back to health, that losing his ship may cost him command of the *Southern Cross,* newest steamship of the Devereaux Line. She goes to Charleston with her cousin Drusilla Alston (Susan Hayward), who is secretly Dan Cutler's girl. They meet Stephen Tolliver (Ray Milland), sea lawyer for Devereaux, and Loxi tries to convince him that Captain Stuart's ship was wrecked by pirates. Tolliver is sent to Key West to break up the pirate ring, carrying Stuart's commission in his pocket. Stuart will get it if his name is cleared.

King Cutler tries to do away with Tolliver. There is a big fight and Cutler and his men are beaten, but in the battle Tolliver loses Stuart's commission to the *Southern Cross.* Stuart believes that the lawyer has double-crossed him, because by now both men are in love with Loxi. Furious, Stuart makes a deal with Cutler to wreck the *Southern Cross* and takes command of the steamship on its maiden run to Key West.

Drusilla, anxious to see Dan again, asks the captain to take her with him to Key West, but Stuart refuses, knowing the ship will not reach its destination in one piece. The girl, unseen by Stuart, hides in a big basket on board.

The *Southern Cross,* hit by a hurricane, strikes the jagged rocks of Key West and sinks. Tolliver suspects it was intentional and accuses Captain Stuart of wrecking the ship. At the trial, a witness reveals that Drusilla Alston was on board and killed in the wreck.

Tolliver and Stuart don diver's suits and go under. Tolliver finds Drisilla's scarf, but the men are then attacked by a giant squid. Stuart realizes that Tolliver's testimony could condemn him and saves his life, losing his own, crushed by the monster.

When Tolliver is brought to the surface, he shows the scarf to Dan, who charges his brother with piracy and with the murder of his sweetheart. King shoots him, and Tolliver then shoots King Cutler to death.

As she comforts the dying Dan Cutler, Loxi looks at Stephen with love.

REVIEWS

"The film is a typical DeMille spectacle, based on what the director calls a free adaptation of Thelma Strabel's novel about the vicious wreckers of Key West.

"The story has given DeMille plenty of exciting situations to direct, and some spectacular sea scenes as background for the action."

Loxi teases Drusilla about her secret romance with Dan Cutler (Susan Hayward and Paulette Goddard)

Dan Cutler gives his Drusilla a mantilla (Susan Hayward and Robert Preston)

NOTES

NEW YORK TIMES *Bosley Crowther*

"After thirty years of making motion pictures, Cecil B. DeMille has pretty well learned the trade. . . . Thus it is not surprising that *Reap the Wild Wind,* his anniversary film, is the essence of all his experience, the apogee of his art and as jam-full a motion picture as has ever played two hours upon a screen. . . .

". . . Susan Hayward and Robert Preston handle lesser roles in true romantic style."

NEW YORK POST *Archer Winsten*

"*Reap the Wild Wind* is a massive and colorful tapestry in which technical proficiency deserves the top honors. Mr. DeMille's thirty years in the industry have been notable for spectacles making the hardest demands upon motion picture technique rather than for artistic merit. . . .

". . . Distinguished performances are not possible in a DeMille pageant. But among those who are adequate and more than adequate in looks are Paulette Goddard, Susan Hayward, Ray Milland and John Wayne."

Susan's sugary role with Robert Preston (they had both been in *Beau Geste*) made a lasting impression. This was also her second movie with Ray Milland (also in *Beau Geste*), although this time they were not the lovers, and it was the only film she ever made under the direction of the "master," Cecil B. DeMille.

The film cost over $2 million and the giant squid, alone, about $12,000. This was one of the great achievements of Paramount's engineering department. Most of the underwater scenes were filmed off the island of Santa Catalina, and a 1-million-gallon tank was built at the Pacific Marine Museum in Santa Monica for the studio shots. They also filmed on location for eight weeks, in South Carolina and Key West, and off the Florida Cape.

After this movie, which was her third important film and the second to open at Radio City Music Hall, Paramount considered that Susan was ready for a starring role in her next movie.

Reap the Wild Wind won two Oscar nominations—for Art and Set Direction and Cinematography—and got the award for Special Effects.

When the movie was re-released in 1954, Wayne and Hayward, by then popular stars, got top billing over Milland and Goddard, whose fame was declining.

71

The Forest Rangers

Paramount, 1942

CAST

Don Stuart, Fred MacMurray; *Celia Huston,* Paulette Goddard; *Tana Mason,* Susan Hayward; *Jammer Jones,* Lynne Overman; *Twig Dawson,* Albert Dekker; *Mr. Huston,* Eugene Pallette; *Frank Hatfield,* Regis Toomey; *Jim Lawrence,* Rod Cameron; *Terry McCabe,* Clem Bevans; *George Tracy,* James Brown; *Ranger,* Kenneth Griffith; *Ranger,* Keith Richards; *Mr. Hanson,* Jimmy Conlin.

CREDITS

Directed by George Marshall. *Screenplay by* Harold Shumate. *Based on a story by* Thelma Strabel. *Technicolor direction by* Natalie Kalmus. *Art Directors,* Hans Dreier and Karl Hedrick. *Film Editor,* Paul Weatherwax. *Photography,* Charles Lang, Jr., A.S.C. *Process photography,* Farciot Edouart, A.S.C. *Color Camera,* William V. Skall, A.S.C. *Special Photographic Effects,* Gordon Jennings, A.S.C. *Sound Recording,* Harry Mills and Richard Olson. *Music score by* Victor Young. *Songs by* Frank Loesser, Joseph Lilley, *and* Frederick Hollander. *Running time, 86 minutes.*

As Tana Mason

Don and Tana prepare to fly with Frank, not suspecting that he is the perpetrator of the fires (Fred MacMurray, Susan Hayward, and Regis Toomey)

THE STORY

When suspicious fires hit Bolderoc National Forest, Don Stuart (Fred MacMurray), district ranger, goes to Hallis, a nearby town, searching for the firebug. Hallis is having its annual frontier fiesta, and Don finds instead Celia Huston (Paulette Goddard), a lovely but pampered debutante, daughter of a retired tycoon from the East (Eugene Pallette). Don marries Celia and takes her back to the ranger station.

Everyone thinks that Don has made a mistake, particularly Jammer Jones (Lynne Overman). Don should have married Tana Mason (Susan Hayward), owner of the Mason Lumber Company, who is in love with him.

Tana's rival in the lumber business, Twig Dawson (Albert Dekker), is suspected of starting the fires, and Don heads for the high Sierras to investigate. Tana drives him and manages to show up Celia as a tenderfoot, which has the desired effect on Don.

When fires break out again, after Twig Dawson has been murdered, Don decides to close the forest to visitors. Tana could lose everything, but she pitches in with the crew when a blaze gets out of control. "Smoke Jumpers," the paratroops of the forest service, are dropped along the fire line to start back fires with flame throwers, and a forest service observation plane, piloted by Frank Hatfield (Regis Toomey), spots the path of the fire for the men on the ground. Hatfield is in love with Tana Mason.

Celia, jealous of Tana's ability to work alongside of Don, drives a truck with food and hot coffee for the firefighters. Tana rides back with her and suddenly they are cut off by the fire. The truck was a two-way radio and they notify Don, who takes off in Hatfield's plane, intending to jump and rescue them. Before they get there, Don finds out that Hatfield is the firebug. Hatfield admits it, but knocks Don unconscious, sets the plane on fire, and jumps out, but his chute carries him into the flames and death.

Don recovers in time to jump out of the burning plane and lands near the girls in the truck. He finds Tana trembling with fear under a soaked tarpaulin while his wife Celia, the tenderfoot, bravely battles the flames with a power pump that had been dropped by parachute. He realizes that he married the right girl after all.

REVIEWS

NEW YORK TIMES *T.S.*

"Put a producer outdoors with a Technicolor camera, and before you can say pyromaniac you have an arsonist on your hands. 'Let's make a bonfire,' he mutters with a slightly mad gleam in his eyes, and reaches for his flint and steel. Thus is born another tale of the tall timbers complete with conflagrations, he-men and women like cats.

"A good deal of film goes over the sprockets while Miss Hayward subjects Miss Goddard to the vicissitudes of frontier life—log jumping and sleeping al fresco with one blanket for three."

Whatever Jammer is saying makes Tana ponder (Lynne Overman and Susan Hayward)

Tana and Celia are trapped by the flames (Susan Hayward and Paulette Goddard)

NEW YORK POST   *Irene Thirer*

"Both girls, Paulette and Susan, are a joy in Technicolor, with the gorgeous Goddard wardrobe, of course, showing to better advantage than the Hayward britches. But Susan's hair wins out."

NEW YORK DAILY NEWS   *Wanda Hale*

"Hayward does fine with her catty, determined female."

NOTES

Director Marshall, a stickler for authenticity, included color shots of real forest fires. Camera crews, equipped with special heat-resistant film magazines, went on location near Missoula, Montana, with the Rangers of the U.S. Forest Service and filmed scenes of the famous "Smoke Jumpers" in action. The crews also flew to Lakeview, Oregon, where they covered an actual forest fire, from both the air and the ground. Not until their heat-resistant film started to smoke did they retreat.

Paulette's hairdo was designed by her Mexican artist-friend Diego (Rivera), and she had a beautiful wardrobe. In contrast, Susan had to wear masculine clothes but, far from putting her at a disadvantage, she looked more beautiful than ever, making MacMurray's scorning of her a bit unbelievable.

This was Susan's second movie with Goddard and the last in which they shared scenes. (In their third, *Star Spangled Rhythm,* they never appeared together.)

The ending is ridiculous. Throughout, Hayward is the strong one, the lumber mill operator who faces all situations like a man—and all of a sudden she's afraid of being trapped by the fire, is saved by the city girl, and suffers an undignified dowsing of her "derrière" by Paulette's hose.

75

Estelle's father introduces Wooley at the party in his honor (Susan Hayward, Robert Warwick, Fredric March, and bit player Bess Flowers seated at the right table)

I Married a Witch

UNITED ARTISTS, 1942

CAST

Wallace Wooley, Fredric March; *Jennifer,* Veronica Lake; *Dr. Dudley White,* Robert Benchley; *Estelle Masterson,* Susan Hayward; *Daniel,* Cecil Kellaway; *Margaret,* Elizabeth Patterson; *J. B. Masterson,* Robert Warwick; *Tabitha,* Eily Malyon; *Town Crier,* Robert Greig; *Martha,* Viola Moore; *Nancy,* Mary Field; *Harriet,* Nora Cecil; *Allen,* Emory Parnell; *Vocalist,* Helen S. Rayner; *Justice of the Peace,* Aldrich Bowker; *His Wife,* Emma Dunn.

CREDITS

Directed and produced by Rene Clair. *Screenplay by* Robert Pirosh *and* Mark Connelly. *Based on a story by* Thorne Smith. *Story completed by* Norman Matson. *Photography by* Ted Tetzlaff. *Editor,* Eda Warren. *Running time, 82 minutes.*

THE STORY

In the year 1690, in New England, two witches were burned at the stake by members of the Wooley family. The witches, a father and his daughter, put a curse on the Wooley family: no male of the breed will ever find happiness in marriage. This proves true for generations.

Around 1940, we find Wallace Wooley (Fredric March), witch-burner's descendant and candidate for governor, about to marry Estelle Masterson (Susan Hayward), the beautiful daughter of an influential publisher who's backing him, J. B. Masterson (Robert Warwick).

During a party in Wooley's honor, lightning strikes the tree where the witches were imprisoned, and they materialize, first as smoke puffs, later taking human form. Daniel (Cecil Kellaway), the father, and Jennifer (Veronica Lake), the daughter, are still planning vengeance on the Wooleys.

When Jennifer meets Wooley, her plans to make him unhappy start to falter. Instead, she starts mixing love potions to woo him and stop him from marrying Estelle. Wooley goes on with his plans, so she and her father interrupt the wedding with a hex-induced hurricane right inside the church. Later, Estelle finds Wooley in Jennifer's arms and calls off the marriage.

Wooley is now under Jennifer's spell and she is in love with him so, on their wedding night, she confesses that she is a witch. He doesn't believe her but, to prove her point, she uses witchcraft on the ballots and Wooley wins an election that was practically lost when he disgraced himself publicly. But Jennifer finds out that love is eroding her powers as a witch.

Daniel is angry at his daughter for revealing her secret to Wooley and threatens her with extinction. She contrives to shut him up in a bottle and begs Wooley to flee with her from the devilment of her father. They try to escape, but at the stroke of midnight, Jennifer's spirit leaves her body, returning to the witches.

Love proves stronger than witchcraft and, years later, Jennifer and Wooley, happily married, watch their children play. Their blonde daughter, wearing her hair over one eye, is riding a broomstick.

REVIEWS

NEW YORK HERALD TRIBUNE   *Howard Barnes*

"Motion picture hocus-pocus is only good when it creates persuasive illusion. *I Married a Witch* wavers back and forth between captivating conceits and conventional Hollywood cliches. The cliches, unfortunately, have the best of it."

Is everything finally ready for the much-interrupted wedding? (Susan Hayward, Robert Benchley, and Robert Warwick)

NEW YORK TIMES   *Bosley Crowther*

"Mr. Clair, in his old pre-Hollywood fashion, has a lot of fun with spooks and camera tricks—a bit stiffly, perhaps, in comparison with the sport of his better French films, but still a high bounce above the usual run of cinematic whimsies."

BROOKLYN DAILY EAGLE   *Jane Corby*

"Susan Hayward is right as the wrong woman for Marsh."

Estelle has a way of winning all her arguments (Fredric March, Susan Hayward, and Robert Benchley)

At the hospital, Estelle is impatient to leave (Fredric March, Susan Hayward, and Robert Benchley)

NOTES

Hayward's billing did not make her at all happy, not after having had a taste of star billing in her previous flick. She felt that she was just standing on the sidelines while other starlets who came after her were making it big. Veronica Lake was one, and she was now a big star at Susan's own home studio. (Miss Lake's popularity was phenomenal during the war years.)

The special effects deserved an award, but they did not receive even a nomination. The music score, however, won an Oscar nomination, the only one for this movie.

Her role, although short, gave Hayward a chance to show her vixenish qualities. As March's fiancée, she was impertinent and obnoxious.

Her violent, exasperated walk up the aisle was one more skillful touch in a movie full of skillful touches.

Star-Spangled Rhythm

PARAMOUNT, 1942

CAST

Pop Webster, Victor Moore; *Jimmy Webster,* Eddie Bracken; *Polly Judson,* Betty Hutton; *G. B. De Soto,* Walter Abel; *Sarah,* Anne Revere; *Mimi,* Cass Daley; *Hi-Pockets,* Gil Lamb; *Mr. Fremont,* Edward Fielding; *Mac,* Edgar Dearing; *Duffy,* William Heade; *Sailors,* Maynard Hoomes, James Millican; *Tommy,* Eddie Johnson; *Playing themselves:* Bob Hope, Bing Crosby, Mary Martin, Fred MacMurray, Franchot Tone, Ray Milland, Dorothy Lamour, Vera Zorina, Dick Powell, Alan Ladd, Paulette Goddard, Veronica Lake, Rochester, William Bendix, Jerry Colonna, Macdonald Carey, Susan Hayward, Marjorie Reynolds, Betty Rhodes, Dona Drake, Lynne Overman, Gary Crosby, Johnnie Johnston, Ernest Truex, Katherine Dunham, Arthur Treacher, Walter Catlett, Sterling Holloway, Slim and Slam, The Golden Gate Quartet, Walter Dare, Wald and company, Cecil B. DeMille, Preston Sturges, and Ralph Murphy.

CREDITS

Directed by George Marshall. *Produced by* Joseph Sistrom. *Screenplay by* Harry Tugend. *Art Directors,* Hans Drier *and* Ernst Fegte. *Editor,* Arthur Schmidt. *Photography,* Leo Tover; *Music,* Robert Emmett Dolan. *Songs,* Johnny Mercer *and* Harold Arlen. *Running time, 99 minutes.*

THE STORY

Jimmy Webster (Eddie Bracken) and his shipmates are on leave in Los Angeles. Jimmy's girlfriend Polly (Betty Hutton) is the telephone operator at Paramount studios, and his father (Victor Moore) is a gateman who has told his sailor boy that he's head of the studio. One thing leads to another and the father "big shot" ends up promising his son that he'll get the Hollywood stars to put on a show for his buddies. Impossible, of course, but somehow it happens—and everybody's happy.

REVIEWS

"All this nonsense is excellent fun. The cast is all-star, even the bits being played by big names."

NOTES

The song "That Old Black Magic," sung by Johnny Johnston and danced by Vera Zorina, won an Oscar nomination.

One of the few advertisements on which you could see Susan's face or name

Eddie Bracken and Susan Hayward

Young and Willing

UNITED ARTISTS, 1943

CAST

Norman Reese, William Holden; *George Bodell,* Eddie Bracken; *Arthur Kenny,* Robert Benchley; *Kate Benson,* Susan Hayward; *Dottie Coburn,* Martha O'Driscoll; *Marge Benson,* Barbara Britton; *Tony Dennison,* James Brown; *Muriel Foster,* Florence MacMichael; *Mrs. Garnet,* Mabel Paige; *Mr. Coburn,* Jay Fassett; *1st Cop,* Paul Hurst; *2nd Cop,* Olin Howlin; *Phillips,* Billy Bevan.

CREDITS

Directed by Edward H. Griffith. *Produced by* Edward H. Griffith. *Screenplay by* Virginia Van Upp. *Based on a play by* Francis Swann. *Director of Photography,* Leo Tover, A.S.C. *Art Director,* Hans Drier *and* Ernst Fegte. *Editor,* Eda Warren. *Sound Recorders,* Harold Lewis *and* Don Johnson. *Costumes,* Edith Head. *Makeup,* Wally Westmore. *Running time, 83 minutes.*

THE STORY

Dottie Coburn's (Martha O'Driscoll) apartment in Greenwich Village is also home for Kate Benson (Susan Hayward), Marge Benson (Barbara Britton), Norman Reese (William Holden), George Bodell (Eddie Bracken), and Tony Dennison (James Brown). The three girls share one bedroom, the three boys the other bedroom.

All are unemployed actors and actresses dreaming of theatrical success, trying to make ends meet by doing demonstrations in store windows and the like. They hear that producer Arthur Kenny (Robert Benchley) has moved into the apartment below them, so they have to get his attention. They start by removing the radiator pipes to get a view of his apartment.

Kate befriends Kenny, who tells her that he used to live in that apartment years ago, before he became successful, and has kept it for sentimental reasons: he wrote his first play there. When he was unable to pay the rent, the landlady, Mrs. Garnet (Mable Paige), had locked him out and confiscated his trunk—with the play in it, probably.

It turns out that the kids have Kenny's manuscript and are rehearsing it, but they don't know who the author is.

Nothing is easy for them. Tony and Marge, secretly married, keep other secrets from each other: Tony has been inducted into the army and Marge is going to have a baby.

Dottie's father (Jay Fassett), who has been paying all the bills, arrives from Hoopsville, Illinois, and, fearing that he might want to take his daughter home, the boys pack up and leave. But Tony, having been away, walks right into the situation. Mr. Coburn is finally placated, but still wants his daughter to come home with him.

Then everybody finds out about Marge's baby and Tony's induction into the army, and things seem hopeless.

Kate is all smiles trying to get all she wants from Kenny (Robert Benchley and Susan Hayward)

Dottie's father and Muriel have their doubts about the girls' living arrangement (left to right: Barbara Britton, Jay Fassett, Martha O'Driscoll, Florence MacMichael, and Susan Hayward)

Producer Kenny doesn't seem too happy with the kids' ideas (left to right: Robert Benchley, Susan Hayward, Martha O'Driscoll, William Holden)

George tries his "acting" on fiancée Kate (Eddie Bracken and Susan Hayward)

Kenny discovers that his neighbors have his play *Mostly Murder* and is excited, so Norman takes advantage of the situation. He tells Kenny that they have lost the manuscript but have memorized all the parts. If he wants his play, therefore, he'll have to record it.

The private performance that follows is a hilarious mess, with cops crashing in to investigate the noise.

Dottie is ready to go back home when Kenny barges in with the news that the play, recorded with all the mixups and interruptions, has turned out to be the murder play burlesque of the season. It will be produced immediately, and all of them will get their chance. Dottie rushes back into Norman's arms.

REVIEWS

NEW YORK POST   *Irene Thirer*

"Not a weighty picture, but a light and laughable lot of histrionics which Edward H. Griffith directed amiably."

VARIETY   *Kahn*

"The four stars, William Holden, Eddie Bracken, Robert Benchley and Susan Hayward, along with the two featured performers, Martha O'Driscoll and Barbara Britton, do as well as can be expected with the lame script."

SCREENLAND

"The younger generation and those who at some time have thought of embarking on a theatrical career will get a lot of laughs out of this fun-filled comedy about would-be actors, who plot to interest a producer enough to have him sit through a rehearsal of their show."

NOTES

Francis Swann, author of the original play on which the movie was based, admitted the story was mostly the true experiences of his sister Lyn ("Kate" in the movie), a young New York actress trying to win fame, so Susan got in touch with Lyn, who was in Hollywood at the time, and obtained first-hand information on how to play her role.

The movie, made in 1942 and released in 1943, was her second with Robert Benchley who, along with Florence Mac-Michael and Mabel Paige, drew the best reviews.

Part of the wall decoration at the apartment shared by the boys and girls consisted of original playbills, such as *La Citta Morta* with Eleanora Duse, *Andrea* with Mrs. Leslie Carter, and *Hamlet* with Edwin Booth—a treasure for nostalgia collectors.

Hit Parade of 1943

Republic, 1943

J. MacClellan Davis joins Rick and Jill in a spontaneous trio (John Carroll, Susan Hayward, and Walter Catlett)

CAST

Rich Farrell, John Carroll; *Jill Wright,* Susan Hayward; *Toni Jarrett,* Gail Patrick; *Belinda Wright,* Eve Arden; *Bradley Cole,* Melville Cooper; *J. MacClellan Davis,* Walter Catlett; *Janie,* Mary Treen; *Westinghouse,* Tom Kennedy; *Joyce,* Astrid Allwyn; *Brownie,* Tim Ryan; *Playing themselves:* Jack Williams, the Harlem Sandman, Dorothy Dandridge, Pops and Louie, Music Maids, 3 Cheers, Chinita, Golden Gate Quartet, Freddy Martin and Orchestra, Count Basie and Orchestra, Ray McKinley and Orchestra.

CREDITS

Directed by Albert S. Rogell. *Produced by* Albert J. Cohen. *Original by* Frank Gill, Jr. *Additional dialogue by* Frances Hyland. *Photography,* Jack Marta. *Editor,* Thomas Richards. *Music Directors,* Walter Scharf, Jule Styne, *and* Harold Adamson. *Songs,* J. C. Johnson *and* Andy Razaf. *Orchestrations,* Marlin Skiles. *Dances,* Nick Castle. *Running time, 90 minutes.*

THE STORY

Like so many young hopefuls, Jill Wright (Susan Hayward) comes to New York from the Midwest hoping to "make it" as a songwriter. Having paid fifty dollars to the Miracle Song Publishing Company to have a song published, she wants to meet the firm's two partners, Rick Farrell (John Carroll) and J. MacClellan Davis (Walter Catlett). She suspects that they are not quite honest and wants to find out what has happened to her song.

Her suspicions are proven right when she discovers that Farrell has stolen her song, changing its name and capitalizing on its success. Jill's cousin, Belinda (Eve Arden), a sophisticated New Yorker, advises her to expose Farrell at once, but when Rick asks Jill to "ghostwrite" his songs, on a fifty-fifty basis, she plans a better form of revenge. She agrees to write the songs for him and, when his name is better known, she will expose him, which will be even more humiliating for him.

Jill had not counted on Rick's charm and, when she gets to know him better, falls in love with him. Toni Jarrett (Gail Patrick), an unscrupulous songstress, who is also in love with Rick, gets insanely jealous.

Rick, who has fallen in love with Jill, plans to reveal her as the true composer of his forthcoming song "Change of Heart," but Toni, not about to give him up, tells Jill that she and Farrell are engaged. Jill is heartbroken and thinks that she must have been right: Rick was a crook and a double-crosser. She refuses to see him.

Believing that he can set things straight if he announces her as the author of the new song, Rick tries to make all the arrangements, but finds that Toni, who has furthered her career through her friendship with Bradley Cole (Melville Cooper), manager of the country's most important bands, has talked Bradley into forbidding his orchestra to play Farrell's songs.

Rick hears that a bond-selling broadcast will play any tune on the air, if whoever makes that request buys a bond. He raises enough money to make the purchase and have them play Jill's song. In the meantime, J. MacClellan Davis, Rick's partner, goes to see Jill. He convinces her that Toni framed Rick, and that Rick really loves her, Jill.

They rush to the broadcasting station and Jill gets there just in time to accompany Rick as he sings her song.

REVIEWS

NEW YORK DAILY NEWS   *Wanda Hale*

"In trying so hard to make *Hit Parade of 1943* a gorgeous musical spectacle, the producers have made only a wasteful, trying picture."

VARIETY   *Abel*

"Miss Hayward registers as the not so naive ingenue who knows how to handle herself in the clinches."

NOTES

The movie has so many musical numbers that it was a miracle there was enough time left for a story at all.

This was Hayward's second movie for Republic (the first was *Sis Hopkins*) and she "sang" in both. Besides "Change of Heart," which was nominated among the "best songs," Susan mouthed "Who Took Me Home Last Night?" and "Harlem Sandman," plus a duet with John Carroll, "That's How You Write a Song."

Eve Arden, Susan's cousin in the movie, had the best lines and displayed her own acid style.

The title was later changed to that of the nominated song, "Change of Heart," perhaps to dissociate it from the "Hit Parade" series, or to bring it up to date by not mentioning the year.

Three famous band leaders and their orchestras were featured: Ray McKinley, Freddy Martin, and Count Basie, plus the Golden Gate Quartet; the film was also nominated for its "music score."

Singer Dorothy Dandridge appeared long before her *Carmen Jones* days; the beautiful "other woman" of the thirties, Astrid Allwyn, had a brief role, the last of her career.

Is this the way to "create" a song? (Mary Treen, John Carroll, and Susan Hayward)

(Top), Jill is driving Belinda crazy with her ideas (Eve Arden and Susan Hayward)

Jack London

UNITED ARTISTS, 1944

CAST

Jack London, Michael O'Shea; *Charmian Kittredge*, Susan Hayward; *Freda Maloof*, Osa Massen; *Professor Hilliard*, Harry Davenport; *Old Tom*, Frank Craven; *Mamie*, Virginia Mayo; *George Brett*, Ralph Morgan; *Mammy Jenny*, Louise Beavers; *Kerwin Maxwell*, Jonathan Hale; *Captain Tanaka*, Leonard Strong; *"Lucky Luke" Lannigan*, Paul Hurst; *Scratch Nelson*, Regis Toomey; *Mike*, Hobart Cavanaugh; *Mailman*, Olin Howlin; *French Frank*, Albert Van Antwerp; *Whiskey Bob*, Ernie Adams; *Red John*, John Kelly; *Captain Allen*, Robert Homans; *Richard Harding Davis*, Morgan Conway; *James Hare*, Edward Earle; *Fred Palmer*, Arthur Loft; *English Correspondent*, Lumsden Hare; *American Correspondent*, Brooks Benedict; *Geisha Dancer*, Mei Lee Foo; *Hiroshi*, Robert Katcher; *American Consul*, Pierre Watkin; *Japanese General*, Paul Fung; *Interpreter*, Charlie Lung; *Japanese Official*, Bruce Wong; *Japanese Sergeant*, Eddie Lee; *Spider*, John Fisher; *Victor*, Jack Roper; *Axel*, Sven Hugo Borg; *Pete*, Sid Dalbrook; *Commissioner*, Davison Clark; *Literary Guests*, Harold Minjir, Roy Gordon, Torben Mayer; *Bit Child*, Charlene Newman; *Bit Father*, Edmund Cobb; *Theodore Roosevelt*, Wallis Clark; *William Loeb*, Charles Miller; *Japanese Ambassador*, Richard Loo; *Cannery Foreman*, Dick Curtis; *Cannery Woman*, Sarah Padden; *Indian Maid*, Evelyn Finley; *Chairman's Secretary*, Rose Plummer.

CREDITS

Directed by Alfred Santell. *Produced by* Samuel Bronston. *Screenplay by* Ernest Pascal. *Based on* The Book of Jack London *by* Charmian London. *Photography by* John W. Boyle, A.S.C. *Art Director*, Bernard Herzbrun. *Film Editor*, William Ziegler. *Sound*, Ben Winkler. *Set Dressing*, Earl Wooden. *Wardrobe*, Maria Donovan *and* Arnold McDonald. *Assistant Director*, Sam Nelson. *Special Effects*, Harry Redmond. *Musical Director*, Fred Rich. *Unit Manager*, Ben Berk. *Dialogue Director*, Edward Padula. *Running time, 92 minutes.*

THE STORY

This is the story of the famous author, war correspondent, and adventurer Jack London (Michael O'Shea).

As an oyster pirate he leads a lawless existence and is involved in a tempestuous romance with Mamie (Virginia Mayo). He is satisfied with his roisterous life until his best friend Scratch Nelson (Regis Toomey) gets killed by the Fish Patrol. This tragedy makes Jack become of age, and he leaves Mamie to sail on a sealing schooner to the Bering Sea.

It was a long, cruel voyage and Jack had to fight for his life, but out of this experience he drew the colorful, interesting characters that made his works so great.

Charmian comforts and encourages London to fight for his ideal (Michael O'Shea and Susan Hayward)

London's publisher and Charmian are proud of London's stories about Japan (Ralph Morgan and Susan Hayward)

Charmian Kittredge, lady in waiting . . . for the love of Jack London (Susan Hayward)

His desire for adventure still strong, he sets out for Alaska and the Yukon gold fields. There he finds trails that help him understand himself, and his Alaskan stories bring him recognition as one of America's best authors.

His life gains real meaning, however, when he meets Charmian Kittredge (Susan Hayward), with whom he falls in love. Charmian was already in love with the author through his books, but is afraid of being disappointed in the man. Jack wins her love, but when a new adventure comes his way, he leaves to become a war correspondent. His publisher, George P. Brett (Ralph Morgan), tries to comfort Charmian during his absence.

The Boer War had just ended when he arrived in London on his way to Africa, so he returns home. He and Charmian make plans for their wedding. Their plans are interrupted by his assignment to cover the Russo-Japanese War. Charmian is disappointed, but realizes that she cannot keep him home.

London arrives in Japan with Richard Harding Davis (Morgan Conway) and Jimmy Hare (Edward Earle) but finds that the Japanese will not let any American correspondent visit the war front. Jack is determined to get there and he does, eluding the thick net of diplomacy. Once there, although constantly watched by Japanese Captain Tanaka (Leonard Strong), he manages to give his eyewitness accounts to the world. He is arrested for taking pictures of atrocities committed by the Japanese and is released only through the intervention of the President of the United States, Theodore Roosevelt.

Home again, he lets America know the menace that Japan poses with its plans to conquer the world. Aided by the love of his Charmian and the cares of Mammy Jenny (Louise Beavers), he dedicates the rest of his life to fighting for the truth.

REVIEWS

MORNING TELEGRAPH   *Leo Mishkin*

"The life of Jack London was a blood and thunder, stirring adventure story. . . . But it is to be doubted exceedingly whether it followed the pattern laid out in the new picture, simply and eloquently titled *Jack London.* For here many of the facts in the author's life are changed, glossed over, or deliberately ignored, and the result comes out not so much the life of Jack London, as just another dreamed up fictional movie biography. . . .

"Susan Hayward makes an appealing Charmian Kittredge, the girl whom London married.

VARIETY   *Kahn*

"Samuel Bronston has brought to the screen one of the great men of American letters, Jack London, and if ever there was a blood-and-guts subject for Hollywood treatment, London has long seemed a natural.

"For box office purposes one of the main snags to *London* is the fact that one of the film's two most important characters—Charmian London, the author's wife—fails to appear until the film has consumed half its running time. Susan Hayward is starred in the role."

NEW YORK HERALD TRIBUNE   *Bert McCord*

"Evincing many of the characteristics of James Cagney, Michael O'Shea is convincing in the title role, while Susan Hayward is quite charming in the part of the fiancee."

NOTES

This was Hayward's first portrayal of a true character, Charmian Kittredge, author of *The Book of Jack London*, on which the movie was based, with whom Susan was photographed in the sets of the movie.

It was said that Susan looked a lot like Mrs. London, but the same thing was said when she later portrayed Jane Froman, Lillian Roth, and even Barbara Graham. Perhaps she did.

This was the first picture she made for United Artists—the two others released under their banner were really Paramount products sold to this studio.

John Garfield was first considered for the role of London but was not available. Michael O'Shea was chosen and, although the reviewers compared him physically with Spencer Tracy and James Cagney, he lacked their personal dynamics.

Virginia Mayo, who had a small role in the movie, eventually married Michael O'Shea.

The film was Hayward's second under director Alfred Santell (the first was *Our Leading Citizen*) and got a music score nomination.

It has been credited as a 1943 release, but it was not released in New York until 1944.

The Fighting Seabees

Dennis O'Keefe and Susan Hayward

REPUBLIC, 1944

Daydreaming? Connie doesn't seem to be interested in writing for the moment (Susan Hayward)

CAST

Wedge Donovan, John Wayne; *Constance Chesley,* Susan Hayward; *Lieutenant Commander Robert Yarrow,* Dennis O'Keefe; *Eddie Powers,* William Frawley; *Johnny Novasky,* Leonid Kinskey; *Sawyer Collins,* J. M. Kerrigan; *Whanger Spreckles,* Grant Withers; *Ding Jacobs,* Paul Fix; *Yump Lumkin,* Ben Welden; *Lieutenant Kerrick,* William Forrest; *Captain Joyce,* Addison Richards; *Joe Brick,* Jay Norris; *Juan,* Duncan Renaldo.

CREDITS

Directed by Howard Lydecker *and* Edward Ludwig. *Produced by* Albert J. Cohen. *Screenplay by* Borden Chase *and* Aeneas MacKenzie. *Original story by* Borden Chase. *Photography by* William Bradford. *Editor,* Richard Van Enger. *Musical Score by* Walter Scharf. *Running time, 100 minutes.*

THE STORY

Donovan (John Wayne) goes to the deck to meet his work crew, returning from a job in the Pacific, only to learn that many of his men were killed or injured by the Japanese. Commander Yarrow (Dennis O'Keefe) explains that the law prohibits arming civilians; this angers Donovan, who decides to do something about it.

In Washington, his efforts to get his men armed are futile and he goes to the island to lead the crew himself. On the ship, he meets Connie (Susan Hayward), Bob Yarrow's girl, who is on her way to join her fiancé. They like each other, but Donovan has more important things on his mind.

Yarrow is in charge of the naval station where he and his crew will be doing the construction, and Connie's presence does not help to ease the situation between the two men. The Japanese attack and Donovan, without Yarrow's permission, arms his crew and fights back. The casualties include Connie, who, thinking she's going to die, confesses to Donovan that she's in love with him. (She recovers from her wound.) This is too much for Yarrow, who accuses his rival of being personally responsible for the tragedy.

Back in Washington, Donovan finally gets his point across. He wants his men to be part of construction battalions—equipped to fight as well as build—attached to the navy. Yarrow, putting his personal dislikes aside, recognizes the merit of this idea and joins forces with Donovan to create this new branch of the services. The Seabees are born, and Donovan becomes the officer in charge.

Again, Donovan and Yarrow are together in the Pacific, and Yarrow instructs him to ignore the snipers and concentrate his efforts on building. Donovan follows orders until one of his pals is killed. Then he orders his men to clear out the Japs. A savage battle ensues, and Japanese troops get reinforcements. The Americans are surrounded and a valuable oil depot is threatened. Yarrow is wounded and tells Donovan that the oil must be saved.

John Wayne and Susan Hayward

What more can a girl ask for? She has two handsome escorts . . . (John Wayne, Susan Hayward, and Dennis O'Keefe)

Donovan rushes into the thick of the battle, sets fire to one of the oil tanks, and the Japanese are wiped out. Donovan dies a hero.

Commander Yarrow is sent back to the States to recover from his injuries. He is reconciled with Connie. Together, they watch the ceremony in which Donovan is awarded the medal of honor, posthumously.

REVIEWS

NEW YORK WORLD-TELEGRAM   *Alton Cook*

"*The Fighting Seabees* takes the screen today back to the spectacular and romantic style of picturing war, a fashion that the movies lately had properly abandoned to such enterprises as a Coney Island side show."

NEW YORK MORNING TELEGRAPH   *Leo Mishkin*

"Now it's the Seabees who come in for their share of credit in the movies. Nothing less than *The Fighting Seabees*. . . .

"There's a girl bouncing in and out of the proceedings, Susan Hayward, no less, playing the role of a newspaper reporter."

NEW YORK POST   *Archer Winsten*

"The performers are not to blame. Miss Hayward didn't put herself on an atoll, nor, doubtless, did she ask to be wounded."

NOTES

Ballyhooed as Republic's most expensive film to date, it was a box office hit. This was the only "war propaganda" picture Susan made during World War II. It was a typical war movie of that time, with the Japanese being called "Japs" or "monkeys." Not until after the war were they considered people again.

Seabees was her second movie with John Wayne (after *Reap the Wild Wind*) and her third and last for Republic. Susan was gaining recognition and this studio couldn't afford her growing salary.

The "happy ending" was absurd: since she couldn't have Wayne, she took second best, O'Keefe. Reviewers complained about the "forced romance triangle."

The movie received an Oscar nomination in the music score category.

Connie is amused by the goings on at a party, but Donovan looks perplexed (left to right: Susan Hayward, Dennis O'Keefe, John Wayne, and William Frawley)

Donovan's men are despondent about not being able to defend themselves from Japanese attacks (left to right): William Frawley, J. M. Kerrigan, Susan Hayward, John Wayne, Grant Withers

The Hairy Ape

UNITED ARTISTS, 1944

CAST

Hank Smith, William Bendix; *Mildred Douglas,* Susan Hayward; *Tony Lazar,* John Loder; *Helen Parker,* Dorothy Comingore; *Paddy,* Roman Bohnen; *Long,* Tom Fadden; *MacDougald,* Alan Napier; *Gantry,* Charles Cane; *Aldo,* Raphael Storm; *Portuguese Proprietor,* Charles La Torre; *Concertina Player,* Don Zolaya; *Waitress,* Mary Zavian; *Police Captain,* George Sorrel; *Doctor,* Paul Welgal; *Musician,* Egon Brecher; *Refugee Wife,* Gesela Werbsek; *Young Girl,* Carmen Rachel; *Water Tender,* Jonathan Lee; *Third Engineer,* Dick Baldwin; *Head Guard,* Ralph Dunn; *Lieutenant,* William Halligan; *Doorman,* Tommy Hughes; *Bartender,* Bob Perry.

CREDITS

Directed by Alfred Santell. *Produced by* Jules Levey. *Screenplay by* Robert D. Andrews *and* Decla Dunning. *Original play by* Eugené O'Neill. *Film Editor,* Harvey Manger. *Music Score,* Eddie Paul. *Running time, 92 minutes.*

THE STORY

Mildred Douglas (Susan Hayward) is a wealthy, spoiled society girl traveling home from Europe in a steam freighter that is carrying a good number of refugees from the war, among them Helen Parker (Dorothy Comingore).

Mildred, who is continually looking for new things to amuse her, picks Tony Lazar (John Loder), the ship's second engineer, for her shipboard romance and proceeds to seduce him. That Helen is in love with Lazar makes the affair all the more interesting.

Mildred persuades Tony to show her the stokehole and, although women are not allowed there, he takes her. She dresses in white for the occasion.

Hank (William Bendix), the chief stoker, has been shoveling coal furiously, trying to keep up with the whistle of the engineers demanding more steam. He is covered with soot and sweat and is near the point of exhaustion, but he is childishly proud of his job, loves the ship, and believes himself as good as if not better than the officers. Hank has the body of a

Mildred is terrified of Hank, and Lazar tries to calm him down (Susan Hayward, John Loder, and William Bendix)

brute and the mind of a child.

Mildred is terrified of Hank, who is cursing the engineers and their whistle. When he sees her watching him, she seems like a vision in a strange dream. He tries to come near her and Mildred screams "You hairy ape!" and runs back to the deck in a panic.

The big man, although hurt by her words, cannot keep her out of his mind. He finds her when they get to New York, but he can't get past the front door of her building as the doorman throws him out with the help of a policeman.

Hank goes to a circus where he sees a big gorilla in a cage. Her words come back—"You hairy ape!"—and he feels that he is really an ape. The gorilla is crushing a tire and Hank decides that he must crush the girl who uttered those words. He goes back to her building and manages to sneak in and up to her apartment. When Mildred sees him she panics and Hank realizes that, in a way, he has crushed her already.

Returning to the ship, Hank finds Lazar drunk and steals his confounded whistle. Now he's happy. He has finally made it and is at peace with himself and with the world.

REVIEWS

NEW YORK HERALD TRIBUNE   *Otis L. Guernsey, Jr.*

"After more than a score of years, Eugene O'Neill has allowed *The Hairy Ape* to be filmed. Its production by Jules Levey has turned out to be an anticlimax; the current film version is disappointing and bears only a shadowy resemblance to O'Neill's powerful social drama.

"Susan Hayward is appropriately hateful as the empty-minded rich girl who is frightened by the animalistic world of the stokehole. She achieves a good deal of villainy in spite of the wealth of corny dialogue that has been included in her scenes."

NEW YORK SUN   *Eileen Creelman*

"In a season noted for musicals and comedies there has now come a good husky drama. *The Hairy Ape,* based on Eugene O'Neill's play, strays far from its original. It still carries a punch, thanks to the forceful playing of William Bendix and Susan Hayward. Even a happy ending seems natural, as the script has made the story lighter and less loaded with social significance.

"Mildred Douglas, played most ably by Susan Hayward, is just an irritatingly self-absorbed girl."

TIME

"William Bendix is a likable and sincere actor, but his natural good temper shines fatally through his industrious soot-&-greasepaint toughness. Susan Hayward, as the girl who drives him crazy, is much tougher—too coarsely so for the size of the girl's penthouse or the height of her social standing—but she is more convincing. She is, in fact, Hollywood's ablest bitch-player."

NOTES

All the critics recognized Hayward as the last of the vamps, a Hollywood species on its way to extinction. Noticeably, the movie was not Paramount's, and she had an excellent role.

The movie was not a box office hit, perhaps because William Bendix, although a good actor, was not the popular "hero" type. Nevertheless, he fit the title perfectly, and this was probably his best performance and one of the few where he got top billing.

Dorothy Comingore, who made such a big impression in Orson Welles' *Citizen Kane,* made one of her rare screen appearances in a brief role.

The film won an Oscar nomination in the music score department.

Lazar tries to satisfy Mildred's every whim (John Loder and Susan Hayward)

Helen and Mildred try to find accommodations in the freighter's quarters (Dorothy Comingore and Susan Hayward)

And Now Tomorrow

Paramount, 1944

CAST

Dr. Marek Vance, Alan Ladd; *Emily Blair,* Loretta Young; *Janice Blair,* Susan Hayward; *Jeff Stoddard,* Barry Sullivan; *Aunt Em,* Beulah Bondi; *Dr. Weeks,* Cecil Kellaway; *Angeletta Gallo,* Helen Mack; *Joe,* Darryl Hickman; *Peter Gallo,* Anthony Caruso; *Dr. Sloane,* Jonathan Hale; *Bobby,* Conrad Binyon; *Patient,* Minerva Urecal; *Hester,* Connie Leon; *Emily —Age 7,* Ann Carter; *Dr. Vance—Age 12,* Merrill Rodin; *Janice—Age 4,* Eleanor Donahue; *Carrie,* Constance Purdy; *Receptionist,* Mae Clark; *Clerk,* Byron Foulger; *Nurse,* Mary Field; *Maid of Honor,* Doris Dowling; *Best Man,* Ronnie Rondell; *Charlie,* Doodles Weaver; *Waiter,* Jack M. Gardner; *Nurse,* Hazel Keener; *Truck Driver,* Jimmie Dundee; *Mr. Meade,* Alec Craig.

CREDITS

Directed by Irving Pichel. *Produced by* Fred Kohlmar. *Screenplay by* Frank Partos *and* Raymond Chandler. *Based on the novel by* Rachel Field. *Photography by* Daniel L Fapp. *Art Directors,* Hans Dreier *and* Hal Pereira. *Editor,* Duncan Mansfield. *Special Effects,* Farciot Edouart. *Music,* Victor Young. *Running time, 84 minutes.*

THE STORY

The Blair family, for generations the owners of textile mills in Blairstown, have just celebrated their daughter Emily's (Loretta Young) engagement to Jeff Stoddard (Barry Sullivan). That same night Emily develops meningitis and, as a result of her illness, becomes deaf.

Emily's sister, Janice (Susan Hayward), who had returned from Europe especially for the party, stays home, and while Emily is slowly recovering, she and Jeff fall in love, possibly because Emily's illness has drawn them together.

The family physician, Dr. Weeks (Cecil Kellaway), sends Emily to one specialist after another, but they cannot find a cure for Emily's deafness. Then a young surgeon from the other side of the tracks, Dr. Marek Vance (Alan Ladd), comes into the picture. He had never forgotten the Blair girls, although he had seen them only once when they were children. To him they were like creatures from another world: the rich world he had never known. He has developed a serum for deafness, but has tried it only on rabbits. He is reluctant to try it on Emily and, aside from that, they don't like each other. She considers him a presumptuous young man, and he thinks of her as a snob. Nevertheless, their association continues and when, in an emergency, she helps Dr. Vance administer the anesthesia when he has to perform a mastoidectomy on the child of mill workers Peter and Angletta Gallo (Anthony Caruso and Helen Mack), their feelings toward each other start to change.

Vance has learned of the growing attachment between Jeff and Janice, but Emily is not aware of it. Her wedding has been postponed because of her illness. She finally convinces Dr. Vance to give her the serum treatment and, although for days she hangs between life and death, when she regains consciousness she can hear again.

Janice, having learned about this, makes Jeff talk about their love and how they must sacrifice if for Emily's sake—right outside of Emily's room.

Emily, learning of their love for each other and the sacrifice they are willing to make for her, examines her own heart and realizes that it is Marek she really lvoes.

REVIEWS

MOTION PICTURE

"Susan Hayward and Barry Sullivan get the juiciest roles of their careers. . . .

"Irving Pichel directs, getting good value out of a romantic story that is slightly familiar . . . but well done."

NEW YORK TIMES   *Bosley Crowther*

"For a film in which the principal character, played by Loretta Young, is deaf, there is certainly a lot of conversation. . . .

"Susan Hayward and Barry Sullivan are a couple who mix up the plot in a thoroughly conventional fashion."

NEW YORK HERALD TRIBUNE   *Otis L. Guernsey, Jr.*

"The Rachel Field novel, *And Now Tomorrow,* about a rich girl who is seemingly doomed to lifelong deafness, has a somewhat shaky outline on the screen. . . . Even with Alan Ladd perfectly cast as a young doctor from the Blairstown slums who thinks he can cure his social enemy, the piece is too long and often only barely believable.

"Susan Hayward plays the sister, another predatory female."

NOTES

For the second time in her career, Susan was represented as a child in a movie. This time Eleanor Donahue played Janice Blair at age four. (Eleanor Donahue acquired TV fame in the fifties as Robert Young and Jane Wyatt's daughter in "Father Knows Best," as *Elinor* Donahue.) The child appeared in one brief flashback sequence and had nothing to say.

Hayward's role promised to be an "other woman" type of role, but, given her talent and capacity for wickedness in these roles, this one proved to be as disappointing as the movie itself. At the end Susan gets Barry Sullivan and Loretta Young gets Alan Ladd, the sisters remain good friends, and everybody lives happily ever after—except the reviewers.

Thus, Susan bid farewell to her Paramount years. It was the end of an era that she gave up with no regrets. She was sorry about the years she had lost there. Although her future was insecure (she left Paramount with no other contract), she had faith in herself and was determined that there would be no more "little sisters" or "other women" of the secondary type. The years to come speak for themselves.

Janice and Dr. Vance watch as Emily and Jeff dance to a waltz (Susan Hayward, Alan Ladd, Loretta Young, and Barry Sullivan)

To her surprise, she was besieged with offers after she left Paramount. Not that she didn't believe in herself, but she never considered herself "lucky enough to be the center of such litigations." She got offers from three very important producers: David O. Selznick, Samuel Goldwyn, and Walter Wanger, but she decided to wait a little to consider which one was best. After all, with twins on the way, she needed time off.

The twins, named Timothy and Gregory, were born prematurely, on February 19, 1945. She was one of the few movie stars ever to be blessed with twins, so the event made hot copy. Photographers and editors were after the proud parents for exclusive shots and stories, but Hayward didn't capitulate that easily. Some editors were so sore about her reluctance to publicize her private affairs that they carried a grudge for years. By the time she finally agreed to let the twins be photographed, they were fourteen weeks old. The photos made the rounds in many different magazines, including *Time*.

With the twins in 1945

Talking about the hectic courtship, she confessed, "I even had an engagement ring once. But when we had a disagreement I gave it back to him. When we made up again, the ring had been sold. Now we have the babies—but still I haven't got a ring!"

She was now ready to consider all the offers and, after serious thought and consulting her horoscope charts, she decided to accept Selznick's offer and went to see him. But when she arrived at his office and was told she'd have to wait an hour to see him, she walked away. She decided to sign with Walter Wanger, and this was a decision she was to be thankful for all her life.

A story went around about why Walter Wanger offered her a contract which was ridiculous and obviously false. Supposedly, the "four Paramount greats" at the time (Lamour, Colbert, Goddard, and Lake) got together and decided to talk Wanger into giving her a contract that would get rid of "scene stealer Hayward once and for all." (It is true, however, that Susan lost a role at Paramount more than once because the top female stars didn't want her in the same movie.)

Wanger not only made her a star, but started to give her mellower roles. If she did get a "bitchy" role, at least she had a chance to prove that she also had a good side. (Her last Paramount movie *And Now Tomorrow* had been that type.)

In 1945, after the twins, she took a rest; the two films she made that year were released in 1946. She was supposed to have played Ann Baxter's part in *The Razor's Edge,* for which Miss Baxter won a supporting actress Oscar. (This was the movie that marked Tyrone Power's return from the war, and Hayward would later star with him twice.)

In the meantime, she was filming at RKO the first movie ever in which she was top billed, *Deadline at Dawn,* based on a novel by William Irish and scripted by Clifford Odets. She was mentioned for Selznick's *Duel in the Sun,* which could have been her oddest role: as Pearl Chavez, the sultry half-breed. Would Susan have dyed her hair a dark brown for this part? (She never wore a wig or dyed her hair a different color. That was probably why she refused pictures in which the role demanded such things.)

Evicted, at the end of 1946

Judge Earl Warren congratulates Susan Hayward after watching *Smash-up*

With Walter Wanger and Martin Gabel

She was a likely candidate for the part of Amber St. Clair in the movie *Forever Amber*. It would have been a perfect part for her, the wench who grew to court prominence in England during the reign of Charles II. (The part went to Peggy Cummings, but the studio thought she looked too young and Amber was finally played by Linda Darnell.) *Deadline at Dawn*, released early in 1946, was considered an above average "whodunit."

Next Susan had her first release under Walter Wanger's tutelage, and her first western *Canyon Passage*, in Technicolor. The picture was filmed on location in Oregon. She was billed third, under Dana Andrews and Brian Donlevy (the Markoff of *Beau Geste*).

Later that year she had the first eviction of a few to follow, caused by her adorable twins, whom landlords didn't find so charming (Claudette Colbert among them).

Finally she got to play the part that was to be the turning point in her career: Angie Evans, the tormented alcoholic singer who sacrifices her career for her husband, a crooner, in *Smash-Up—The Story of a Woman*, originally called "A Woman Destroyed." The movie was filmed in 1946, and should have been released that year in order to be considered for the Oscars of 1947; yet it was released early in 1947, perhaps to put more time between this movie and *The Lost Weekend*, a similar story of an alcoholic that won the Oscar for Ray Milland in 1946. Hayward was "heard," dubbed again, this time by Peg La Centra, "singing" two songs: "I Miss the Feeling" and "Hush-a-bye Island." For the first time she felt she had arrived. She worked in an intensive promotion campaign for the movie, including a special screening for an audience of legislators at the California State Senate in Sacramento.

It was rumored that the movie was a left-handed biography of one of the country's top crooners and his troubled wife (Bing Crosby and Dixie Lee?). Susan's leading men were Lee Bowman and Eddie Albert. Her reviews were great. *Photoplay* chose her for their "Best Performances of the Month" column. *Life* magazine chose the film as "The Movie of the Week," and it was said that it would probably earn her an Academy Award nomination. *Silver Screen* again dedicated their page "We Point with Pride" to her, and they wrote: "One of the finest actresses in pictures, Susan Hayward, has a role in *Smash-Up*, which shows emphatically that they don't come any finer." And the *Daily Mirror* selected the film as movie of the week.

Smash-Up was a role in a million that Hayward played superbly. It was one of the strongest roles any actress had played up to that time, and it put her on the "map" as an actress.

After *Smash-Up*, she was finally a big star, which meant no more third or fourth billings and better movies. Wanger was proud of his "red-headed Bette Davis," as he tagged her. Joan Bennett, Wanger's wife during those years, was also her booster, and Susan and her husband attended all their parties, though the Barkers were not partygoers and Susan prized her privacy.

Producer Joan Harrison, Alfred Hitchcock's ex-assistant, sought her for *They Won't Believe Me*, an above-average thriller that was underrated. Hayward played scheming Verna Carlson to Robert Young's playboy Larry Ballantine, in a part that fitted her to perfection, except for the brevity of her footage (Young had two other leading ladies: Jane Greer and Rita Johnson). Susan was dispatched early by the plot; burned beyond recognition, she died in a car accident.

After the completion of the movie, she announced that she was through with posing for "pinup art." She had done a lot of it for this picture, and being now the proper mother of two-year-old twins, she was unwilling to continue this kind of publicity. (Nevertheless, she later posed for a few more "leg art" photos.) Her vital statistics at the time were weight: 110 lbs.; bust: 36"; waist: 24½; hips: 35½. They were to vary little during all the years to come. As late as 1952 she was still being praised for her figure and legs, and a magazine chose her among Hollywood's twelve most Leg-o-Genic actresses. (Yet the photograph in their display was one of the many taken in 1947 for *They Won't Believe Me*.) Susan herself considered her legs too thin and short. (She was short for a model anyway, only 5'3", and in some photos she looked as if she were four inches shorter.)

In 1947 she was reunited with Charles Boyer to do "Gaslight" on another radio show, CBS's "Screen Guild Players," in the role that Ingrid Bergman played in the movie version.

Her last movie released that same year was another underrated one: the exquisitely filmed version of Henry James' novel *The Aspern Papers*, entitled *The Lost Moment*. Her performance, as beautiful Tina Borderau, the split-personality guardian of her 105-year-old aunt Juliana, played by Agnes Moorehead (unrecognizable under the marvelous makeup of Bud Westmore), is one of the most brilliant of her roles during the forties. She was photographed to best advantage by Hal Mohr's camera, and it is regrettable that the movie wasn't filmed in Technicolor, but perhaps color would have detracted from the eery atmosphere of the musty Venetian sets. While she was making this movie she received an honorary membership card, presented to her by the First Families of Brooklyn, as a loyal Brooklynite.

Moment was her only movie that Martin Gabel directed. Their temperaments clashed from the beginning; Gabel wouldn't let anyone speak to her on the set to keep her in an "out-of-this-world" mood. They argued about this. Once, during a difficult take, Susan had a long speech and he kept stopping her just as she got to a certain word. On the twelfth take, she said, "Listen, my fine-feathered friend, I have been saying that word exactly as you told me to. If you stop me once more, I'm going to punch you right in the nose." He stopped her again, and she picked up a lamp and threw it at him.

Her private life was also troubled. She and Barker were on the verge of divorce, but were reunited by a marriage counselor.

By late 1947 she and Barker decided to purchase a home. They found a beautiful one in the San Fernando Valley, with a pool and tennis court. They erected a fence around the pool to prevent any kind of accident with the twins, like the one in which Lou Costello's little boy drowned in his pool.

Susan declared in a frank interview: "I know many people consider me a very temperamental and hard person. I don't think I'm temperamental. Oh, yes, I fight for the things I think are right. I point out mistakes around me, involving my work. I try to do my job as best as I can. I'm never late and I

The "last" of her cheesecake poses, for *They Won't Believe Me*

At her dressing room during shooting of *The Saxon Charm* in 1948

Frederic Wakeman (left), author of *The Saxon Charm,* visits with Audrey Totter and Susan Hayward on the set; producer Joseph Sistrom and scenarist-director Claude Binyon are standing

don't delay productions. People that are that unprofessional make me very angry: I can't stand them. When I work I want to work. If that is being temperamental, then I am. I haven't forgotten how I was kicked and pushed around when I first came to Hollywood. I should forgive, but I'm only human. Maybe I'm a bit too defensive. People I have known made me that way. Were they so friendly to me when I was a nobody?"

Early in 1948 she saw her dreams realized: she won an Academy Award nomination for her 1947 performance in *Smash-Up.* She got so excited that she bought a new gown to attend the award presentation. Loretta Young won for *Farmer's Daughter* over her friend Rosalind Russell, who was the favorite, for *Mourning Becomes Electra,* Dorothy McGuire, for *Gentlemen's Agreement,* Joan Crawford, for *Possessed,* and Hayward. Her much publicized gown, however, merited a few lines in movie magazines, which didn't stop Susan from wearing it again to the following year's Academy Awards. (This time she had to accept from Arlene Dahl an Oscar awarded for the musical score and art direction of *The Red Shoes.*) Some reviewers still feel that Hayward should have won her first Oscar for *Smash-Up.*

She went on location to North Carolina for her next movie venture, which was the closest she ever got to what made her go to Hollywood in the first place: *Gone With the Wind.* In this film, based on James Street's bestseller *Tap Roots,* she played "spitfire" southern heroine Morna Dabney. The movie was popular but the reviews were mixed. It suffered from comparisons with *Gone With the Wind.* She was photographed in "glorious Technicolor" again, and her leading man was Van Heflin. Among others in the cast was a very young Julie London in a "bitchy younger sister" role that resembled some of Hayward's old Paramount s roles.

This was her last movie with director George Marshall, with whom, apparently, she got along well. (Given the prologue he wrote, years after, for Doug McClelland's *The Divine Bitch,* a paperback that was the first book written about her.)

Her next film was *The Saxon Charm,* released almost immediately after *Tap Roots,* and based on a novel by Frederic Wakeman. The alienating main character, Matt Saxon, a Broadway producer, was played by Robert Montgomery, though Hayward's leading man was John Payne, another "victim" of "the Montgomery charm." Her Janet Bush was the weakest of all her roles at Universal. This could be because it was not a Walter Wanger production. She allowed them to cut her hair short for this role. Montgomery got the best reviews in this movie.

In an interview she said, "I can't stand people who come to me with a chip on the shoulder and demand that I do things. But I'm a softie for friends who treat me like a human being, and for them I'll do anything within reason. The only time my temper rises is when I get the phony approach—the snide, hypocritical attitude. Frankly, life is too short to bother with the insincere and the phony."

The following year she made her last movie under Wanger's contract, *Tulsa,* a 1949 release, one of her best adventure yarns. Hayward had been the original choice to play *Anna Lucasta* at Columbia Pictures, prior to the filming of *Tulsa,* but at the last minute Paulette Goddard was selected to play the controversial heroine. (The film had mixed reviews, on the bad side.)

Tulsa was one of the first movies where you could see some of the real Susan Hayward: ambitious, fighting all the way to the top. (There would be other heroines close to her own self: *I Can Get It for You Wholesale*—a scheming career-woman role; *The Lusty Men*—fighting for her man and her beliefs; *Untamed*—determination and bouncing back from misfortune; and *Valley of the Dolls*—a ruthless, aging star fighting to stay on top.)

Wanger, who had money troubles at the time because of his *Joan of Arc* with Ingrid Bergman, decided, regretfully, to sell her contract to Darryl F. Zanuck, the top 20th Century-Fox mogul, for $200,000, which was approximately what she would get annually under her new seven-year contract with Fox. Loyal as ever to her astrological signs, Susan declared in an interview: "I signed my contract with 20th at precisely 2:47 a.m. on the date that was presumably most advantageous. I had Western Union phone me a wire waking me up in time to stagger to my desk where I had the paper and the pen ready." Wanger commented, "When I sold Susan's contract it was with a mixture of relief and regret."

Between 1949 and 1950, 20th Century-Fox began to drop from their payroll the long reigning queens of the studio, due to changing currents, television, the beginning of the end of the studio era, and the belief that new faces were the answer to lure audiences back to the movies.

Nevertheless, Hayward, already an established star, had enough potential to carry her along, in spite of the decline of such Fox favorites as Linda Darnell, Gene Tierney, Anne Baxter, June Haver, Jeanne Crain, and Betty Grable, whose latest movies were not too successful at the box office.

Marilyn Monroe, soon to be labeled a "new" Betty Grable, was yet to become the most photographed star of the fifties; she and Hayward became the two top figures at Fox during the decade.

The trouble was not only Fox's: all the names from the two preceding decades were fizzling out. The careers of Davis, Hepburn, Garson, Fontaine, and Crawford were starting to sag. Irene Dunne, Loretta Young, and Margaret Sullavan could not survive the early fifties.

Beauties like Bennett, Lamarr, and Goddard were slipping, with personal problems or career slumps. The glamour of Montez, Lake, Lamour, Sheridan, and others was losing its appeal.

Even ex-child stars like Durbin, Garland, and Temple had had it by then.

Vivacious Carmen Miranda was showing signs of fatigue in her undemanding "specialty" roles. Hayworth had briefly retired with husband Aly Kahn, Ingrid Bergman exiled herself in Italy, and Esther Williams drowned on land by the mid-fifties. Jennifer Jones put her fire on ice in this decade (*Splendored Thing* aside), Merle Oberon never again found suitable roles, Yvonne de Carlo was trying hard to prove what a good comedienne she was, and Arlene Dahl looked like a good bet for stardom but never got there.

Few really interesting personalities were products of the fifties, like Marilyn Monroe, Elizabeth Taylor, Ava Gardner, and later, Audrey Hepburn, Kim Novak, and Shirley Mac-Laine. Actors fared better, but they always had.

The early fifties specialized in "sweet and innocent" actresses like June Allyson, Ann Blyth, Jane Powell, Debbie

Susan and husband Jess Barker don evening clothes and join the dinner crowd at Restaurant Chanteclair, in Hollywood, 1947

Reynolds, and Doris Day, all far from Hayward's film personality. There were also Deborah Kerr and Jean Simmons. And then there were Jane Wyman, a remnant of the thirties still popular, but never like Hayward, and Jane Russell, popping out of Hughes' brassieres and occasionally making movies.

Susan Hayward was an almost unique exception: a beautiful woman with more than ten years in the business who made the transition successfully. (Lana Turner was another exception.) Hayward went to greater glories in the fifties, no small feat, considering the times.

Zanuck was interested in getting her because "she has the two qualities most desired in any actress: she is beautiful, and she can act." She was considered some kind of "missing link" between the beauties and the actresses. As a beauty, she garnered yet another title in 1949: "The most beautiful girl in the world," from the American Beauticians Congress in San Francisco. As an actress, she had another disappointment when she lost a big role to Olivia de Havilland: the lead in Anatole Litvak's *The Snake Pit*. (Wanger and Zanuck had talked about giving this role to Susan, before her contract was sold, but the talks never materialized.)

In *Tulsa*, which was distributed by Eagle Lion by mid-1949, her beauty was at its peak, photographed in Technicolor, and she had one of her best "spitfire" roles as the ambitious oil queen Cherokee Lansing, "part Indian." Her co-stars were Robert Preston and Pedro Armendariz. The climactic fire was one of the best special effects in any movie of the forties, being used again and again, as stock footage, in numerous productions.

June and Alex are surprised by Gus at Edna's apartment
(Paul Lukas, Susan Hayward, and Bill Williams)

Deadline at Dawn

RKO RADIO, 1946

CAST

June Goffe, Susan Hayward; *Gus,* Paul Lukas; *Alex,* Bill Williams; *Bartelli,* Joseph Calleia; *Helen Robinson,* Osa Massen; *Edna Bartelli,* Lola Lane; *Lester Brady,* Jerome Cowan; *Sleepy Parsons,* Marvin Miller; *Collarless Man,* Roman Bohnen; *Man With Gloves,* Steven Geray; *Babe Dooley,* Joe Sawyer; *Mrs. Raymond,* Constance Worth; *Lieutenant Kane,* Joseph Crehan.

CREDITS

Directed by Harold Clurman. *Produced by* Adrian Scott. *Screenplay by* Clifford Odets. *Based on a novel by* William Irish. *Photography by* Nicholas Musuraca. *Editor,* Roland Gross. *Music Director,* C. Bakaleinikoff. *Music,* Hans Eisler. *Running time, 82 minutes.*

THE STORY

Alex (Bill Williams) is a young sailor on leave in New York City from Norfolk, Virginia. On his last night in the city, he gets involved in a poker game with a bunch of crooks at Bartelli's (Joseph Calleia) café.

Bartelli's sister, Edna (Lola Lane), lures Alex into her apartment and slips him a mickey. When he wakes up, Alex finds fourteen hundred dollars in his pocket that he believes he took from the girl's apartment. He walks around the city, not knowing quite what to do, and in a dancehall meets June (Susan Hayward), who works there. The girl is tired of her job as a dancing partner; her outlook on life is far from rosy. But Alex's honesty disarms her. She persuades Alex to return the money to Edna, but when they get there, they find Edna has been murdered.

Gus (Paul Lukas), the cabdriver who took them there, surprises them in Edna's apartment, but promises to help them prove Alex's innocence. Mrs. Raymond (Constance Worth) sneaks into the apartment trying to steal some letters accusing her of maintaining illicit relations with Lester Brady (Jerome Cowan). Later, at Lester's apartment, Bartelli, who heard about his sister's murder, knocks Alex unconscious with the butt of his gun.

Alex has only a few hours left before he has to go back to Norfolk. Together at the murdered girl's apartment, June, Gus, Bartelli, and Lester examine clues and speculate on the possible murderers. They eliminate them one by one. Following a lead—a white carnation—they go to a nightclub where Sleepy Parsons (Marvin Miller), Edna's former husband, plays the piano. He is blind and is finally proved innocent, but dies of a heart attack while pleading with Bartelli not to hurt him.

Finally Alex is arrested, but at the police station, with only a few minutes left, he is saved by the murderer's confession. It was Gus the taxi driver, who killed Edna because she was making his daughter miserable by having an affair with her husband. Gus had repeatedly asked her to stop seeing his son-in-law, but she wouldn't listen.

Alex goes back to the naval base in Norfolk, Virginia, taking June with him to meet his mother.

REVIEWS

NEW YORK TIMES   *Bosley Crowther*

"Plainly, the first essential of a first-class mystery film is that it catch and excite audience interest in the telling of its uncertain tale. And the longer it keeps the audience guessing the more intriguing it is likely to be. Those two desirable essentials are eminently satisfied by RKO's latest thriller *Deadline at Dawn*.

"And the performances are thoroughly engaging. Bill Williams is winning as the gob, Susan Hayward is spirited as a night-moth who assists him, and Paul Lukas plays a taxi driver well."

SCREEN GUIDE

"Suspense, stepped up by sharp performances and alert direction, puts this RKO murder thriller a notch above the usual whodunit.

"Susan Hayward and Paul Lukas score acting hits, both in roles that take them far out of their routines."

Edna's ex-husband, a blind pianist, is the latest suspect, and June questions him (left to right: Marvin Miller, Susan Hayward, Paul Lukas, Joseph Calleia, Jerome Cowan, and Bill Williams)

Bill Williams and Susan Hayward

NOTES

This was Hayward's first "free-lance" movie after Paramount, and her first for RKO Radio Pictures; it was also her first after having her twins. She was billed over Paul Lukas, who had won an Oscar for *Watch on the Rhine,* made in 1943.

Susan, as June Goffe, a young and innocent-looking lady of the night, was a tough cookie who made sailor Williams look like a baby lost in the big city. She wore one dress for almost the entire eighty-two minutes of the picture's unreeling: everything was supposed to happen in one night.

It was filmed in an RKO studio, but the atmosphere of cheap cafés in the lower part of New York City was well created.

The movie marked the end of Lola Lane's career. (She was the sister of Priscilla and Rosemary.) Ominously, Lola finished the movie as a corpse.

Susan Hayward and Brian Donlevy

Canyon Passage

UNIVERSAL, 1946

CAST

Logan Stewart, Dana Andrews; *Camrose*, Brian Donlevy; *Lucy Overmire*, Susan Hayward; *Hi Lennet*, Hoagy Carmichael; *Ben Dance*, Andy Devine; *Honey Bragg*, Ward Bond; *Caroline*, Patricia Roc; *Jonas Overmire*, Stanley Ridges; *Mrs. Overmire*, Fay Holden; *Johnny Steele*, Lloyd Bridges; *Vane Blazier*, Victor Cutler; *Lestrade*, Onslow Stevens; *Marta*, Rose Hobart, *Mrs. Dance*, Dorothy Peterson; *Clenchfield*, Halliwell Hobbes; *Gray Bartlett*, James Cardwell; *Neil Howison*, Ray Teal; *Liza Stone*, Virginia Patton; *Asa Dance*, Tad Devine; *Bushrod Dance*, Denny Devine; *Cobb*, Francis McDonald; *Judge*, Erville Alderson; *Stutchell*, Ralph Peters; *Teamster*, Jack Rockwell; *Miners*, Joseph P. Mack, Gene Stutenroth, Karl Hackett, Jack Clifford, Daral Hudson, Dick Alexander; *MacIvar*, Wallace Scott; *Indian Spokesman*, Chief Yowlachi.

CREDITS

Directed by Jacques Tourneur. *Produced by* Alexander Golitzen. *Screenplay by* Ernest Pascal. *Based on the story by* Ernest Haycox. *Technicolor Director*, Natalie Kalmus. *Director of Photography*, Edward Cronjager. *Special Photography*, D. S. Horsley. *Technicolor Associate*, William Fitsche. *Art Directors*, John B. Goodman *and* Richard H. Riedel. *Film Editor*, Milton Carruth. *Sound Director*, Bernard B. Brown. *Technician*, William Hedgcock. *Set Decoration*, Russell A. Gausman *and* Leigh Smith. *Costumes*, Travis Banton. *Director of Makeup*, Jack B. Pierce. *Hair Stylist*, Carmen Dirigo. *Assistant Director*, Fred Frank. *Musical Director*, Frank Skinner. *Dialogue Director*, Anthony Jowitt. *Running time, 92 minutes.*

THE STORY

It is the year 1856, and Logan Stewart (Dana Andrews), at the request of his close friend Camrose (Brian Donlevy), prepares to make a trip and take his friend's fiancée, Lucy Overmire (Susan Hayward), from Portland to Jacksonville, Oregon, to join Camrose.

Logan, a transient mule-train owner who has a store in Jacksonville, is in love with Lucy, but avoids her out of loyalty to his friend, and courts Caroline (Patricia Roc), daughter of nearby settlers, Mr. and Mrs. Dance (Andy Devine and Dorothy Peterson).

Their first stop is the Dances' cabin, and Caroline is not exactly thrilled to see Logan in Lucy's company. After a rest, Logan and Lucy resume their journey to Jacksonville.

Meanwhile, Camrose, losing a lot of money at poker, steals from miners' pokes entrusted to him in order to pay his debt, and ends up killing one of the miners.

Arriving in Jacksonville, Lucy and Logan learn that Camrose has been accused of murder and a friend of the slain miner, Johnny Steele (Lloyd Bridges), is rousing the crowd to hang Camrose. Logan intervenes, convincing them that the man should have a trial, saving his friend from lynching.

The trial is postponed when Honey Bragg (Ward Bond), Logan's enemy, incites an Indian uprising by killing a young Indian girl.

Logan organizes a company to defend the settlement, but the invading Indians burn Jacksonville. In the battle, Camrose is killed, Ben Dance and his son Asa (Ted Devine) are massacred, and Logan's store is destroyed.

Caroline, who has escaped with her brother Bushrod (Denny Devine), and fled to the hills, returns home and realizes that she could never be happy with the restless Logan.

At last Logan and Lucy are free to love each other. They head for San Francisco to get the money to rebuild the store—and their lives.

REVIEWS

NEW YORK TIMES   *T.M.P.*

"Walter Wanger spared nothing, least of all his actors, in producing *Canyon Passage*. Miles of beautiful outdoor scenery in stunning Technicolor is lavishly punctuated with rough and tumble episodes, moments of tender romance and a smattering of folk customs. . . .

". . . and there is Susan Hayward and Patricia Roc to remind the boys . . . that love is a wonderful thing."

TIME

"Unlike bridge, alcohol, the ponies and other popular forms of escape, this brilliantly engineered movie is non-habit-forming and has no nagging aftereffects.

"*Canyon Passage* has all this and more—plus better-than-average dialogue and competent players (Dana Andrews, Susan Hayward, Brian Donlevy, Britain's Patricia Roc)."

NOTES

Hayward's first movie for Walter Wanger was this beautiful

They arrive in Jacksonville and find that Camrose is in trouble (Susan Hayward and Dana Andrews)

Happy to make her acquaintance? Not Lucy: she is Logan's sweetheart, Caroline (Dana Andrews, Susan Hayward, and Patricia Roc)

and different western, which is unjustly ignored when discussing western films and "how the west was won." Filmed on location, mostly at the Umpqua National Forest, the Oregon scenery was shown in all its splendid beauty.

Susan, a good rider, had to learn how to ride sidesaddle for this movie, which was her second with Brian Donlevy, and the last where she got third billing. From now on it was strictly first or second billing for her.

Patricia Roc, an English import and newcomer to American films, was boosted to stardom, but she didn't click despite her fresh beauty, which reminded one of Deanna Durbin.

Hoagy Carmichael's music was an added attraction; his "Ole Buttermilk Sky" won an Oscar nomination.

Ken is away and Angie panics when the doctor tells her her little girl is very sick (Carl Esmond and Susan Hayward)

Smash Up-The Story of a Woman

UNIVERSAL INTERNATIONAL, 1947

CAST

Angie Evans, Susan Hayward; *Ken Conway,* Lee Bowman; *Martha Gray,* Marsha Hunt; *Steve,* Eddie Albert; *Dr. Lorenz,* Carl Esmond; *Mr. Elliott,* Carleton Young; *Mike Dawson,* Charles D. Brown; *Miss Kirk,* Janet Murdoch; *Edwards,* Tom Chatterton; *Angelica,* Sharyn Payne; *Mr. Gordon,* Robert Shayne; *Emcee,* Larry Blake; *Wolf,* George Meeker; *Farmer,* Erville Alderson.

CREDITS

Directed by Stuart Heisler. *Produced by* Walter Wanger. *Screenplay by* John Howard Lawson. *Based on a story by* Dorothy Parker *and* Frank Cavett. *Film Editor,* Milton Carruth. *Music,* Frank Skinner. *Orchestrations,* David Tamkin. *Additional dialogue,* Lionel Wiggam. *Running time, 103 minutes.*

THE STORY

Angelica Evans (Susan Hayward), a popular nightclub singer, abruptly ends her career to marry Ken (Lee Bowman), songwriter and song plugger. Mike Dawson (Charles D. Brown), her agent, pleads with her to continue her singing career, but she believes one singer in the family is enough and wants nothing interfering with her happiness as Ken's wife. For Angie's sake, Dawson gets Ken and his pal Steve (Eddie Albert), also a struggling songwriter, jobs in radio.

Ken makes it big in radio. He gets a secretary, Martha (Marsha Hunt), who is lovely and efficient.

Angie thinks that her happiness is complete when she gives birth to a daughter. However, after they move to their country home, Ken is so tied up with recording sessions and radio programs that they have to get a penthouse in the city, which Martha selects for them.

Hairdos shouldn't be that perfect (Susan Hayward and Marsha Hunt)

Steve tries to comfort Angie, but his words don't help much (Eddie Albert and Susan Hayward)

Lonely and depressed, Angie finds solace in alcohol, and the more Ken's stature grows in radio, the more Angie drinks. But Ken is too busy to notice his wife's disintegration.

Ken goes on a tour and tells Angie to join him, but she is drunk and misses the plane. While he's away the baby gets sick and, after calling the doctor, she gets Ken on the phone and overhears the sounds of a party going on in his room. He comes home and tries to convince her that her suspicions are unfounded, but she doesn't believe him.

Ken gives a party and for a while Angie behaves, but at the sight of Martha she starts to drink. She follows her to the powder room and starts a violent fight with her.

Ken assails Angie's intemperance and divorce proceedings follow, with Ken given custody of their child.

Unable to bear the separation, Angie goes to the park where her daughter plays, watched by a governess, and when the woman is distracted, kidnaps the child.

Angie hides in the country with her child. One day she accidentally drops a lighted cigarette, while drunk, and starts a fire. She rescues the child, but is severely burned.

When she regains consciousness at the hospital and finds Ken and her daughter at her side, she thinks that perhaps there is still hope for them.

REVIEWS

TIME

"*Smash-Up* (Walter Wanger: Universal-International) could be mistaken, on its surface, for just another of those wife-v.-secretary 'problem' movies which are called, with unconscious contempt, 'woman's pictures.' But beneath its soap-opera surface, it takes some perceptive looks at a marriage going to pieces."

CUE

"Miss Hayward gives the best performance of her career."

NEW YORK HERALD TRIBUNE   *Howard Barnes*

"A female alcoholic takes her place in the screen's gallery of psychiatric cases. *Smash-Up—The Story of a Woman* is a somewhat savage account of dipsomania. John Howard Lawson, Dorothy Parker and Frank Cavett have written sequences which are literate and terrifying, while Stuart Heisler has staged them with ominous underlining. Since Susan Hayward plays the afflicted heroine with considerable power, the production is definitely disturbing."

NEW YORK DAILY MIRROR   *Jack Thompson*

"Walter Wanger has produced a fascinating study of a lady drunk in *Smash-Up,* a Universal-International picture.

"Miss Hayward gives a remarkably fine performance as the lady who drinks."

Angie wakes up in a strange room (Susan Hayward)

NOTES

If *The Lost Weekend* had not been released the year before, Hayward might have won the Oscar and *Smash-Up* would probably be a classic today.

Smash-Up was by far the best movie Stuart Heisler ever directed for Hayward and, besides her nomination as best actress, the movie won another Oscar nomination as best original story.

The highlight was her big battle with Marsha Hunt in the powder room, one of the most violent fights between two women in film history.

The film was recommended in various women's organizations as an effective aid in the fight against alcoholism.

They Won't Believe Me

RKO RADIO, 1947

Between these two secretaries, it is obvious who is getting the best job (Robert Young, Susan Hayward, and Lovyss Bradley)

CAST

Larry Ballentine, Robert Young; *Verna Carlson*, Susan Hayward; *Janice Bell*, Jane Greer; *Gretta Ballentine*, Rita Johnson; *Trenton*, Tom Powers; *Lieutenant Carr*, George Tyne; *Thomason*, Don Beddoe; *Cahill*, Frank Ferguson; *Judge Fletcher*, Harry Harvey; *Patric Gold*, Wilton Graff; *Susan Haines*, Janet Shaw; *Parking Lot Attendant*, Glen Knight; *Tough Patient*, Anthony Caruso; *Highway Cop*, George Sherwood; *Police Stenographer*, Perc Launders; *Mortician*, Byron Foulger; *Nick*, Hector Sarno; *Chauffeur*, Carl Kent; *Detective*, Lee Frederick; *Maid*, Jean Andren; *Mr. Bowman*, Paul Maxey; *Sheriff*, Herbert Haywood; *Mrs. Bowman*, Elena Warren; *Mrs. Hines*, Lillian Bronson; *Sailor*, Martin Wilkins; *Emma*, Dot Farley; *Court Clerk*, Milton Parsons; *Bailiff*, Lee Phelps; *Patrick Collins*, Frank Pharr; *Screaming Woman*, Ellen Corby; *Tiny Old Man*, Matthew McHugh; *Officer Guarding Larry*, Bob Pepper; *Waiter*, Ira Buck Woods; *Woman*, Irene Terow; *Untidy Woman*, Berta Ledbetter; *Girl at Newsstand*, Lida Durova; *Hotel Clerk*, Bob Thom; *Bartenders*, Ivan Browning, Jack Gargan; *Mrs. Roberts*, Madam Borget; *Rancher*, Harry Strang; *Driver*, Bud Wolfe; *Gus*, Sol Gorss; *Miss Jorday*, Lovyss Bradley; *Fisherman*, Harry D'Arcy; *Tour Conductor*, Jack Rice; *Spinster*, Netta Packer.

CREDITS

Directed by Irving Pichel. *Produced by* Joan Harrison. *Executive Producer*, Jack J. Gross. *Screenplay by* Jonathan Latimer. *Story by* Gordon McDonnell. *Photography by* Harry J. Wild. *Art Director*, Albert S. D'Agostino *and* Robert Boyle. *Editor*, Elmo Williams. *Sound*, John Tribby. *Set Decorators*, Darrell Silvera *and* William Matinetti. *Assistant Director*, Harry D'Arcy. *Special Effects*, Russell A. Cully. *Music Director*, C. Bakaleinikoff. *Music*, Roy Webb. *Running time, 95 minutes.*

THE STORY

Larry Ballentine (Robert Young) relates the story from the witness stand in a courtroom where he's being tried for murder.

A charming man, he plays at being a Wall Street broker while married to Gretta (Rita Johnson), who is wealthy. He meets a young writer, Janice (Jane Greer), but after a few dates she realizes that she's in love with Larry and decides to go to Montreal to end the affair. Larry tells her he will get a divorce and follow her.

Gretta finds out and fights to keep her husband. She buys him a partnership in a brokerage firm in Los Angeles and he forgets Janice and goes to Los Angeles with his wife.

There, Larry meets Verna Carlson (Susan Hayward), the gold-digging secretary who works for Trenton (Tom Powers), his partner. He incurs Trenton's enmity when he wins Verna away from him, and Gretta again tries to keep Larry by means of her money. This time she buys an isolated ranch. Larry gives in but can't break away from Verna and continues seeing her.

Finally, Larry plans to elope with Verna, after cleaning out his wife's bank account. But Verna, originally attracted to Larry's money, has a change of heart at the last minute and wants nothing to do with Gretta's money.

On the way back to return Gretta's money, they have an accident and Verna's body is burned beyond recognition. When Larry recovers consciousness he learns that the authorities have assumed that the burned body is that of his wife. He goes to the ranch and finds that Gretta committed suicide after reading his farewell letter. He abandons her body in a remote mountain pool.

In possession of his wife's money, he goes to Jamaica and tries to drown his memories in alcohol. But he finds Janice and falls in love with her again. They return to Los Angeles and

Janice meets Larry and Verna by chance; not a very happy encounter for former lovers Larry and Janice (Robert Young, Susan Hayward, and Jane Greer)

Larry and Verna meet again at a bar (Robert Young and Susan Hayward)

Rehearsing a scene while camera and lights wait to do their stuff are co-stars Robert Young and Susan Hayward

Janice, who is only playing a part and wants Larry to pay for what he did to her, tells Trenton that he should look into Larry's case. An investigation is started and Gretta's body is discovered, but it is beyond identification. Trenton declares it to be Verna's body and Larry is arrested for murder.

The trial proceeds after Larry finishes his account of the happenings; things don't look good for him.

When the jury files back to render a verdict, Larry loses his nerve and makes a dash for the window but is killed by the police. The jury then returns its verdict: NOT GUILTY.

REVIEWS

TIME

"*They Won't Believe Me* (RKO) is a skillful telling of a pretty nasty story about a man (Robert Young) who loves money and women almost equally well, and finds that they get in each other's way. . . .

"Susan Hayward proficiently sells her special brand of sexiness."

SCREEN GUIDE

"The title of this picture couldn't be more apt. All through the 95 minutes of running time, you'll feel that something drastic is going to happen. In the last three minutes of the film something does: the smash, unexpected ending.

"The ending is exciting and worthy of producer Joan Harrison's training with the master, Alfred Hitchcock."

SILVER SCREEN

"The explosive action will best remain the film's secret until seen, and it's worth seeing. Young is a believable rotter-plus; Jane Greer does her best acting to date even though she remains a bit on the frozen-faced side, and Rita Johnson's work will remind you that she's still quite an actress. But save your loudest applause for Susan Hayward, the one-time model who has learned to project an intense personality."

NOTES

The title of the film was a very appropriate one as far as Robert Young's fans were concerned: they didn't believe his Larry Ballentine. Larry just wasn't Young's type. The script does not help the credibility of Robert Young's Larry, or of Hayward's Verna either, with scenes like the one where after being money worshippers all their lives, they decide that they don't want the money that Young has taken from his wife.

Hayward was again the "other woman," but this time with class and star billing. This time there were two "other women." The other one was Jane Greer, who also got star billing and looked promising for a few years at RKO, but never really achieved success as a star.

Rita Johnson played the part of Robert Young's wife, a year before the accident that almost ended her life (a hair dryer fell on her head in her own home).

Lewis cannot believe that this beautiful girl at the piano is the stern, withdrawn Tina he has been seeing every day (Susan Hayward)

Like a ghost, she roams through the palace during one of her spells. (Susan Hayward)

CAST

Lewis Venable, Robert Cummings; *Tina Borderau,* Susan Hayward; *Juliana Boderau,* Agnes Moorehead; *Amelia,* Joan Lorring; *Father Rinaldo,* Eduardo Ciannelli; *Charles,* John Archer; *Pietro,* Frank Puglia; *Maria,* Minerva Urecal; *Vittorio,* William Edmunds.

CREDITS

Directed by Martin Gabel. *Produced by* Walter Wanger. *Screenplay by* Leonardo Bercovici. *Based on the novel* The Aspern Papers *by* Henry James. *Photography,* Hal Mohr, A.S.C. *Editor,* Milton Carruth. *Music,* Daniele Amfitheatrof. *Orchestrations,* David Tamkin. *Running time, 89 minutes.*

THE STORY

An American publisher, Lewis (Robert Cummings), gets interested by his friend Charles (John Archer) in obtaining the missing love letters written by a mysteriously disappeared poet in Venice to his fiancée.

Lewis, under an assumed name, goes to the eerie Borderau mansion to try to solve the mystery of the poet and the love letters.

There he meets Juliana (Agnes Moorehead), the 105-year-old fiancée of the poet, and recipient of the letters, and her niece Tina (Susan Hayward). Tina treats him harshly from the moment they meet.

But Lewis stays and finds out, during a conversation with Juliana, that she is blind. He also meets Amelia (Joan Lorring), the maid, who agrees to help him in spite of her fear of Tina and the old house.

At night Lewis hears someone playing the piano and investigates. Tina, in a trance, is playing the piano; when she sees Lewis, she thinks he is the lost poet. He goes along with the farce; Tina believes herself to be Juliana and encourages his lovemaking.

Bewildered, Lewis goes to see the parish priest, who informs him that Tina's mind is unbalanced because of the love letters and the mystery of the poet.

Lewis wants to help Tina and takes her out to dine and dance, but cannot resist the temptation to steal the letters from the hiding place Juliana had revealed to him earlier. When Tina, in another trance, cannot find the letters, she tries to kill her aunt, thinking she has taken them. Lewis comes in and stops her by dropping the letters on the floor, and Juliana then confesses that she had killed her lover because he was going to leave her. Tina faints and Lewis carries her outside to the garden. In the meantime, Juliana, groping for the letters, accidentally starts a fire.

Lewis rescues her, but too late, and Juliana dies.

Tina—shaken out of her trance forever—and Lewis witness the scene in silence.

Lewis tries a different approach and invites Tina out to dinner (Robert Cummings and Susan Hayward)

Co-stars Susan Hayward and Robert Cummings share a garden rendezvous with director Martin Gabel, hand outstretched, and his camera crew

121

Tina is not happy having Lewis as a boarder, but Juliana wants it this way (Susan Hayward and Agnes Moorehead)

At the moment Tina has a softer look in her eyes (Robert Cummings and Susan Hayward)

REVIEWS

NEW YORK HERALD TRIBUNE   *Otis L. Guernsey, Jr.*

"It is always difficult to produce sharp screen values out of a leisurely, conversational, confined drama, but *The Lost Moment* has worked the trick better than might be expected. Based on Henry James's *The Aspern Papers,* its action is almost wholly limited to a house in Venice as it gradually reconstructs an eerie story out of the past. The scenario by Leonardo Bercovici is a literate, slangless outline of emotional stresses at the turn of the century, and Martin Gabel's direction keeps the camera moving within the house's four walls. With nicely controlled performances by Robert Cummings and Susan Hayward . . . *The Lost Moment* manages to insert style and suspense where pace and photographic variety are missing."

NEWSWEEK

"Susan Hayward, in a baffling role, is better than the producers had a right to expect."

VARIETY   *Hobe*

"Susan Hayward, who played another psychotic character in *Smash-Up,* also for Walter Wanger, is effective in both facets of the present part."

NOTES

Hayward's characterization of Tina Borderau was one of her finest acting jobs. The subtle romantic mood she projected as Juliana, during her nighttime trance, was in sharp contrast with the austerity and harshness of her everyday Tina. She was so alluring during her spells that it was hard to believe that Cummings could think of the letters when they were together.

Her publicity stills were gorgeous. Yet Susan hated the movie, perhaps because of her quarrel with director Gabel.

The makeup job that made Agnes Moorehead look 105 years old was a masterpiece. The studio's Venice sets, although well done, didn't look anything like the real Venice (the setting for Hayward's *The Honey Pot* almost twenty years later).

Morna's flirting with Keith doesn't make Clay happy
(Van Heflin, Susan Hayward, and Whitfield Connor)

Tap Roots

UNIVERSAL INTERNATIONAL, 1948

CAST

Keith Alexander, Van Heflin; *Morna Dabney,* Susan Hayward; *Tishomingo,* Boris Karloff; *Aven Dabney,* Julie London; *Clay MacIvor,* Whitfield Connor; *Hoab Dabney,* Ward Bond; *Bruce Dabney,* Richard Long; *Reverend Kirkland,* Arthur Shields; *Dr. MacIntosh,* Griff Barnett; *Shellie,* Sondra Rodgers; *Dabby,* Ruby Dandridge; *Sam Dabney,* Russell Simpson.

CREDITS

Directed by George Marshall. *Produced by* Walter Wanger. *Screenplay by* Alan LeMay. *Based on the novel by* James Street. *Directors of Photography,* Lionel Lindon, A.S.C., *and* Winton C. Hoch, A.S.C. *Technicolor Color Director,* Natalie Kalmus. *Associate,* Morgan Padelford. *Production designed by* Alexander Golitzen. *Art Director,* Frank A. Richards. *Film*

Editor, Milton Carruth. *Sound,* Leslie I. Carey *and* Glenn E. Anderson. *Set Decorations,* Russell A. Gausman *and* Ruby R. Levitt. *Costumes,* Yvonne Wood. *Makeup,* Bud Westmore. *Hair Stylist,* Carmen Dirigo. *Assistant Director,* Aaron Rosenberg. *Second Unit Director,* George Templeton. *Music,* Frank Skinner. *Orchestrations,* David Tamkin. *Additional Dialogue by* Lionel Wiggam. *Running time, 109 minutes.*

THE STORY

Hoab Dabney (Ward Bond) is determined that Lebanon County, Mississippi, is going to remain independent, and when Mississippi secedes from the Union, Lebanon County secedes from the state. Hoab had promised his father Sam (Russell Simpson) to defend the land where Sam and Tishomingo (Boris Karloff) had first settled.

Dabney and his family—his daughters Morna (Susan Hayward) and Aven (Julie London) and his son Bruce (Richard Long)—are joined in their rebellion by the notorious newspaper publisher and famous duelist, Keith Alexander (Van Heflin). Keith writes editorials in favor of the Lebanon cause, and backs them up with his dueling pistols, but his main interest is the beautiful, red-haired Morna. She's engaged to Clay MacIvor (Whitfield Connor), but the wedding is postponed when Morna falls from a horse and one leg becomes paralyzed.

Clay, who has been seeing Aven, Morna's sister, secretly, declares his intention to leave Lebanon and fight for the Confederacy as soon as the Civil War starts. Hoab kicks him out of the house and he and Aven elope while Morna is unable to walk. Keith can now openly try to win the beautiful redhead for himself.

Hoab and his son, Bruce, together with Reverend Kirkland (Arthur Shields), start campaigning to recruit followers for the secession of Lebanon, and Tishomingo heals Morna's leg with Indian curative methods.

Lebanon is doomed when the Confederate army sets out to crush the rebellion. Clay, now a major, leads the soldiers and Reverend Kirkland is slain when they retreat into the swamp. Morna tries to help, but Dabney is wounded, and Bruce is killed when he tries to launch a counterattack. Keith, who is now really fighting for Morna and her people, confronts Clay in the swamp and kills his rival.

Keith helps the wounded Hoab to a cabin and Morna joins them. Keith and Morna will face the future together with more faith than ever in their tap roots.

REVIEWS

NEWSWEEK

"*Tap Roots* is a pleasantly romanticized account of . . . the bold refusal of the people of Lebanon Valley to secede from the Union and the way they barricaded themselves against the Confederate Army. . . .

". . . the film owes its effectiveness mostly to the unobtrusive accuracy of its background and the expert performances of Bond, Karloff, Heflin, and especially Miss Hayward, who should more than compensate the bedraggled warrior who ultimately finds himself in her arms for the tactical loss of even so pleasant a valley as Lebanon."

NEW YORK TIMES   *T.M.P.*

"Susan Hayward, generously endowed by nature and further endowed by Technicolor, is, however, defeated at almost every turn by the script."

NEW YORK HERALD TRIBUNE   *Joe Pihodna*

"Of course, Susan Hayward is also visually exciting as a latter-day Scarlet O'Hara."

Susan Hayward as Morna Dabney

The sisters get ready for an important visitor: Keith Alexander, the notorious duelist whom they are dying to meet (Susan Hayward and Julie London)

The bells are tolling and Clay and Morna know why: Mississippi has seceded from the Union (Whitfield Connor and Susan Hayward)

NOTES

After eleven years in Hollywood, Susan played a role similar to the one she had lost and longed to play. Morna Dabney was almost another Scarlett O'Hara, a southern spitfire, and Susan played it with nerve and vitality, despite some clichés.

It was planned to be a big spectacle, and no money was spared to achieve this end. The costumes were superb as were the settings, with tremendous battles, hundreds of extras, and a big fire (an important element in most of Hayward's Universal films: cottages burned by the Indians in *Canyon Passage;* her own fire that destroyed her home in *Smash-Up;* a fire in the Venice palace in *The Lost Moment;* and now, the burning of her plantation home by Union soldiers). Most of the outdoor scenes, including the fire, were shot on location in North Carolina.

Boris Karloff played the Indian Tishomingo, which was quite a deviation from his usual monster roles.

Waiting to meet "wonder boy" Saxon, Janet makes conversation with Alma, Saxon's girl, and the Humbers (left to right: Harry Von Zell (standing); sitting: Audrey Totter, Cara Williams, and Susan Hayward)

The Saxon Charm

UNIVERSAL INTERNATIONAL, 1948

CAST

Matt Saxon, Robert Montgomery; *Janet Busch*, Susan Hayward; *Eric Busch*, John Payne; *Alma*, Audrey Totter; *Hermy*, Henry Morgan; *Zack Humber*, Harry Von Zell; *Dolly Humber*, Cara Williams; *Captain Chatham*, Chill Wills; *Vivian Saxon*, Heather Angel; *Peter Stanhope*, John Baragrey; *Abel Richman*, Addison Richards; *Ingenue*, Barbara Challis; *Jack Bernard*, Curt Conway; *Mrs. Noble*, Fay Baker; *Chris*, Philip Van Zandt; *Manager*, Martin Garralaga; *Proprietor*, Max Willenz; *Headwaiter*, Fred Nurney; *Mrs. Maddox*, Archie Twitchell; *Mrs. Maddox*, Barbara Billingsley; *Harassed Secretary*, Eula Guy; *Bald Man*, Al Murphy; *Mr. McCarthy*, Clarence Straight; *Mr. Noble*, Bert Davidson; *Mrs. McCarthy*, Maris Wrixon; *Cyril Leatham*, Peter Brocco; *Flower Girl*, Donna Martell; *Designer*, Mauritz Hugo; *Agent*, Anthony Jochim; *Nurse*, Kathleen Freeman; *Soubrette*, Blanche Obronska; *Buxom Nurse*, Laura Kasley Brooks; *Blonde*, Vivian Mason; *Character Man*, Basil Tellou; *Leading Man*, Robert Spencer; *Waiter*, Paul Rochin; *Headwaiter*, Lomax Study; *Bus Boy*, Robert Cabal.

CREDITS

Directed by Claude Binyon. *Produced by* Joseph Sistrom. *Screenplay by* Claude Binyon. *Based on the novel by* Frederic Wakeman. *Photography by* Milton Krasner. *Editor*, Paul Weatherwax. *Music*, Walter Sharf. *Running time, 88 minutes.*

THE STORY

Eric Busch (John Payne) is delighted when Matt Saxon (Robert Montgomery), the eccentric producer, agrees to produce his new play. To celebrate, Saxon gives a dinner party for Eric and his wife Janet (Susan Hayward), his backer, Zack Humber (Harry Von Zell), Dolly Humber (Cara Williams), and Saxon's girlfriend Alma (Audrey Totter).

When Saxon flies into a rage at the start because the food is not to his liking, Janet has a premonition and later asks Eric to break with Saxon. Eric seems convinced, but the next evening they meet Saxon again in a nightclub where Alma is auditioning for a place in the floor show. Eric and Janet are amazed at the influence Saxon has on Alma and the way he guides her in her routines. Janet again pleads with Eric not to let Saxon dominate him, but Eric doesn't listen.

When Saxon tells Eric that he should rewrite the third act, but that he should be by himself and not let Janet disturb him, Eric prevails upon Janet to go to their summer home alone. Soon after, Saxon calls Eric from Mexico City and tells him to join him there to meet their new backer, who turns out to be Saxon's wealthy ex-wife Vivian (Heather Angel). The woman is no longer wealthy and Saxon flies to Hollywood to sign a well known actor, Peter Stanhope (John Baragrey), to play the lead. Eric returns to New York to find Janet drunk. They quarrel and decide to separate.

Eric wants Janet to understand Saxon, but she's giving him a hard time (John Payne and Susan Hayward)

Things get interesting when Alma and Janet meet Stanhope while enjoying a cocktail at a nightclub (left to right: Audrey Totter, Susan Hayward, and John Baragrey)

Alma gives Janet food for thought about Saxon (Susan Hayward and Audrey Totter)

Good news? You can't tell by the expression on Janet's face (Susan Hayward)

One night Janet and Alma meet Peter Stanhope in a nightclub, where he has gone with a stage producer, Abel Richman (Addison Richards). Stanhope tells them about turning down Eric's play when Saxon approached him in Hollywood. Meanwhile, Alma receives a call from Hollywood telling her that her contract has been canceled because of false rumors that Saxon spread about her. Janet begs Stanhope and Richman to read her husband's original version of the play and they finally agreed.

When Saxon returns to New York, Alma, waiting in his office, tells him what she thinks of him and walks out. Saxon then goes to see Eric. He's suggesting new changes to Eric's play when Eric receives a call from Richman telling him that they liked the original version and Stanhope wants to do the play. Eric happily throws Saxon out and goes looking for Janet. He finds her in a nightclub and they are reconciled.

REVIEWS

NEW YORK HERALD TRIBUNE   *Otis I. Guernsey, Jr.*

"Based on Frederic Wakeman's novel, *The Saxon Charm,* it examines at close range a pathetic and cruel individualist—a Broadway theatrical producer whose contempt for the whole human race includes even himself. Claude Binyon's screen play and direction are crisp and concise, and Robert Montgomery's interpretation of Matt Saxon is exactly the right combination of honey and acid."

NEWSWEEK

"Some humorous exaggeration of his influence and sumptuous surroundings disguises the fact that he is basically not a very likely character. And Payne, Miss Hayward, and Audrey Totter as a night club singer who also succumbs to the Saxon 'charm' nicely offset his sophisticated comedy by playing their roles straight and looking very much like genuine human beings."

NEW YORK TIMES   *T.M.P.*

"John Payne is convincing as the author and Susan Hayward is nicely subdued and appealing as his wife."

NOTES

Although she had a lot of footage, Hayward's role was not as important as Robert Montgomery's or even John Payne's parts. This was her least exciting and popular movie for Universal, and the last she made for that studio during this period.

There were no fires in this movie—not even her own fire to light up the role of Janet. But the role of an ordinary housewife did not fit Hayward's temperament.

Robert Montgomery's performance was recognized as the best in the movie, and Audrey Totter's was next.

As Cherokee Lansing, the cattle lady who became an oil queen (Susan Hayward)

Cherokee is disappointed when her "oil well" turns out to be just water (Susan Hayward and Robert Preston)

CAST

Cherokee Lansing, Susan Hayward; *Brad Brady*, Robert Preston; *Jim Redbird*, Pedro Armendariz; *Bruce Tanner*, Lloyd Gough; *Pinky Jimpson*, Chill Wills; *Johnny Brady*, Ed Begley; *Steve*, Roland Jack; *Nelse Lansing*, Harry Shannon; *Homer*, Jimmy Conlin; *Tooley*, Paul E. Burns; *Charlie Lightfoot*, Chief Yowlachie; *Winters*, Pierre Watkin; *Cab Driver*, Tom Dugan; *Mr. Kelly*, Lane Chandler; *Candy Williams*, Lola Albright; *Osage Indian*, Iron Eyes Cody; *Joker*, Dick Wessel; *Oilmen*, John Dehner, Selmer Jackson; *Oil Worker*, Fred Graham; *Governor*, Larry Keating; *Judge McKay*, Joseph Crehan; *Man with Newspaper*, Nolan Leary; *Winslow*, Thomas Browne Henry.

CREDITS

Directed by Stuart Heisler. *Produced by* Walter Wanger. *Associate Producer*, Edward Lasker. *Screenplay by* Frank Nugent and Curtis Kenyon. *Suggested by a story by* Richard Woemser. *Technicolor Director*, Natalie Kalmus. *Associate Color Director*, Richard Mueller. *Director of Photography*, Winton Hoch, A.S.C. *Art Director*, Nathan Juran. *Film Editor*, Terrell Morse. *Decorations*, Armor Marlowe and Al Orenbach. *Costume Designer*, Herschel. *Makeup*, Ern Westmore and Del Armstrong. *Hair Styling*, Joan St. Oegger and Helen Turpin. *Assistant Director*, Howard W. Koch. *Special Photographic Effects*, John Fulton. *Sound*, Howard Fogetti. *Musical Director*, Irving Friedman. *Music Conductor*, Charles Previs. *Orchestrations*, David Tamkin. *The song "Tulsa" by* Mort Green and Allie Wrubel. *Production Supervision*, James T. Vaughn. *Running time, 90 minutes.*

THE STORY

After the death of her father, Nelse Lansing (Harry Shannon), in an explosion at an oil field, Cherokee Lansing (Susan Hayward) is determined to demand retribution from oil lord Bruce Tanner (Lloyd Gough).

She's getting noplace and decides to enlist the aid of her cousin Pinky Jimpson (Chill Wills). On her way to see him, she meets "Crude Oil" Johnny Brady (Ed Begley), whom she has befriended after rescuing him from a street bully. Brady is grateful to her and, after several drinks, signs some oil leases over to her.

Cherokee plans to return the papers to Crude Oil Johnny the next day, but learns he has been killed in another brawl. This makes her the lawful owner of the oil leases. When Tanner makes her an offer for the leases she realizes that they must be valuable and starts drilling with the help of her Indian friend, Jim Redbird (Pedro Armendariz), who lends her the money.

At the drilling site she is visited by Brad Brady (Robert Preston), the son of Crude Oil Johnny. He is a geologist and can help her.

The money is running out and Cherokee asks Tanner for a loan. They make a deal: if by a certain date she has not gotten any oil, the leases are his.

Cherokee Lansing enjoys the triumph of her first gusher that is to lead her to wealth and power (Susan Hayward)

Brad cannot share Cherokee's elation about her plans to expand the oil fields (Robert Preston, Pierre Watkin, Susan Hayward, and Pedro Armendariz)

131

When she's about to lose all hope of saving her leases, oil bursts out. From then on things keep going up, up, up for Cherokee, now called the "Oil Queen" of Tulsa.

Oil towers are booming across the land, despite the protests of people like Jim Redbird, who claim they are destroying prime grazing land. An Indian spokesman, getting royalties from Cherokee's oil leases, demands that she drill as many oil wells as Tanner has so that everybody can get more money. Afraid of losing the Indian's support, Cherokee agrees, though she realizes the danger of polluting the grazing lands.

Brad doesn't like the idea, but Cherokee persuades him to stay. They are falling in love. She becomes wealthy and plans to marry Brad, but cannot resist the temptation of merging with Tanner, only to realize, too late, that they have agreed to supply more oil than she can produce. Brad, enraged, breaks their engagement.

To produce the extra oil, Tanner suggests that they drill on Redbird's property. Jim refuses to give them permission, but Tanner brings him before a judge. He's threatened with being declared mentally incompetent if he does not consent. Cherokee, heartbroken, refuses to side with Tanner, even if it means losing her oil empire.

Jim flees to his ranch and finds dead cattle near a stream. Lighting a match, he throws it in the stream, which flares up because of the oil in it. Wind spreads the flame to a nearby oil field, starting a vast conflagration.

They band together to fight the huge fire—Brad, Cherokee, Tanner. But Cherokee, who has seen Jim trying to save some of his cattle, runs over to him, and both are trapped by the falling oil towers. Brad gets a bulldozer and rescues them.

Finally, the fire under control, they view the ruins. Brad and Cherokee plan to build again.

REVIEWS

TIME

"*Tulsa* (Walter Wanger; Eagle Lion) like a damp fuse, provides a loud bang at the end of a long splutter. Its plot is so rambling and logy with clichés that its climax—a big fire scene —seems wonderfully good.

"The girl who gets rescued from the fire, and who indirectly caused it, is Susan Hayward. Pretty enough to spark all sorts of explosions."

MOVIE STARS PARADE

"Susan Hayward plays a rags-to-riches girl who builds an empire on black gold.

"The technicolor photography of the landscape in general and especially of two spectacular scenes: a 'gusher' and an oil well fire, is a vivid sight.

"Miss Hayward and Preston team perfectly in presenting a very exciting chapter in our country's history. There was never a dull moment in the city of Tulsa nor are there any in this movie."

NOTES

In this last Walter Wanger production, Susan had to fight still another fire, one of the biggest of all "her fires"; entire oil fields burned.

The ads promised: "Meet Cherokee Lansing, Half Wildcat . . . Half Angel . . . All Woman!" And Cherokee Lansing really was one of Hayward's most exciting roles of the decade. It was a truly "Hayward-type" heroine: tough on the outside, but with a soft heart beneath the armor; fighting all the way to the top and making mistakes along the way, but finally righting her wrongs.

It was a messy film for Susan, who spent a large part of it "covered with oil." It was make-believe oil, but still messy.

This was Hayward's fourth—and last—movie with Preston (if you count *Star Spangled Rhythm*).

It was her only film for Eagle Lion (she was in at least one picture made by every important company during the forties and fifties), and it was this company's most elaborate production and top money grosser during its short life. It was also Hayward's last movie directed by Stuart Heisler.

Starlet Lola Albright had another bit part in this movie, but although she looked promising, major roles eluded her for most of her career.

Tanner tries to convince Cherokee to drill on Redbird's property (Susan Hayward and Lloyd Gough)

Leaving her marks for posterity, at Grauman's Chinese Theater; she is assisted by Ralph Hathaway (August 10, 1951)

It wasn't long before Susan started her first Fox feature, *House of Strangers* (first called "Collision" and then "East Side Story"), a story about a "vendetta" among the members of an Italian family. The main character was played with gusto by Edward G. Robinson, who was awarded the best actor honors at the Cannes festival. Richard Conte, one of his sons in the movie, was the axis around which the plot revolved, and Hayward was his girl. Her scenes were brief but sharp and lacerating, and her wardrobe (by Charles LeMaire, one of Fox's main designers), the most impressive of any of her movies to date. The director, Joe Mankiewicz, wanting her to cut her hair, tried the psychological approach: "Your hair is beautiful, but don't you think it's a little too long? After all, everybody is wearing a short bob." Nice try, but it didn't work!

During the filming she upset Mankiewicz—who was noted for his informal approach to everybody—by continually addressing him as "Mr. Mankiewicz." In contrast, he used to call her "Susie." Finally, as the picture was winding up, Susan completed a scene and asked, "How was that, Joe?" Mankiewicz, startled, answered: "It was fine, Miss Hayward."

The movie was such a popular success that it was remade in 1954 as *Broken Lance*, a western, with Spencer Tracy, Robert Wagner, and Jean Peters in the main roles, and again in 1961, as *The Big Show*, about a circus, with Esther Williams and Cliff Robertson in the leads.

Before the end of the year she had yet another rushed release, so it could compete at the Academy Awards of 1949, Samuel Goldwyn's *My Foolish Heart*, although the official release date was early 1950. She had the part of a "nice girl," Eloise Winters, in a poignant love story that made Victor Young's title song popular—or vice-versa. Goldwyn also tried to get her to cut her long tresses, to no avail. She knew that her hair was one of her best assets. (A clause in her contract, stating that her hair could not be cut, made it easy for her to have her way.)

Her reviews were outstanding. Take a *Look* movie review: "Susan Hayward and Dana Andrews, as troubled lovers, dominate the large cast. In her best screen job to date, Miss Hayward shakes off some old distracting mannerisms and makes the tragedy of a girl in love in wartime very real indeed." But there were dissidents: the *New York Times* critic wrote: "Susan Hayward, foolish? . . . In any case, Miss Hayward is emphatically not the sadly confused and innocent schoolgirl (college) type depicted here." Her co-star in this J. D. Salinger story was Dana Andrews, who was billed over her, though his role was secondary. Robert Keith, as Hayward's father, gave a memorable performance.

In a magazine article she reminisced about the night of the movie première and how it had brought back the memory of her father's words at the time of her first screen test, and how right he had been!

She got her second Academy Award nomination for her sensitive performance. She graced the Academy night festivities, an occasion that she rarely missed. What she missed was getting an Oscar, which went to Olivia de Havilland for *The Heiress*. The other losers were Jeanne Crain, for *Pinky*; Loretta Young, for *Come to the Stable*; and Deborah Kerr, for *Edward, My Son*.

Hayward had her first suspension from Fox when she refused the title role in *Stella*, which was played by Ann Sheridan. She had a few other suspensions through the years, when she believed that the roles offered were not up to standards she had set.

By midyear, *Newsweek* magazine echoed a publicity bit on "real" red-headed beauties: "Carrot Top: the world's sexiest women are redheads, according to Frank, of Frank & Joseph's beauty salons in Hollywood, who dye film stars' hair. 'A woman hasn't lived until she is a redhead,' he said. 'A man may whistle at blondes and leer at brunettes, but he sits up and goes "Arf" when a redhead wriggles by. Take Rhonda Fleming, Susan Hayward and Ann Sheridan. They're real—and gorgeous.' " And *Esquire* ran a full-page photo of Susan, in color, with the caption: "All this and acting ability too, won favor for Susan Hayward in Eagle Lion's 'Tulsa.' "

Her marital life seemed peaceful, although magazines were remarking how Susan's star had soared, in contrast with Barker's. They were seen, apparently happy, at a few social events. Barker's main business seemed to be authoring articles for fan magazines about his ever more famous wife. (Ironically, a very private person, she never authorized a fan club of her own.) In a magazine interview, talking about her marriage, she said: "In cases I have known, it is the husband who is often possessive and demanding. When the situation is reversed, however, it is, but definitely, a rough deal, because no one can hold on tighter or become more unreasonable than a very possessive wife. I don't want to feel that I own my husband. I want to feel that I share with him. And I like to think that I can understand him and he can understand me."

She continued filming all year, but the movies were released in 1951.

For *I'd Climb the Highest Mountain*, her first release that year, she went to Georgia. Barker and his mother visited her on location. He said, "She had the soul of a ballerina and the appetite of a truckdriver."

During the filming she discovered a nearby waterfall and decided to take some pictures from a high point to get a good view of the countryside. She and a native guide "climbed the highest mountain." She adjusted her camera and crept to a ledge. Then she started to slip, but the guide grabbed her and both steadied themselves on the edge of the precipice, miraculously spared from falling to their deaths. A few days later, she calmly said to the company publicity man, "Oh, I forgot to tell you—I was nearly killed the other day!"

Both *Modern Screen* and *Movieland* magazines chose the film as the best of the month, but it failed to attract audiences: it was the least popular of all her releases for 1951. (Ironically, the first movie in which she played under director Henry King's guidance, and the least ambitious of the four in which he directed her, it is considered today the best one of the King-Hayward combination.)

Susan Hayward and Jane Froman at 1952 presentation of USO citation to Froman

The two most popular movie stars in the world for 1952, according to the Foreign Press Association; the trophies are Henriettas (John Wayne and Susan Hayward)

After the movie was released, she re-created her role, along with co-star William Lundigan, for CBS's "Lux Radio Theatre."

In her next release Susan was co-starred with 20th Century-Fox's long-standing king Tyrone Power for the first time, in a kind of "western thriller" that was much above average: *Rawhide.* She and Power were very good in this nerve-wracking movie, although they had competition for acting honors from villainous Jack Elam. The movie was directed briskly by Henry Hathaway, who was at his best.

Next she had a part that looked fitting for her: Harriet Boyd, the beautiful, devilish model-designer who stopped at nothing to get to her goal in Jerome Weidman's novel *I Can Get It for You Wholesale,* which featured Dan Dailey and George Sanders. If there was ever a movie character that could compare to Susan in her own drive for recognition, this was it. Most of the film was shot on location in Manhattan, and she was photographed shopping and dining in different places around town. She had excellent reviews and *Cosmopolitan* magazine chose her for "Best Feminine Performance" of the month.

By this time her tremendous popularity plus her acting laurels could no longer go unnoticed by film people, and on August 10, 1951, she was invited to imprint her footsteps at Grauman's Chinese Theatre, side by side with the legends of past and present Hollywood.

A few days later came her most important release that year, *David and Bathsheba,* but the expectancy didn't survive reality. The movie was Gregory Peck's, and the acting laurels went to him. Hayward was "pure Hollywood," looking beautiful, with nothing to do. It was the biggest money maker for Fox that year, though it was more a character study than a spectacle.

Look magazine dedicated its "Movie Review" to the film, and *Life* magazine had an article about the movie, especially the "sexy" aspect of it, since Hayward had her first and only biblical bath. They printed a large color photo of her behind a glass screen, not completely translucent, so you couldn't see too much of the Hayward figure. Nevertheless, this was considered too "hot," so the screen was replaced with a wooden one for the movie.

For the filming of this "bath" scene she had to spend the whole day in a waist-high tub, while a female slave poured water on her. Although the temperature of the water was controlled, the air on the sound stage was not, and shooting had to be interrupted by Susan's fits of sneezing. By the time the scene was finished, she had caught a cold.

The publicity for the movie was colossal, even giving away color brochures before the picture was released. There was the catch phrase "This is the year of *David and Bathsheba,*" and the publicity line that Hayward, as Bathsheba, put the accent on the "bath." *Esquire* magazine dedicated another color page to her, as Bathsheba, and this time it was an even larger photograph (a foldout).

Hayward was seen at the première signing autographs, which she didn't do often, with Jess Barker by her side.

In spite of this being one of her best years, she could not escape her paradoxical fate: she learned that she had been considered for the annual "award" as "worst actress of the year" by the *Harvard Lampoon,* for *I Can Get It for You Wholesale* and *David and Bathsheba.* (The "honor" finally went to Ava Gardner for *Showboat,* when she should have been nominated for the Oscar.) Susan laughed the whole thing off: "As long as they go to see my movies."

She wanted to do *My Cousin Rachel.* Olivia de Havilland got the role. It wasn't the only time Miss de Havilland played a role that Susan had coveted.

Hayward's star status, increasing each year, was noticed when *Look* magazine announced, early in 1952, the "Movies twenty top ticket sellers," according to *Motion Picture Herald* magazine, where her name appeared for the first time as number nineteen. Also, a national magazine carried a cover story entitled "Susan Hayward's $ucce$$ $tory." But she was number six on a list of the ten worst dressed movie stars in Hollywood. (The others were, in this order, Rita Hayworth, Shelley Winters, Bette Davis, Jane Russell, Betty Grable, Pier Angeli, Esther Williams, Lana Turner, and Janet Leigh.) It seems her main "faults" were that she showed too much of her anatomy, and that she always seemed to be peering from under her tresses.

Her next movie was the one that really did it for her, giving her the "little push" that she needed to become the new "America's sweetheart." It was the successful *With a Song in My Heart,* based on the life of singer Jane Froman, which gave her another rich part to play, and the "best dubbing job" since the Larry Parks–Al Jolson *The Jolson Story.* For the first time, she adorned the cover of *Look* magazine. Both *Modern Screen* and *Motion Pictures* magazines also selected the film "The Movie of the Month," and *Silver Screen* again dedicated the "We Point with Pride" page to her. For this role she permitted her hair to be cut.

Her leading men were Rory Calhoun and David Wayne, and they were superbly supported by Thelma Ritter (who won a supporting actress nomination). In a bit part, Robert Wagner was much noticed, and it marked the real beginning of his career. But the movie was one of Hayward's greatest personal triumphs. She danced and "sang" the most beautiful popular tunes of the thirties and forties, including "Blue Moon," "Tea for Two," "I'll Walk Alone," "That Old Feeling," and the title song. Capitol released a 10-inch "long-playing" record with most of the music from the film, which was a best seller.

As a promotion for the movie in New York, the "Brooklyn Bernhardt" came back to that city in triumph, and was invited to speak at her old school, now called Prospect Heights High School, which she had not visited since 1935. At the school auditorium, Governor Dewey honored her with a "Special Award." And right there, before forty-five hundred students she declared, "I'm going to tell the truth. Your yearbook states that I was a member of Arista, the honorary scholastic society, but I never made Arista. I lived at 2568 Bedford Avenue, and things weren't too prosperous at home. I did some modeling while going to school, but was rather handicapped as I had only one good blouse and one good skirt."

After the Jane Froman role, Hayward started crowding Betty Grable for first place in fan mail at Fox. She was so pleased with the movie that she let her twins see her on the screen for the first time.

Susan was assigned to what looked like another good role, as

Getting popularity award from Spanish magazine *Cine-Mundo*

one of Gregory Peck's wives in Ernest Hemingway's *The Snows of Kilimanjaro.* But another "wife" had the better romantic part. After all Susan's scenes were filmed, Ava Gardner stepped into the role of Cynthia, the best loved wife. Susan's script was originally twice as long as it was in the final print. But since Gardner and Hayward didn't share any scenes in the film, this came as a surprise—she found out just before the movie was released. What she and Miss Gardner did share was a *Look* magazine cover (separate photos, of course).

Hayward was billed right after Peck, but what other way could they bill her? She was Fox's top movie star by then (Marilyn Monroe's career was just beginning). That she was far from pleased with her role was evident when she said that her "best histrionic moments were shared with a hyena."

The movie had mixed reviews, but it was one of director Henry King's personal favorites. It was a tremendous hit at the box office, Susan's third in a row.

Her next assignment was a loanout to RKO for Nicholas Ray's highly rated *The Lusty Men,* a story about rodeo people which, during the shooting, had been titled "This Man Is Mine." (To show how titles get twisted around in different languages, the Spanish title of this movie was not translated, but radically changed to *La Mujer Codiciada,* which means "The Coveted Woman.")

As Louise in this movie, Hayward's points of view were almost the same as her own in real life. She tried to stick to her marriage, fighting for their happiness together—in the movie and in reality—and it could have been Susan instead of Louise who said, "Men, I'd like to fry them all in deep fat."

Her co-stars were Robert Mitchum, who gave one of his best performances, and Arthur Kennedy. The movie had excellent reviews and rated another *Look* movie review page, but it wasn't as big a box office hit as its predecessors.

With Darryl F. Zanuck and husband Barker in the background

Dining out with agent and friend Ned Marin

At the end of 1952, Hayward's hit role as Jane Froman paid off and she was named the world's favorite actress, with John Wayne as favorite actor, by the Foreign Press Association of Hollywood, who presented them with oversized Henriettas. Susan also received the "Golden Globe Award" from them for the "best performance by an actress in a musical or comedy." *Motion Picture,* in a popular contest among its readers, selected her the "Best Actress of 1952." She also got the *Photoplay* Gold Medal as the most popular actress of the year, with the film earning the medal as the most popular movie of 1952, and she received the *Britain's Picturegoer* Best Actress, as well as being named the favorite female star in a poll in the Rocky Mountain states. *Song* was rated as one of the top grossing films for 1952 by *Motion Picture Daily.*

Zanuck had so much money invested in Susan over that year and forthcoming ones, that she was called "Fox's twelve-million-dollar baby." But it was paying off; her pictures were all box office hits. In the *Motion Picture Herald* poll, she jumped from nineteenth place in 1951 to number nine among the ten top box office stars in 1952 (only other woman was Doris Day, number seven). *Boxoffice* magazine also chose her as the most popular feminine star. Hayward movies for this year grossed more than $11 million! Also, she got another Academy Award nomination for *With a Song in My Heart.* She repeated her role as Jane Froman early in 1953 for "Lux Radio Theatre" with Rory Calhoun and Thelma Ritter repeating their roles too.

She did not attend the Academy Awards presentation in 1953 as she finally embarked on a long-postponed European vacation with her husband. But she didn't miss what she didn't get, the Oscar that went to Shirley Booth for *Come Back, Little Sheba.* (The other actresses nominated were Bette Davis, *The Star*; Joan Crawford, *Sudden Fear*; and Julie Harris, *Member of the Wedding.*

The Barkers traveled to Spain, Italy, and France. They were mobbed by fans everywhere.

Meanwhile, back in the States, they released *The President's Lady,* one of Hayward's best acting jobs in the fifties. Her Rachel Donelson Robards, maligned wife of Andrew (Charlton Heston) Jackson, was a completely different role for her. Her characterization of this pathetic woman was subtle and brilliant, although underrated. This was the only time that she grew old for the cameras and died a natural death.

The famous portrait painter, Peter Fairchild, included her in a group of four beautiful women (with Ava Gardner, Lana Turner, and Lizabeth Scott). According to Mr. Fairchild, these four beauties were the only ones left in Hollywood since Garbo. Said Susan, "It was kind of Mr. Fairchild, but physical beauty comes by the grace of God and your parents. It's what you achieve on your own that counts."

When the Barkers came back from abroad, Susan did some shopping in New York for articles she could not find in Europe. They were happy to be back in the States. While shopping, she wore dark glasses to avoid recognition (unsuccessfully).

Back in Hollywood, Susan found out that changes had taken place during her absence: the movie industry, trying to recapture the audiences that were staying home since television emerged in the late forties, had developed new "weapons" to fight back; 3-D and CinemaScope. The first one was a Warner Bros. development, and the second belonged to Fox.

Soon she was emoting in front of the CinemaScope cameras in what was to be a sequel to the first CinemaScope movie *The Robe,* then titled "The Story of Demetrius." Fox had such hopes for *The Robe* and the new system that both movies were filmed almost simultaneously.

Early in July, her last movie produced under the old studio system was released: *White Witch Doctor,* which reunited her with former co-star Robert Mitchum. This African adventure failed, not only because of a rather thin story, but because the difference between the real Africa exteriors and the "studio Africa" scenes was apparent. Susan was a doctor who had to fight not only jungle diseases, but a tarantula, a witch doctor, spears, and wild animals. According to one reviewer, "the best acting job came from a man that played a gorilla!"

Susan hit the headlines when, just a few days after their ninth wedding anniversary, she and Barker had such a fight that the neighbors called the police. Things had not been smooth for them, and the pressure had been growing for years. The trip to Europe did not really help. Barker had been referred to, in a scandal magazine, as the "best paid movie star consort" and was receiving a "Mr. Hayward" treatment. This, together with his reversed role in the family (Susan working, he at home, taking care of the children) had been a time bomb, and the explosion was powerful.

The newspapers reported that Barker slapped Susan, and dumped her into the pool completely nude. The scandal magazines said that Susan had triggered Jess when, in the middle of an argument, she said, "I think you're very queer." They said Susan tried to put out a cigarette in Jess's eyes, but missed. Susan declared that he was so enraged that she was afraid for her life. "Jess wanted to get my face," she said, "the very means by which I earn my living."

At the Cocoanut Grove, Hollywood, Hayward presents award to Gregory Peck during Annual Presentation Ceremonies co-sponsored by Hollywood Foreign Correspondents Association and Foreign Press Association

Susan, Jess, and his attorney during divorce trial

With director Henry King, at a Hollywood party, early in 1955

Celebrating "The King's" birthday, with Buddy Adler, during filming of *Soldier of Fortune* in February 1955

The children and a guest, her close friend Martha Little, were in the house. Miss Little came out when she heard the screams. She was being treated for cancer, at Susan's expense.

Susan came out of the battle with a black eye, which she had to hide under dark glasses for a while. Then Barker left the house, and the divorce proceedings started. Ironically, one magazine that had just hit the newsstands carried an article on her saying, "This star knows how to stay married." And a few days earlier, *Look* magazine dedicated a third cover to her, with a story about her screen roles, her favorite movie (*Gone With the Wind*), her favorite author (Thomas Wolfe), and her "idyllic marriage to Barker."

The movie magazines told of Hayward's troubles. Louella Parsons, Susan's long-time friend, wrote an article for *Modern Screen* on the failure of Susan Hayward's marriage. Susan confessed to Louella, "In every marriage breakup there are two sides, and I'm not pretending to paint myself as an angel and Jess as a devil. I have a temper and a hot tongue, and I work so hard I'm frequently tired and almost sick with nerves. Movie stars are never easy to live with, and no one knows that better than I. My heart aches very much but it is closed forever on the past."

Susan was going to Nevada to establish residence with her brother Wally and her two children, and to file for divorce as soon as possible. Barker wanted to come back to her but couldn't get to first base. They met a few times, to discuss the future and the children, but there was no hint of a reconciliation. They were together again in the "Children's Court of Conciliation," with Judge Georgia Bullock, who had herself photographed with them and then turned the whole business over to conciliator Margaret Harpstrite. Miss Harpstrite complained, "Georgia gets all the publicity and I have to do all the work." Susan and Jess ordered lunch for Miss Harpstrite, had their picture taken with her, and then Susan and Barker went their own separate ways. The photographs showed a weary Hayward who had not bothered to touch up her hair.

After that she was seen alone or with different dates, at premières, like the one for *The Robe*, with her agent Ned Marin, and at parties. She dated Jeff Chandler (her old friend Ira Grossel of Brooklyn) and Robert Wagner, a few years her junior. But most of the time she went out with friend and agent Marin. The magazines were hinting that a serious romance could develop between Susan and Jeff Chandler, both of whom were separated or divorced—but in vain.

She was mentioned to play Desirée (which would have given her her only opportunity to co-star with Marlon Brando, who played Napoleon), but the part went to Jean Simmons.

Then she went on location to Mexico to film *Garden of Evil*; Barker broke into the house, but "only to see his children."

Susan's popularity seemed undimmed in spite of the bad publicity, because she was again among the "ten top box office stars" for 1953, getting the same number nine spot she had the year before. This time the only other woman was Monroe, who in one year had catapulted from a Fox starlet to number seven among the grossers.

Susan leaves Cedars of Lebanon Hospital completely recovered

In 1954 Hayward started filming *Untamed*, which co-starred her again with Tyrone Power. Richard Egan was also in the movie and they dated. Egan, curious about Susan pushing herself so hard, asked her why she did it. "Have you ever been hungry, Richard?" she replied.

The divorce proceedings, meanwhile, were on their way, with Susan and Jess in and out of courtrooms. She offered Barker a settlement of $100,000, but he refused. Instead he went to the Superior Court and demanded half of the community property, which amounted to more than a quarter million dollars. Jess's lawyer claimed, "He doesn't want a divorce. If Miss Hayward is willing to try and make it work, he's willing to renounce all his rights to their community property." Since Hayward had made him sign an agreement renouncing his rights to her property when they were married, there was no point to the whole thing. (This was almost unprecedented at the time they did it, 1944, and it had remained unpublicized until the hearing for the divorce.) Jess's lawyer called Susan an "icy woman" and an "absentee mother."

On the other hand, Susan's income was about $374,000 in 1951–52, while Jess's was $665 for the same period, but Susan stated that Jess didn't want to work and spent most of his time sleeping, and that he tagged her "a good meal ticket." He even refused her permission to take the boys along with her to Utah, on a location trip. Yet, despite everything that he tried to do to prevent it, she finally obtained a divorce, more than a year after the initial blowup. Susan was awarded all the community property in her name (more than a million dollars), the right to her annual earnings, and the custody of her nine-year-old twins. Barker got the family station wagon and the right to visit his sons.

Almost simultaneously, by midyear, she had her two releases for 1954: first *Demetrius and the Gladiators*, a sequel to *The Robe*, but with values of its own, being more of a spectacle (sex and action) than the first picture, which was more mythical and religious. She played Messalina to husband Claudius (Barry Jones), but her real interest was Demetrius (Victor Mature). *Motion Picture* selected it as "The Movie of the Month," and *Silver Screen* magazine praised it. The picture was put down by many critics, but it was a box office hit.

Her second release was *Garden of Evil*, a "Mexican western." She had Gary Cooper and Richard Widmark as leading men in this one, and it was her second CinemaScope movie, photographed in Technicolor. CinemaScope was specializing in landscapes from every corner of the world, to take advantage of the long, long, narrow screen. But they could have chosen better ones than the barren lands in which most of the picture was filmed. Susan essayed a few words in Spanish at the beginning that, with her husky voice, made her sound like an American Maria Felix (the top star in Mexico).

In the same year, and about the time *Garden* was released, Hayward started working in one of her poorest movies, *The Conqueror*. It was made for RKO, the troubled Howard Hughes company, and she dated the mysterious multimillionaire, to the displeasure of her studio. Asked why she bothered to star in films that brought no luster to her career,

she said simply, "For the money." At the time she was Hollywood's best paid actress, drawing $6,000 per week.

She was working constantly that year. She lost weight and looked tired and drained, so no one was surprised that illness forced her to rest at home. Martha Little, still her house guest, brought some books for her to read, among them *I'll Cry Tomorrow*. As soon as she read the book, she started a campaign to get the role of Lillian Roth. She convinced her new boss at Fox, Buddy Adler (Zanuck had resigned), to loan her out to MGM, which had the rights to the book, if she was okayed to play Roth by the Metro moguls. She would be loaned to Metro on a deal that would bring Spencer Tracy to 20th for *Broken Lance*.

Although she had won her divorce legally, Barker was still attempting actions against her. He needed $10,000 to pay his lawyer to appeal his case. The judge told a baffled Susan, "Give it to Jess; he needs it to fight for custody of your kids." Barker interfered again when she was preparing to go to Hong Kong to film *Soldier of Fortune*, and planned to take her sons with her. When the boys could not go because of Barker's action, she canceled the trip. (She had replaced Grace Kelly, who got married to Prince Rainier that year and said goodbye to Hollywood for her Monaco princedom.) When Susan couldn't go to China, she was ready to decline the role, but Fox, dreading another replacement and counting on the box office power of Hayward and her leading man—Clark Gable—decided to shoot her scenes on the home lot.

In February, looking much better, Susan helped celebrate Gable's birthday during the shooting at Fox's studio, but her laughs were strictly for the camera. She and Gable didn't get along at all well during the filming—perhaps because of her health and all the troubles with Barker.

She was seen frequently at parties, a far cry from the Hayward of earlier times. She was a presenter at the Foreign Press Association annual banquet, handing Gregory Peck the award as the most popular male movie star. At the same party, she was seen enjoying a vivid conversation with that other Hollywood rebel, Marlon Brando. She was present too, with agent Marin, at one of Sonja Henie's glittering parties, a costume ball, chatting with Liberace and dancing with John Carroll, her old flame.

Untamed was released in March and the reviews were quite bad, in spite of a story not unlike *Gone With the Wind*. Susan's role was similar to Vivien Leigh's role and, perhaps because of that, the reviewers were reluctant to find good qualities in the movie. And it wasn't a hit at the box office either. It was in CinemaScope and De Luxe Color (her first), one of the many setbacks of the system, with its purplish, bluish, brownish hues and dull colors.

Unfortunately, this was Hayward's last association with Henry King, the great director, who got a "best acting" performance out of her. Years later, in the book *The Hollywood Professionals*, Volume II, where the director was profiled by Clive Denton, the author pointed out that he had gotten some of the most breathtaking shots of Susan Hayward, or of any

At the divorce proceedings, wearing dark glasses

actress, in movies like *David and Bathsheba* and *Untamed*.

The role of Katie O'Neill in *Untamed* was one of the most physically exhausting that Susan had ever played: she had to ride horses and drive wagons, take a severe beating from Richard Egan, fight tropical storms and Zulus—she even helped "amputate" Egan's leg. She got to be famous for "punching bag" roles, as an article proclaimed: "But the thing she does best of all—better than anybody since Garbo, Bette Davis or Joe Louis—is take a punch. Perhaps never before in the history of the cinema has an actress been kicked, cuffed and slapped around so much. Susan's average may well be one black eye per picture. Fortunately, on her it looks good."

She hit the headlines again when, on April 26, 1955, after swallowing a handful of sleeping pills, she was rushed to North Hollywood Hospital. Her mother had phoned the police to tell them that her daughter had just called her and, because of the way she sounded, she was afraid for her life. An ambulance was dispatched to her house. She had had a meeting with Barker just hours before, and this probably contributed to her mental depression. She had also suffered two severe blows: her friend Martha Little had died in March, and about the same time her agent and friend Ned Marin died of a heart attack. Marin had been a constant companion to her after her separation from Barker. She had also been studying the *I'll Cry Tomorrow* script, not the kind of literature one should read when depressed. (She had finally convinced Dore Schary, then top man at Metro, that she was the right actress to play the part.)

When Barker heard about the suicide attempt, he too made headlines, sobbing, "I love her! I love her!" But as soon as Susan regained consciousness (she was out almost twenty-four hours), she said she didn't want to see him.

In an article in *Photoplay* magazine, later, she talked about the faith that pulled her together again. She reminisced about her father and something he told her once: "As long as you believe, an angel sits on your shoulder and looks after you."

In May, *Soldier of Fortune* was released. This one was also badly treated by the reviewers. Susan had little to do in this adventure movie. The film was Gable's. Anyway, it was good box office.

A few days after the release of *Soldier,* Susan reported to Metro to start working on what was to be her best dramatic part: the life of the once alcoholic singer Lillian Roth. A host of MGM stars wished Susan good luck on the first day of shooting: Howard Keel, Ann Blyth, Vic Damone, Dolores Gray, Cyd Charisse, Lana Turner, Marisa Pavan, Roger Moore, Debbie Reynolds, Esther Williams, Gene Kelly, Robert Taylor, George Murphy, Eleanor Parker, and Glenn Ford. It was the largest turnout of Hollywood personalities to watch a star perform on an MGM set.

I'll Cry Tomorrow was directed by Daniel Mann, who would become Susan's favorite director (she would make two more movies with him). Magazines started to issue reports from the sets at Metro, about how good her role was and how she was getting the most out of it. Another sure Academy Award nomination was predicted before she even finished the film.

Susan wasn't going out too much. She occasionally dated millionaire Bob Neal, without much fanfare or publicity. Everything was coming up roses, when on November 5 she hit the headlines again. Starlet Jil Jarmyn had gone to actor Don "Red" Barry's apartment for a visit, early in the morning, and found Hayward, in pajamas, on the spot. Barry had a little part in *I'll Cry Tomorrow.* The women got entangled in a brief battle with Susan the victor. She broke a broom on Jil's head and bit her finger. Later, Susan said that Jarmyn "made a nasty remark, and, being a redhead, that infuriated me." Miss Jarmyn filed assault and battery against Hayward, but later dropped the charge "for the sake of Susan's children." Coincidentally, Jil's attorney was the same that Jess Barker had engaged. Jil's photos showing the bruises inflicted by Hayward were in all the newspapers.

Both Susan and Jil claimed that they had just dropped by Barry's to have a cup of coffee, and jokes about this made the rounds in Hollywood. Marlene Dietrich commented, "That Don Barry must make awfully good coffee." At a special preview of *I'll Cry Tomorrow,* the powers that be decided to cut a scene where Hayward, as Roth, goes to Alcoholics Anonymous, and is offered a cup of coffee by Barry. Sometime later Susan again made the cover of another slander magazine, which carried the headline: "Nude in the garden, but pajamas in bed." (Years later, Don Barry would say about Susan, "If a man is lucky enough to know a woman like Susan Hayward, he is a lucky man. She's one of the finest ladies I've ever known.")

I'll Cry Tomorrow was rushed into a prerelease before the end of the year so it could qualify for the 1955 Oscars. The movie showed a rather different Hayward: more mature; more womanly; a bit matronly, perhaps, yet with a new kind of beauty. But then, a lot had happened to her, and unhappiness leaves its mark.

Max and Irene are meant for each other: they are both tough and know what they want (Richard Conte and Susan Hayward)

Irene begs Gino to leave Max alone (Edward G. Robinson and Susan Hayward)

CAST

Gino Monetti, Edward G. Robinson; *Irene Bennett*, Susan Hayward; *Max Monetti*, Richard Conte; *Joe Monetti*, Luther Adler; *Pietro Monetti*, Paul Valentine; *Tony Monetti*, Efrem Zimbalist, Jr.; *Maria Domenico*, Debra Paget; *Helena Domenico*, Hope Emerson; *Theresa Monetti*, Esther Minciotti; *Elaine Monetti*, Diane Douglas; *Lucca*, Tito Vuolo; *Victorio*, Albert Morin; *Waiter*, Sid Thomack; *Judge*, Thomas Browne Henry; *Prosecutor*, David Wolfe; *Danny*, John Kellogg; *Woman Juror*, Ann Morrison; *Nightclub Singer*, Dolores Parker; *Bit Man*, Mario Siletti; *Pietro's Opponent*, Tommy Garland; *Guard*, Charles J. Blynn; *Bat Boy*, Joseph Mazzuca; *Cop*, John Pedrini; *3rd Applicant*, Argentina Brunetti; *Bit Man*, Maurice Samuels; *Cop*, George Magrill; *Neighbors*, Mike Stark, Herbert Vigran; *Referee*, Mushy Callahan; *Preliminary Fighters*, Bob Cantro, Eddie Saenz; *Doorman*, George Spaulding, *Taxi Driver*, John "Red" Kullers; *Detectives*, Scott Landers, Fred Hillebrand.

CREDITS

Directed by Joseph L. Mankiewicz. *Produced by* Sol G. Siegel. *Screenplay by* Philip Yordan. *Based on the novel by* Jerome Weidman. *Photography by* Milton Krasner. *Art Director*, Lyle Wheeler *and* George W. Davis. *Editor*, Harmon Le Maire. *Set Directors*, Thomas Little *and* Walter M. Scott. *Special Effects*, Fred Sersen. *Music*, Daniele Amfitheatrof. *Running time*, 101 minutes.

THE STORY

Max Monetti (Richard Conte) is free after serving seven years in jail. He returns to New York and goes straight to Little Italy, in lower Manhattan. First stop is his father's "bank." It is now the Monetti Trust Company, and the names embedded in the stone are those of his three brothers. He meets them inside: Joseph (Luther Adler), Antonio (Efrem Zimbalist, Jr.), and Pietro (Paul Valentine), the President, first vice president, and second vice president of the bank.

There is no love lost between Max and his brothers. He had rotted in jail for seven years while they were enjoying life with the profits of the bank they had taken from their father. They offer Max money. Max throws it in a wastebasket and leaves to visit his mother (Esther Minciotti).

Then Max goes to a fancy apartment on Central Park West. He finds the key in the customary place. She hasn't forgotten! And Max has not forgotten Irene Bennett (Susan Hayward) either. Theirs is a happy reunion in the beginning, but Max has plans for revenge. He slaps Irene when she expresses anger at his father: "his hate," she tells him, "was the only legacy he left you." He will not listen.

His last visit is to the now darkened Monetti Mansion, where the memories come back. . . .

In 1932, Gino Monetti (Edward G. Robinson) had been the "king" of his loan office. He was quick-tempered and obstinate. Max had his law office in the same building. His brothers complained that Max was Papa's favorite and that Papa didn't like them. Max would remind them that one day they would run Papa's business, but they wanted immediate benefits. But when Max asked Papa to give Joe a raise, Gino would talk about how he made very little money in the beginning. Perhaps Papa was inflexible with the boys, and perhaps Max was his favorite son. He used to call Pietro, the youngest, "dumbhead."

At home, Gino presided over the dinner table. Maria (Debra Paget) was there too—she was engaged to Max and her mother (Hope Emerson), a stern chaperone, never left her side. But Max forgot about her after he met Irene.

Irene Bennett had walked into his office to seek legal advice for "a friend." This was the start of a torrid love affair and soon the whole family, and Maria, knew about it. Maria's mother wanted her to break the engagement, but Gino wouldn't hear of it. Irene learned of his engagement and broke up with Max.

Max went to Gino, but Gino had troubles of his own: the government was examining his books and they were not finding the right answers. Max was too preoccupied with Irene to help.

Gino's business was closed down and he was indicted. His sons deserted him; only Max stood by his father and ended up going to jail.

Gino visited Max in jail and built in him a strong desire for revenge that grew with the years. When Gino died and Max attended the funeral, under guard, he swore his brothers would pay. . . .

Back in the present, Max realizes that all he wants is a little happiness. He'll leave his brothers alone.

But his brothers, fearing Max's revenge, come looking for him at the mansion. They give Max a beating, but end up fighting among themselves, and, finally, it is Max who saves Joe from being strangled by Pietro.

Max flees the mansion and falls into Irene's waiting arms. They will make a fresh start.

REVIEWS

"Except for a wobbly beam or two . . . a well-constructed movie. Into its making went an intelligent screen play by Playwright Philip (*Anna Lucasta*) Yordan; some distinguished lighting effects and camera work by Milton Krasner; and Director Joseph (*A Letter to Three Wives*) Mankiewicz's talent for handling atmosphere and sets as effective projections of character."

NEW YORK TIMES   *Bosley Crowther*

"As a sizzling and picturesque exposure of a segment of nouveau-riche life within the Italian-American population, this film, directed by Joseph Mankiewicz and based on a Jerome Wiedman novel, has its decidedly entertaining points."

Wardrobe test for *House of Strangers*

NOTES

In her first movie at 20th Century-Fox, Hayward had a good role which, although subdued to Robinson's and Conte's, marked the beginning of her best years.

This was starlet Debra Paget's second movie, but she and Hayward didn't share any scenes. Most of Hayward's scenes were with Conte.

Susan's wardrobe did not reflect the times when the action occurs (the thirties) but was pure 1949. This was the trend of the American cinema until recently. They updated the clothes (plus hairdos and makeup) from past decades, especially in films depicting the period from the thirties to the sixties, probably with an eye on female moviegoers seeking the latest fashion.

As Eloise Winters (Susan Hayward)

My Foolish Heart

RKO RADIO, 1949

CAST

Walt Dreiser, Dana Andrews; *Eloise Winters,* Susan Hayward; *Henry Winters,* Robert Keith; *Lew Wengler,* Kent Smith; *Mary Jane,* Lois Wheeler; *Mrs. Winters,* Jessie Royce Landis; *Ramona,* Gigi Perreau; *Miriam Ball,* Karin Booth; *Her Escort,* Tod Karns; *Sergeant Lucey,* Philip Pine; *Night Club Singer,* Martha Mears; *Dean Whiting,* Edna Holland; *Usher,* Jerry Paris; *Grace,* Marietta Canty; *Receptionist,* Barbara Woodell; *Mrs. Crandall,* Regina Wallace.

CREDITS

Directed by Mark Robson. *Produced by* Samuel Goldwyn. *Screenplay by* Julius J. Epstein *and* Philip G. Epstein. *Based on a story by* J. D. Salinger. *Art Director,* Richard Day. *Film Editor,* Daniel Mandell. *Sound Recorder,* Fred Lau. *Set Decorations by* Julia Heron. *Costumes by* Mary Wills. *Miss Hayward's gowns designed by* Edith Head. *Makeup by* Blagoe Stephanoff. *Hair Stylist,* Marie Clark. *Special Photographic Effects by* John Fulton, A.S.C. *Musical Direction by* Emil Newman. *Music by* Victor Young. *Musical Arrangements by* Leo Shuken *and* Sidney Cutner. *Lyrics by* Ned Washington. *Running time, 99 minutes.*

THE STORY

Lew Wengler (Kent Smith) and his wife Eloise (Susan Hayward) are about to be divorced. She is moody and resentful, and is seriously considering revealing to her husband that he is not the father of her child, a lovely daughter named Ramona (Gigi Perreau). But Mary Jane, a former schoolmate, who comes to see her after a long separation, prevents the disclosure.

Getting ready to pack her things and leave Lew, Eloise comes across an old evening gown that brings back memories of her poignant past. . . .

Eloise Winters has been snubbed at a dance in a New York hotel ballroom and is brooding about it in the lobby. Walt Dreiser (Dana Andrews), who has crashed the party, takes advantage of the opportunity and consoles her. When they go out on a date, shortly, Walt takes her to his apartment, but although he is an expert at this sort of thing, his advances are repulsed.

Dana Andrews and Susan Hayward

(Left) Eloise's father reminisces about his love affair with her mother and their mistakes (Robert Keith and Susan Hayward)

Eloise is always happy when she is with her father: their relationship is ideal (Susan Hayward and Robert Keith)

Mother is not too happy about Eloise's relationship with Walt (Jessie Royce Landis and Susan Hayward)

(Left) Eloise is shocked when she learns that her sweetheart has been killed in an airplane crash (Susan Hayward)

Eloise and Walt continue to see each other, whenever she can steal away from her boardingschool. Walt also visits her in school; when they are discovered kissing in the school elevator, she is expelled. Her parents come to New York to investigate. Her father, Henry Winters (Robert Keith), a World War I veteran, is understanding. But Mrs. Winters (Jessie Royce Landis) is worried that her daughter might have been compromised. But when the father has a serious talk with Walt and he swears that nothing has happened, they laugh off the whole affair. Her parents intended to take Eloise back home, but she wants to stay in New York. Now they are free to see each other as often as they want. When World War II breaks out, however, Walt is called to duty in the air force; they spend the last evening before his departure together. The next day, just before he takes off in a practice flight, he writes Eloise a letter asking her to marry him. But he is killed in a plane crash before she receives his letter.

Her grief is even greater because she is going to have Walt's baby. In desperation, fearing that she will be exposed, she lures her schoolmate's fiancée into marriage, knowing that Mary Jane and Lew Wengler were about to be married.

When her child is born, Lew believes it is his. Mary Jane goes away and she and Eloise never see each other again until . . .

The old gown still in her hands, Eloise realizes that she has betrayed not only an innocent husband, but an innocent friend. She tells Lew that he can go ahead with the divorce and take the child too, if he wants her, but Lew lets her keep Ramona. As Lew and Mary Jane leave together, Eloise hugs Ramona.

REVIEWS

NEW YORK TIMES *Bosley Crowther*

"Every so often there comes a picture which is obviously designed to pull the plugs out of the tear glands and cause the ducts to overflow. Such a picture is Samuel Goldwyn's latest romance, *My Foolish Heart*."

SCREEN GUIDE

"Susan Hayward and Dana Andrews are tops, and there is an unforgettable performance by Robert Keith. Women will love this picture."

PHOTOPLAY

"Susan Hayward packs plenty of emotion in her portrayal of impetuous youth."

NEWSWEEK

"This is very much Susan Hayward's picture, and she makes the most of her first chance at an honest, demanding characterization by realizing it with an admirable sincerity and understanding."

NOTES

This was Susan's second movie with Dana Andrews, her third with RKO Radio Pictures, the third to open at Radio City Music Hall, and her only one for Samuel Goldwyn.

Her role as Eloise Winters brought her rave reviews from all the critics, who claimed that this was the second best movie in her career.

It was the third hit in a row for director Mark Robson, the first two being *Champion* and *Home of the Brave*. Robson always used the system of preproduction rehearsal. These rehearsals were aimed toward a finer, more polished production with a quality achieved through advance briefing.

The title song was nominated among the best songs of the year.

This movie was released late in 1949 to meet the "Oscar" deadline, but the general release was in 1950.

Lew tries to be nice to Eloise (Kent Smith and Susan Hayward)

Tears designed to trick Lew into marriage (Kent Smith and Susan Hayward)

Mary Jane can't understand why Eloise hasn't told Walt that she is pregnant, but Eloise doesn't want him to feel obligated to marry her (Lois Wheeler and Susan Hayward)

151

I'd Climb the Highest Mountain

20th CENTURY-FOX, 1951

CAST

Mary, Susan Hayward; *William Asbury Thompson,* William Lundigan; *Jack Stark,* Rory Calhoun; *Jenny Brock,* Barbara Bates; *Mr. Brock,* Gene Lockhart; *Mrs. Billywith,* Lynn Bari; *Glory White,* Ruth Donnelly; *Mrs. Brock,* Kathleen Lockhart; *Salter,* Alexander Knox; *Mrs. Salter,* Jean Inness; *Dr. Fleming,* Frank Tweddell; *George Salter,* Jerry Vandiver; *Bill Salter,* Richard Wilson; *Martha Salter,* Dorothea Carolyn Sims; *Pike Boys,* Thomas Syfan, Crady Starnes; *Martin Twins,* Kay and Fay Fogg.

CREDITS

Directed by Henry King. *Produced by* Lamar Trotti. *Screenplay by* Lamar Trotti. *Based on a novel by* Corra Harris. *Technicolor Consultant,* Monroe W. Burbank. *Director of Photography,* Edward Cronjager, A.S.C. *Art Directors,* Lyle Wheeler *and* Maurice Ransford. *Film Editor,* Barbara McLean. *Sound,* Eugene Grossman *and* Roger Heman. *Set Decorations,* Thomas Little *and* Al Orenbach. *Wardrobe Direction,* Charles LeMaire. *Costumes designed by* Lionel Newman. *Makeup,* Ben Nye. *Technical Adviser,* Rev. Wallace Rogers, D.D. *Special Photographic Effects,* Fred Sersen. *Music,* Sol Kaplan. *Orchestration,* Edward Powell. *Running time, 88 minutes.*

THE STORY

In a country church in the Blue Ridge Mountains of Georgia, Reverend William Asbury Thompson (William Lundigan) marries his fiancée, Mary (Susan Hayward). It is the year 1910.

Mary, city-bred, knows it's not going to be easy for her to adjust to her life as the wife of a young circuit rider, but she is determined to work hard at being Mrs. Thompson, and feels that her love for William will overcome her difficulties.

Her new neighbors are Mr. and Mrs. Brock (Gene and Kathleen Lockhart) and their daughter Jenny (Barbara Bates), whom she meets at a party. Mr. Brock, the owner of the general store, is a powerful man in the community. He's also a church steward and a big contributor.

Mr. Salter (Alexander Knox), on the other hand, is a confirmed atheist and is raising his children out of the church. He is a challenge to William, who rides his circuit with faith, conviction, and courage. Mary is her husband's constant companion and helpmate. She shows her courage and conviction when, during an epidemic, it becomes her duty to help lay out and dress the dead.

Jenny Brock is brought to the hospital with a fever and in her delirium calls for Jack (Rory Calhoun). Jenny's father dislikes the boy intensely, and when Jack comes to the hospital, Brock tries to hit him and is only stopped by William, who promises him that with the Lord's help Jenny will recover. And she does.

Mrs. Billywith gets the picture; she is no longer welcome at Mary's home (Lynn Bari and Susan Hayward)

William prays that Mary learns to understand him and his vocation (Susan Hayward and William Lundigan)

The Reverend and his beautiful wife (Susan Hayward and William Lundigan)

Mr. and Mrs. Brock and daughter Jenny meet Reverend Thompson's wife (left to right: Barbara Bates, Gene Lockhart, Kathleen Lockhart, Susan Hayward, and William Lundigan)

The Reverend does not fare so well when he takes the Salter children to a church picnic without their father's permission: George Salter falls in the mill pond and drowns. William's faith is shaken, but he and Mary continue their good work.

Jack Stark and Jenny Brock come to William to be married despite Mr. Brock's objections. Although hesitant at first, William performs the ceremony.

When Christmas comes, William and Mary decide that every child in the hills should have a present. They ride through the countryside on Christmas Eve, dropping gifts at every house, including the house of the Salters. When the children happily tell their father that Santa Claus brought them the presents, Mr. Salter knows that he has lost a major point.

Spring comes and William is ordered to a new post. When he and Mary bid the people farewell, they realize that their faith and hard work have inspired in his congregation the true love of God.

Sometimes William has to remind Mary that he is the boss in their house (William Lundigan and Susan Hayward)

REVIEWS

NEW YORK HERALD TRIBUNE   *Joe Pihodna*

"Susan Hayward photographs beautifully in Technicolor as the parson's wife in a part which gives her ample opportunity at comedy and pathos."

NEWSWEEK

"What emerges is not a closely woven narrative but an episodic, now-dramatic, now-light story that will probably have most appeal for nonurban audiences. It is not a serious study of a God-fearing, life-moving man in the Georgia of 1910. But it is a wholesome and colorful film."

NEW YORK TIMES   *Bosley Crowther*

"Outside of the slight improbability of Susan Hayward's appearance as the wife of a Methodist circuit-rider in the red-clay Georgia Hills, there is character and general plausibility in 20th Century-Fox's amiable film about a horse-and-buggy preacher.

"The flavor of the Georgia hill country has been captured by Director Henry King by shooting much of his picture—the exteriors—in the genuine locale."

NOTES

Hayward stepped into this role to replace Jeanne Crain, originally slated to play the part. It was a different role for her, that of a hard-working, dedicated preacher's wife. It also provided her an opportunity to show her comic vein, especially in the scenes that had to do with the "other woman," Lynn Bari.

For the first time, Hayward's voice was used to narrate parts of the story.

Susan got to be so popular in Georgia that, upon completion of the film, she was officially named an "Adopted Daughter" of Georgia by a resolution of the State Senate.

William Lundigan had one of his rare starring roles in an "A" movie. As Reverend Thompson, Hayward's husband, his performance was moving.

The movie acquired importance through the years and is today considered one of director Henry King's best films.

Vinnie burns damaging evidence (Tyrone Power and Susan Hayward)

Rawhide

20th CENTURY-FOX, 1951

CAST

Tom Owens, Tyrone Power; *Vinnie Holt,* Susan Hayward; *Zimmerman,* Hugh Marlowe; *Yancy,* Dean Jagger; *Sam Todd,* Edward Buchanan; *Tevis,* Jack Elam; *Gratz,* George Tobias; *Luke Davis,* Jeff Corey; *Tex Squires,* James Millican; *Fickert,* Louis Jean Heydt; *Gil Scott,* William Haade; *Dr Tucker,* Milton R. Corey, Sr.; *Wingate,* Ken Tobey; *Cilchrist,* Dan White; *Miner,* Max Terhune; *Billy Dent,* Robert Adler; *Callie,* Judy Ann Dunn; *Chickering,* Howard Negley; *Mr. Hickman,* Vincent Neptune; *Mrs. Hickman,* Edith Evanson; *Flowers,* Walter Sande; *Hawley,* Dick Curtis.

CREDITS

Directed by Henry Hathaway. *Produced by* Samuel G. Engel. *Written by* Dudley Nichols. *Director of Photography,* Milton Krasner, A.S.C. *Art Directors,* Lyle Wheeler *and* George W. Davis. *Film Editor,* Robert Simpson. *Sound,* Eugene Grossman *and* Roger Heman. *Set Decorations,* Thomas Little *and* Stuart Reiss. *Wardrobe Direction,* Charles LeMaire. *Costumes designed by* Travilla. *Makeup,* Ben Nye. *Special Photographic Effects,* Fred Sersen. *Musical Direction,* Lionel Newman. *Music,* Sol Kaplan. *Orchestration,* Edward Powell. *Song: "A Rollin' Stone," Music by* Lionel Newman, *Lyrics by* Bob Russell. *Running time, 89 minutes.*

It is now Vinnie's turn to dig the hole under the bed, which might be their only way out (Susan Hayward)

THE STORY

At the lonely Rawhide Relay Station, in the year 1880, Sam Todd (Edgar Buchanan) and young Tom Owens (Tyrone Power) greet the Overland Stagecoach. Vinnie Holt (Susan Hayward) and her little orphaned niece Callie (Judy Ann Dunn) are about to board the stagecoach, but word comes that four escaped killers are in the neighborhood, and they are not allowed to leave: it's too dangerous. Vinnie protests, but has no choice but to wait for the next stagecoach.

When the stage leaves, a man rides in alone, claiming to be Sheriff Miles, from Huntsville, looking for the outlaw. But Sam recognizes him as Zimmerman (Hugh Marlowe) and when the outlaw realizes it, he draws his gun and calls the other three, who had been out of sight: Tevis (Jack Elam), Gratz (George Tobias), and Yancy (Dean Jagger).

The outlaws announce that they plan to stay at Rawhide until the next day, when the east-bound stagecoach is due, which they know is carrying $100,000 in gold. Soon Tevis discovers that there is a woman about and Sam, who fears for Vinnie, tries to warn her and is killed by Tevis. Zimmerman, believing that Vinnie is Tom's wife, locks them up together in a room.

Tom is sure that once they rob the stage the next morning, the outlaws will dispose of the three of them, so that it is necessary to devise a way of escaping. Every attempt is thwarted either by Zimmerman or, worse, by Tevis, who is half crazed. Finally, Tom manages to dig a hole in the adobe wall with a knife he had smuggled in. The hole is almost finished by morning.

Zimmerman orders him to hitch up the relay team and, meanwhile, unnoticed, Callie slips into the hole. When Vinnie realizes that Callie is gone she begins to pound on the door. Tevis opens it and she struggles with him trying to get out. Zimmerman believes that Tevis is trying to molest Vinnie and, rushing over, knocks him down. Tevis shoots Zimmerman and then kills Gratz. Yancy runs.

Tom tries to take advantage of the situation by getting a pistol he had hidden in the corral, but Tevis sees him and grabs Callie, threatening to kill her if Tom doesn't come out. Tom is about to give up when Tevis falls dead, killed by a bullet from Vinnie's rifle.

When the stage arrives the driver wants to know what happened. Tom looks at Vinnie with a smile: "Just learning the business," he replies, "just learning the business."

REVIEWS

NOTES

Rawhide was a Hathaway western with touches of Hitchcock's suspense. A real thriller. However, the ads showing Tyrone Power trying to subdue a wild Susan Hayward, wearing a half-torn blouse and screaming, "I'll kill you, Owens. . . . For this I'll kill you!" suggest things that are happening in movies of the seventies, the era of real violence and sex, but that never happened in this movie.

The exteriors were filmed on location at Lone Pine, California, where the temperature dropped so that the actors were shivering, though the action was supposed to take place in a warm locale.

Hayward and Power made a beautiful couple, physically. Hayward's hair looked glorious.

The music heard in the previews had been used before by 20th Century-Fox, in prestigious westerns like *Brigham Young* and *Yellow Sky,* and was yet to be used in not-so-prestigious westerns like *The Silver Whip.*

Tyrone Power and Susan Hayward

Vinnie and Tom feel helpless while Zimmerman orders everybody around (Hugh Marlowe, Susan Hayward, and Tyrone Power)

George Sanders, Susan Hayward, and Dan Dailey

I Can Get it for You Wholesale

20th CENTURY..Fox, 1951

CAST

Harriet Boyd, Susan Hayward; *Teddy Sherman,* Dan Dailey; *Noble,* George Sanders; *Cooper,* Sam Jaffe; *Marge,* Randy Stuart; *Four Eyes,* Marvin Kaplan; *Savage,* Harry Von Zell; *Ellie,* Barbara Whiting; *Hermione Griggs,* Vicki Cummings; *Ray,* Ross Elliott; *Kelley,* Richard Lane; *Mrs. Boyd,* Mary Philips; *Fran,* Benna Bard; *Bettini,* Steve Geray; *Pulvermacher,* Charles Lane; *Ida,* Jan Kayne; *Terry,* Marion Marshall; *Models,* Jayne Hazard, Aline Towne; *Miss Marks,* Eda Reis Merin; *Louise,* Marjorie Hoshelle; *Nurse,* Doris Kemper; *Secretary,* Elizabeth Flournoy; *Bartender,* Jack P. Carr; *Mrs. Cooper,* Tamara Shayne; *Tiffany Joe,* Ed Max; *Speaker,* David Wolfe; *Elevator Man,* Harry Hines; *Blondes,* Diana Mumby, Shirlee Allard, Beverly Thompson.

CREDITS

Directed by Michael Gordon. *Produced by* Sol C. Siegel. *Screenplay by* Abraham Polonsky. *Adaptation by* Vera Caspary. *Based on the novel by* Jerome Weidman. *Director of Photography,* Milton Krasner, A.S.C. *Art Direction,* Lyle Wheeler *and* John De Cuir. *Film Editor,* Robert Simpson. *Sound,* Winston H. Leverett *and* Roger Heman. *Set Decorations,* Thomas Little. *Wardrobe Direction,* Charles LeMaire. *Makeup,* Ben Nye. *Special Photographic Effects,* Fred Sersen. *Musical Direction,* Lionel Newman. *Music,* Sol Kaplan. *Orchestration,* Earle Hagen. *Running time, 91 minutes.*

THE STORY

Harriet Boyd (Susan Hayward) is a model at the dress house of Put-Bel-Kel, located on the famous Seventh Avenue, the garment center of New York. She is also a designer and decides to open her own dress business, taking with her, as partners, Teddy Sherman (Dan Dailey), the best salesman in the industry, and Sam Cooper (Sam Jaffe), the top "inside man" at Put-Bel-Kel.

Sherboyco Dresses Inc. is born from the partners' savings, and starts to function with Harriet's cold, calculating mind. Teddy, however, disregarding her attitude, falls in love with her.

When J. F. Noble (George Sanders) is introduced to Harriet at the Garment Makers Ball, things start to change. Noble, who is the owner of the powerful and prestigious Noble Department Store, convinces Harriet that he can make her one of America's leading designers of fine evening gowns, known as "Harriet of Noble's." This is a tempting offer for ambitious Harriet.

Teddy is opposed to making evening gowns: Sherboyco manufactures commercial dresses, and that's the way it should stay. Harriet, lured by the prestige Noble promises, tries to dissolve the partnership, but Teddy, infuriated with her relationship with Noble, will not release her.

Harriet, angry, forgets Teddy in her pursuit of fame, and enters into a secret agreement with Noble to produce evening gowns for his store. She also informs Teddy that if the company refuses to deliver the gowns she will see that it goes bankrupt. She accomplishes nothing with her threats, however, because Teddy and Sam agree that bankruptcy is better than eating dirt.

Harriet plans to sail to Europe with Noble. At the pier, Noble realizes that she's only going with him out of spite, and that she really loves Teddy. He advises Harriet to go back to Teddy and beg his forgiveness.

Finally, Harriet realizes how wrong she has been. Taking Noble's advice, she rushes back to Sherboyco, where Teddy greets her with open arms. Sherboyco is in business again.

REVIEWS

NEW YORK HERALD TRIBUNE *James S. Barstow, Jr.*

"Romance and the dress business are turned out in a slick combination from 20th Century-Fox. There's more of the former in *I Can Get It For You Wholesale,* as an ambitious dress designer takes her partners for a ride along Seventh Avenue, and much of the garment industry flavor of the Jerome Weidman novel gets lost during the trip. But with Susan Hayward, Dan Dailey and Sam Jaffe nimbly catching the occasional sparks in Abraham Polonsky's screenplay under the smooth direction of Michael Gordon, a familiar boy-meets-girl routine looks nice and fancy in the new setting.

"Miss Hayward is just right in playing a conventional role fast and sassy on her double-crossing climb from $10.95 models to Paris creations; she's nasty-nice enough almost to carry the contrived, good-girl-after-all conversion of the climax."

Susan Hayward as Harriet Boyd

Cooper consults Harriet before making a decision (Susan Hayward and Sam Jaffe)

Teddy is full of ideas, but Harriet is more interested in her own (Susan Hayward and Dan Dailey)

Harriet makes up a story to get money from Ray and her sister (Ross Elliott, Susan Hayward, and Randy Stuart)

Cooper and Harriet try the new fabrics on a model (Sam Jaffe, Marion Marshall, and Susan Hayward)

TIME

"Actor Dailey's breeziness and Actress Hayward's fire, brighten the old scenario about the ruthless career woman who is redeemed by the love of a good man."

NOTES

Fox filmed most of the exteriors right in the garmet center on New York's Seventh Avenue to catch the real local flavor. Director Gordon even filmed some scenes with Hayward and Dailey amidst unsuspecting garment workers going about their daily business (how Hayward could go unnoticed is a mystery). It was a different story when they filmed at Bonwit Teller, where the onlooking crowd tied up traffic for hours.

Hayward was perfectly cast, projecting all of Harriet's acidity and distrust. She also had a chance to match her wit with that of the master of sarcasm: George Sanders. And the ads didn't let Hayward down this time: "The spectacular rise of a woman in a man's world'"; "She made good—with a plunging neckline and the morals of a tigress"; "Never promise what you can't deliver."

The title was changed to *Only the Best* for TV showings, to differentiate it from the 1962 Broadway production, which starred Lillian Roth, Elliot Gould (portraying the character that Susan played in the movie, which was a man in the novel), and Barbra Streisand, who became a Broadway star as a result of this show.

Character actor Sam Jaffe was notified, during the last stages of the filming, that he had been honored with an award at the Venice International Film Fesitval: Best Actor, for his performance in *The Asphalt Jungle.*

David and Bathsheba

20th CENTURY-FOX, 1951

Bathsheba feels as guilty as David but they can not change their feelings (Gregory Peck and Susan Hayward)

CAST

David, Gregory Peck; *Bathsheba*, Susan Hayward; *Nathan*, Raymond Massey; *Uriah*, Kieron Moore; *Abishai*, James Robertson Justice; *Michal*, Jayne Meadows; *Ira*, John Sutton; *Joab*, Dennis Hoey; *Goliath*, Walter Talun; *Adulteress*, Paula Morgan; *King Saul*, Francis X. Bushman; *Jonathan*, Teddy Infuhr; *David (as a boy)*, Leo Pessin; *Specialty Dancer*, Gwyneth Verdon; *Absolom*, Gilbert Barnett; *Priest*, John Burton; *Old Shepherd*, Lumsden Hare; *Egyptian Ambassador*, George Zucco; *Amnon*, Allan Stone; *Samuel*, Paul Newlan; *Jesse*, Holmes Herbert; *Executioners*, Robert Stephenson, Harry Carter; *Jesse's First Son*, Richard Michelson; *Jesse's Second Son*, Dick Winters; *Jesse's Third Son*, John Duncan; *Court Announcer*, James Craven.

CREDITS

Directed by Henry King. *Produced by* Darryl F. Zanuck. *Written for the screen by* Philip Dunne. *Technicolor Color Consultant*, Leonard Doss. *Director of Photography*, Leon Shamroy, A.S.C. *Art Direction*, Lyle Wheeler *and* George Davis. *Film Editor*, Barbara McLean. *Sound*, E. Clayton Ward *and* Roger Heman. *Set Decorations*, Thomas Little *and* Paul S. Fox. *Wardrobe Direction*, Charles LeMaire. *Costumes designed by* Edward Stevenson. *Makeup*, Ben Nye. *Biblical Technical Adviser*, Dr. C. C. McCown. *Special Photographic Effects*, Fred Sersen. *Music*, Alfred Newman. *Orchestration*, Edward Powell. *Choreography by* Jack Cole. *Running time, 116 minutes.*

THE STORY

Three thousand years ago, King David (Gregory Peck), having stormed the walls of Rabgah, saved the life of one of his captains, Uriah (Kieron Moore), and received a flesh wound, returns to Jerusalem. Back at his court, David attends to matters of state and listens as Nathan the Prophet (Raymond Massey) praises his plan to bring the sacred Ark of the Covenant from Philistia. But the King is lonely. His first wife, Michal (Jayne Meadows), complaining of neglect, has berated him for being a "shepherd's son" and taunted him with the greatness of her father, King Saul (Francis X. Bushman). David goes out onto the terrace and sees a beautiful woman bathing in an adjacent house, attended by two female Nubian servants. He finds out that this beautiful woman is Uriah's wife, Bathsheba (Susan Hayward).

Sending for her, the King discovers that she, too, is unhappy in her marriage. It is not long before they admit their love for each other and enter into unholy wedlock.

When the caravan bringing the Ark of the Covenant reaches the city gates, David goes to greet it. The Ark sways on its cast and when a soldier attempts to hold it, he drops dead on the spot. Nathan declares that God has considered the moving untimely and directs that a tabernacle be built for the Ark in that very place.

Bathsheba is being dressed for the wedding (Susan Hayward)

David gives Bathsheba a token of his love for her (Gregory Peck and Susan Hayward)

Apparently, Abishai brings David "bad news" from the city (James Robertson Justice, Gregory Peck, and Susan Hayward)

The lovers fear God's wrath is upon them (Susan Hayward and Gregory Peck)

When a drought sweeps the land and there is danger of famine, David suspects that the Lord is punishing him and his people for his sin. But when Bathsheba tells David that she is with child and fears that she may be stoned to death according to the law of Moses, David thinks of nothing else but saving her. He plans to send Uriah to the battle's forefront to be killed.

Uriah is indeed killed in battle and King David marries his beloved Bathsheba in full regal splendor. God punishes them again when Bathshba's child dies soon after birth. Meanwhile, famine has spread throughout the land and the Israelites, prompted by Nathan, blame the King for their plight. They storm the palace and demand that Bathsheba pay for her sin.

David pleads that he should be punished and goes to the Ark to pray for forgiveness. He confesses his sin and places his hands on the Ark: with a clap of thunder King Saul appears before his eyes, and he sees his battle with the giant Goliath and how he saved the Israelites. Then as lightning flashes the tabernacle is enveloped in an unearthly radiance. Overwhelmed, David starts reciting the twenty-third Psalm: "The Lord is my shepherd . . ." Suddenly he hears a drop of rain on the roof of the tent, then another, until it becomes a steady patter. God has forgiven them: the drought has ended!

King David goes to Bathsheba, who is exhausted by her vigil over her dead child. They vow that goodness and mercy shall be with them all their lives and that they shall dwell forever in the house of the Lord.

REVIEWS

NEWSWEEK

"Under the rather trying circumstances in which they find themselves, both Peck and Miss Hayward bring considerable dignity and conviction to their roles."

MOVIELAND

"Susan Hayward is beautiful as Bathsheba but she makes a rather wooden temptress—and the highly ballyhooed bath scene is, to say the least, disappointing. But the picture belongs to David, due mainly to Gregory Peck's memorable performance."

TIME

"*David and Bathsheba* takes itself much more seriously than *Samson and Delilah*. Scripter Philip Dunne has made a literate adaptation of the story from the second book of Samuel. His characterizations of David (Gregory Peck), a national hero grown cynical, lax and unpopular, and Bathsheba (Susan Hayward), a proud, shrewd charmer, are thoughtful and thorough. And Peck's performance carries surprising authority."

The lovers enjoy a peaceful moment on the fields (Gregory Peck and Susan Hayward)

NOTES

This was the most grandiose film that Fox made in 1951, probably trying to cash in on the popularity and box office returns of Paramount's *Samson and Delilah*. The Bible, revived again by Cecil B. DeMille, was paying off. *David and Bathsheba,* although panned by the critics, was one of Hollywood's major earners in 1951 and won Oscar nominations in the following categories: Music Scoring, Art and Set Direction, Cinematography, Story and Screenplay, and Costume Design. The movie, however, was slow and tedious.

The role of Bathsheba didn't earn Hayward any acting laurels, but she looked beautiful in her first biblical film, her second with director Henry King.

The ballyhooed sequence of Bathsheba's bath was brief and disappointing. She was not naked, of course, and the shots could have been closer.

Dancer Gwyneth Verdon (later Gwen Verdon, famous as Lola in both the Broadway and film versions of *Damn Yankees*) was seen in a special dance number in the court of King David. Francis X. Bushman, ex–silent screen idol, had a brief part as King Saul. And Jayne Meadows was King David's first wife, in her final movie role, prior to going on to a full-time television career.

With a Song in My Heart

20th CENTURY-FOX, 1952

CAST

Jane Froman, Susan Hayward; *John Burn*, Rory Calhoun; *Don Ross*, David Wayne; *Clancy*, Thelma Ritter; *GI Paratrooper*, Robert Wagner; *Jennifer March*, Helen Westcott; *Sister Marie*, Una Merkel; *The Tenor*, Richard Allan; *Guild*, Max Showalter; *Radio Director*, Lyle Talbot; *General*, Leif Erickson; *Diplomat*, Stanley Logan; *USO Man*, Eddie Firestone; *Texas*, Frank Sully; *Muleface*, George Offerman; *USO Girl*, Beverly Thompson.

CREDITS

Directed by Walter Lang. *Produced by* Lamar Trotti. *Written by* Lamar Trotti. *Technicolor Color Consultant*, Leonard Doss. *Director of Photography*, Leon Shamroy, A.S.C. *Art Direction*, Lyle Wheeler *and* Joseph C. Wright. *Film Editor*, J. Watson Webb, Jr., A.S.C. *Sound*, Arthur L. Kirbach *and* Roger Heman. *Set Decorations*, Thomas Little *and* Walter M. Scott. *Wardrobe Direction*, Charles LeMaire. *Makeup*, Ben Nye. *Special Photographic Effects*, Fred Sersen *and* Ray Kellogg. *Musical Direction*, Alfred Newman. *Vocal Direction*, Ken Darby. *Orchestration*, Herbert Spencer *and* Earle Hagen. *"Montparnase," Music by* Alfred Newman, *Lyrics by* Eliot Daniel; *"Jim's Toasty Peanuts" by* Ken Darby. *Dances staged by* Billy Daniel. *Technical Adviser*, Jane Froman. *Color by* Technicolor. *Running time, 117 minutes.*

THE STORY

Jane Froman (Susan Hayward) is being honored as "the most courageous entertainer of the year" at the Newspapermen's Annual Ball in New York. John Burn (Rory Calhoun) and Clancy (Thelma Ritter) are in the audience.

John recalls her story as she sings.

In 1936 Jane goes to audition at a radio studio. She mistakes Don Ross (David Wayne) for the program director and sings for him. He suggests that she try the song again, less flamboyantly. The real director (Lyle Talbot) comes in and, although he likes her, suggests that she give the song more flamboyancy. Jane and Don laugh over the incident and she signs her contract.

Jane's success takes her to Radio City and the Paramount Theatre in New York. Don keeps asking her to marry him, but she is not sure that she loves him. When they finally marry, there is friction. Don is a failure as an artist and even when Jane sings his songs he claims that people applaud her, not his songs. Jane tries to be patient, but when the United States enters the war, she is among the first to go abroad to entertain the troops.

Jane boards the plane to Lisbon and meets Captain John Burn, who asks her to help him demonstrate the "Mae West" lifesavers. As the plane approaches Lisbon, it crashes, and they

Susan Hayward as Jane Froman

Jane is on her way: no more "jingles," only romantic songs

are thrown into the water. Jane is badly hurt, but John saves her life. In the Lisbon hospital she meets the caustic, big-hearted Clancy, who becomes her friend.

The doctors fear that Jane will never walk again; her left knee is shattered and her right leg was almost severed. They even talk about an amputation so, when John declares his love, she brushes him off jokingly, despite her feelings for him.

Don comes to take her back to America where she undergoes operation after operation. Clancy, who has come back with her and who keeps spurring her on, and Don, who hires a piano for her, help Jane sing again.

Jane makes a comeback in *Artists and Models,* still in a hip-high cast, and she's magnificent, but soon she has to return to the hospital for yet another operation. Clancy gives her the courage to keep fighting, and finally she's ready to try the stage again.

She gets an engagement at La Riviera Club in New York. John is there, but Jane still avoids him. Don, who has learned about him, has a showdown with John at the club.

Jane, still on crutches, goes back to Europe to entertain the troops. She tours GI camps and hospitals, traveling 30,000 miles with Clancy at her side.

When Jane is getting ready to return home at the end of her tour, Don telephones John to say he won't be waiting for her at the airport—their marriage ended long ago. So John welcomes her and makes her his own.

REVIEWS

NEW YORK TIMES   *Bosley Crowther*

"The courage and perseverance that Jane Froman has shown in surmounting crippling injuries received in an airplane crash in 1943 have been the inspiration for a virtual legend of the entertainment world—a legend that aptly illustrates the great tradition of 'The show must go on.' "

LOOK

"In *With a Song in My Heart,* Susan Hayward steps into the character of singer–World War II heroine Jane Froman—and makes her so alive that from now on the two women may be one in the public's mind.

"All in all, Susan Hayward, with the warmth and range of the artist she has become, makes the Froman story a convincing experience."

MODERN SCREEN

"*With a Song in My Heart* uses *The Jolson Story* technique —that is, Susan Hayward plays Jane Froman, but whenever Susan opens her mouth to sing the voice that comes out is actually Miss Froman's. It works fine, since the synchronization is expert and Miss Hayward has just the right sultry, torchy look that goes with Miss Froman's sultry, torchy singing voice."

Dancing and singing "On the Gay White Way" in one of her films (Susan Hayward)

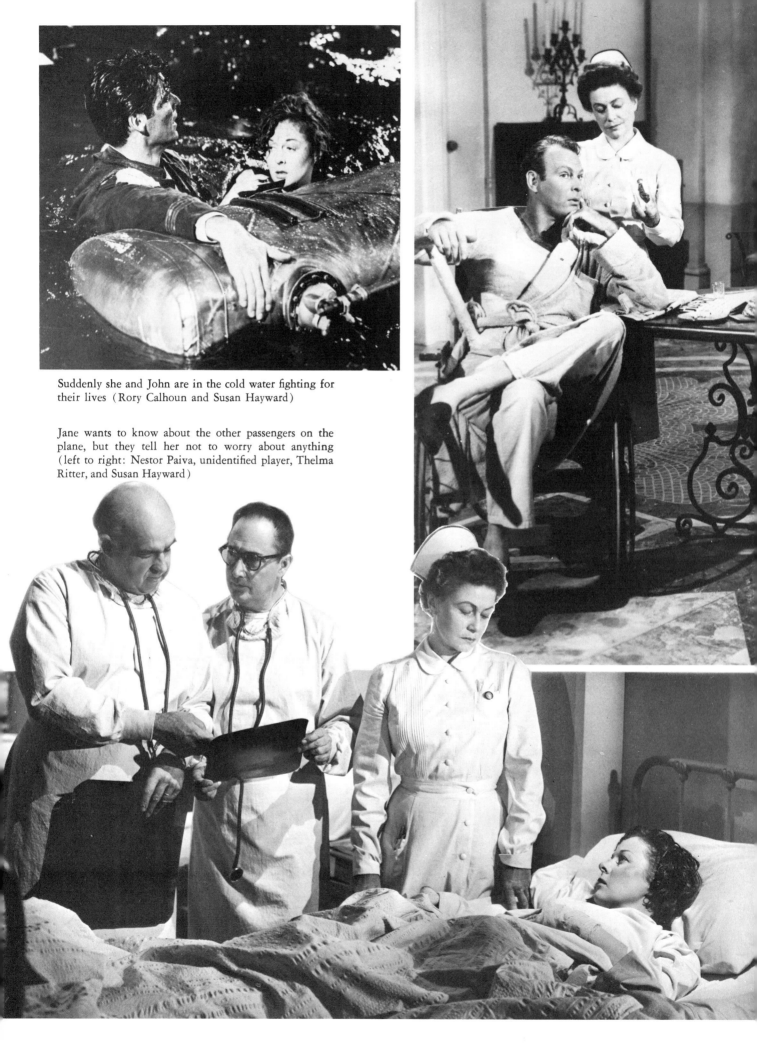

Suddenly she and John are in the cold water fighting for their lives (Rory Calhoun and Susan Hayward)

Jane wants to know about the other passengers on the plane, but they tell her not to worry about anything (left to right: Nestor Paiva, unidentified player, Thelma Ritter, and Susan Hayward)

The general plays a joke on Clancy, to the amusement of John and Jane (Leif Erickson, Thelma Ritter, Rory Calhoun, and Susan Hayward

NOTES

Jeanne Crain wanted desperately to play Jane Froman, but the singer preferred Susan, who looked a little like her. Jane and Susan got along fabulously and were photographed chatting with Jane's mother on the set. Froman said of Hayward, "She looks and acts like a singer, like myself, but she has some tricks of her own."

Jane recorded about twenty-six songs for the movie, which Susan was supposed to mimic in front of the cameras, but Hayward really sang at the top of her lungs instead of just pretending.

Top-flight musical groups in the scoring and recordings were: The King's Men, The Four Girlfriends, The Modernaires, The Melody Men, The Starlighters, and The Skylarks. "On the Gay White Way," a full-scale musical number, with dancers on a stage, was an outstanding achievement, yet it is rarely mentioned; and the film title number was also beautifully staged—"early forties style."

As a result of the promotion for this movie, Susan appeared on the cover of music magazines like *Hit Parade* and *Music Dealer*.

The scene in which the boys at one of the hospitals give Jane Froman a farewell card is a memorable one. She is visibly moved when she reads it: "To Jane Froman, a great soldier who, though wounded herself, didn't forget us wounded."

The wardrobe for the movie was expensive: Hayward wore forty-two different outfits. They had to uphold Froman's tradition as one of the "Ten Best Dressed Women in America."

The sound and the music score were nominated for awards, and it won the Oscar for the latter category.

Jane is ready for a comeback, but her legs are not: she has to be propped up (left to right: Thelma Ritter, Susan Hayward, and David Wayne, way back in the background)

175

The Snows of Kilimanjaro

20th CENTURY-FOX, 1952

CAST

Harry, Gregory Peck; *Helen,* Susan Hayward; *Cynthia,* Ava Gardner; *Countess Liz,* Hildegarde Neff; *Uncle Bill,* Leo G. Carroll; *Johnson,* Torin Thatcher; *Beatrice,* Ava Norring; *Connie,* Helene Stanley; *Emile,* Marcel Dalio; *Guitarist,* Vicente Gomez; *Spanish Dancer,* Richard Allan; *Dr. Simmons,* Leonard Carey; *Witch Doctor,* Paul Thompson; *Molo,* Emmett Smith; *Charles,* Victor Wood; *American Soldier,* Bert Freed; *Margot,* Agnes Laury; *Annette,* Janine Grandel; *Compton,* John Dodsworth; *Harry (Age 17),* Charles Bates; *Venduse,* Lisa Ferraday; *Princesse,* Maya Van Horn; *Marquis,* Ivan Lebedeff.

CREDITS

Directed by Henry King. *Produced by* Darryl F. Zanuck. *Screenplay by* Casey Robinson. *Based on the story by* Ernest Hemingway. *Technicolor Color Consultant,* Leonard Doss. *Director of Photography,* Leon Shamroy, A.S.C. *Art Direction,* Lyle Wheeler *and* John De Cuir. *Film Editor,* Barbara McLean, A.C.E. *Sound,* Bernard Freericks *and* Roger Heman. *Set Decorations,* Thomas Little *and* Paul S. Fox. *Wardrobe Direction,* Charles LeMaire. *Makeup,* Ben Nye. *Special Photographic Effects,* Ray Kellogg. *Music,* Bernard Herrmann. *Choreography,* Antonio Triana. *Running time, 114 minutes.*

THE STORY

Harry Street (Gregory Peck), the famous novelist and big-game hunter, lies dangerously ill in a hunting camp at the foot of the Kilimanjaro in Africa. His wife Helen (Susan Hayward), who had arranged this hunting trip in the hopes of winning his love, takes care of him faithfully and prays for his recovery. Harry is semidelirious and fears that he's going to die.

His feverish mind goes back to his youth. He recalls his uncle Bill Swift (Leo G. Carroll), who guided his life in those early years; Connie (Helene Stanley), the first girl he was interested in; and his wandering around the world looking for something that he never seemed to find.

Once again he finds himself at the little bistro in the Montparnasse in Paris, where he first met Cynthia (Ava Gardner). Inspired by her love, he writes his first novel *The Lost Generation,* making her the central character without conscious planning. Their affair progresses and she is with him when his book is accepted. Harry's only thought is going to Africa, in search of new adventures, instead of establishing a home with Cynthia. Cynthia's love is so great that, despite her disappointment, and hiding from him the fact that she is going to have a baby, she goes with him.

From Africa they go to Spain: first the bullfights in Madrid, then the fiesta in Pamplona. Cynthia keeps following him, afraid of losing his love. She loses her baby, however, and

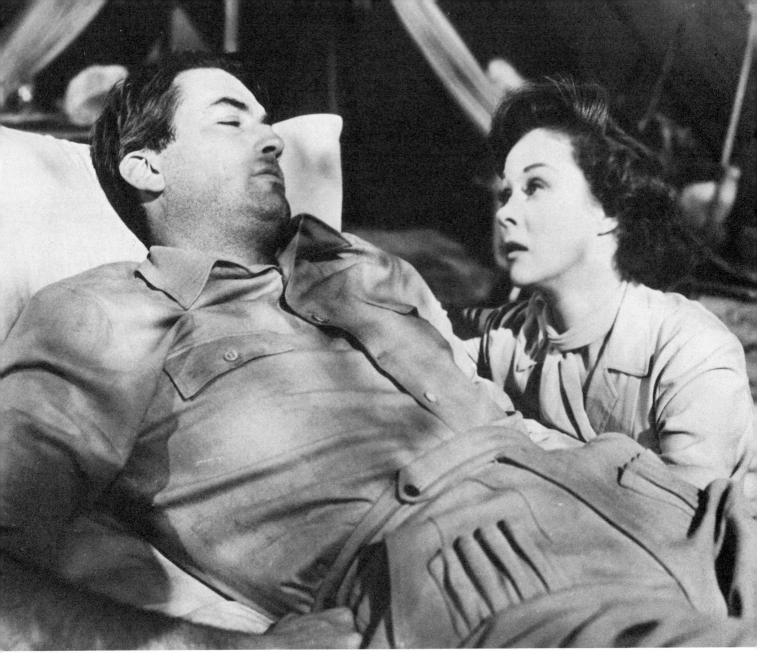

Helen watches anxiously over Harry, who is delirious at times (Gregory Peck and Susan Hayward)

when Harry is not concerned with her plight but only with an offer he had received to cover the war between the Syrians and the French, Cynthia, close to a nervous breakdown, leaves him.

Harry covers the fighting as a war correspondent and then goes off to the French Riviera, where he meets the Countess Liz (Hildegarde Neff), a sculptress who patronizes and fascinates him. But Harry is not content and when royalties and fame start coming, he goes back to Madrid in search of Cynthia.

Unable to find her, he gerts involved in the Spanish Civil War, joining the Loyalist Army. One day, during a battle, an ambulance is hit and the driver is badly wounded. As he seeks to help, he realizes that the driver is Cynthia. She dies.

Returning to Paris, he tours the cafés, drinks too much, and dreams of going to the snow-covered Kilimanjaro, about which he has been reading. One evening, quite drunk, he meets Helen and mistakes her for Cynthia. She is a lonely, rich widow and it doesn't take her long to fall for Harry. She marries him, feeling that her money can at least buy her companionship.

At the hunting camp, Harry awakens to find Helen at his side with the news that a rescue plane is about to land. Looking at his wife, he feels that, for the first time, his life has taken on real meaning.

Helen, through her great love and self-sacrifice, has reached her husband's heart as no one could before.

REVIEWS

NEWSWEEK

"The succinct and vivid qualities associated with Hemingway are rarely evoked, and what has been substituted is for the most part meandering, pretentious, and more or less maudlin romance."

NEW YORK HERALD TRIBUNE   *Otis L. Guernsey, Jr.*

"Miss Gardner is sultry, Miss Hayward self-possessed and Miss Neff irritating as is required in this triptych of romantic memory."

(Gregory Peck and Susan Hayward)

"Produced by Darryl Zanuck and vaguely based on the Ernest Hemingway short story, the movie is a Technicolor travelogue that ranges from Africa to Europe to backwoods Michigan, a sort of scenic railway running through a Tunnel of Love.

"The acting honors are easily captured by a herd of hippopotami plunging like dolphins in an African river, and by a Hollywood hyena whose night prowling about the camp has a superbly eerie quality."

NOTES

This film marked two important events: director Henry King's fortieth anniversary in the movies, and Darryl F. Zanuck's twenty-fifth anniversary as a producer of fine films. It was also one of King's own favorites.

It was Hayward's third movie directed by Henry King and her second with Gregory Peck, as well as her second blockbuster and top grosser for 20th Century-Fox in 1952.

Hayward and Peck's scenes at the foot of Kilimanjaro are constantly interrupted by flashbacks and this, plus the fact that most of their sequences in France were left on the cutting room floor, made Hayward's part sort of "evaporate" from everybody's mind. However, she does have strong dramatic scenes at the end of the movie—laughing hyena and all! (When director King imitated the hyena's laugh from behind the camera, it sounded so good that they decided to use it in the film soundtrack instead of the real thing.)

Anne Francis was replaced by Ava Gardner because Francis didn't look too much like Susan Hayward and Peck had to mistake Hayward for Gardner twice in the story.

Hayward, Peck, and Gardner never set foot in Africa, only in the one created at the Fox lot. Nevertheless, the film got two Oscar nominations: for Art and Set Direction and Cinematography.

(Left), Helen throws the witch doctor out; he is the one doctor she doesn't need now (Susan Hayward and Gregory Peck)

Photographing the hippopotamus before Harry has his accident (Susan Hayward and Gregory Peck)

The Lusty Men

RKO Radio, 1952

Louise seems despondent because things are not going the way she had planned (Susan Hayward)

CAST

Louise, Susan Hayward; *Jeff*, Robert Mitchum; *Wes Merritt*, Arthur Kennedy; *Booker Davis*, Arthur Hunnicutt; *Al Dawson*, Frank Faylen; *Buster Burgess*, Walter Coy; *Rusty*, Carol Nugent; *Rosemary Maddox*, Maria Hart; *Grace Burgess*, Lorna Thayer; *Jeremiah*, Burt Mustin; *Ginny Logan*, Karen King; *Red Logan*, Jimmy Dodd.

CREDITS

Directed by Nicholas Ray. *Produced by* Jerry Wald. *Screenplay by* Horace McCoy *and* David Dortort. *Based on a story by* Claude Stanush. *Director of Photography*, Lee Garmes, A.S.C. *Associate Producer*, Thomas S. Gries. *Art Directors*, Albert S. D'Agostino *and* Alfred Herman. *Film Editor*, Ralph Dawson, A.C.E. *Sound*, Phil Brigandi. *Set Decorations*, Darrell Silvera *and* Jack Mills. *Wardrobe*, Michael Woulfe. *Makeup*, Mel Berns. *Hair Stylist*, Larry Germain. *Musical Director*, C. Bakaleinikoff. *Music by* Roy Webb. *Running time, 113 minutes.*

THE STORY

Jeff (Robert Mitchum) gets thrown and gored by a Brahma bull. Rodeo is his life. Away from it he's nothing, and physically and emotionally spent, he limps across the empty rodeo arena, unable to continue his profession because of his injuries.

He searches desperately for something on which to build a new life. Looking for what he thinks he has lost, he returns to the home he had once escaped, now owned by a garrulous old man. Remembering a childhood cache that he had hidden under the floor, he retrives it: an old rodeo program and two nickels. This is all he has after twenty years of rodeoing.

Later, he meets Wes Merritt (Arthur Kennedy) and his wife Louise (Susan Hayward), who want to buy his old place. Recognizing the former rodeo star, Wes gives him a job at his ranch, and since he has won some rodeo events himself, they decide to form a partnership with Jeff as Merritt's manager.

Jeff's interest in Wes Merritt, however, includes his wife. Louise disapproves of her husband's decision, but understands and shares his ambitions, and his dissatisfaction with their present way of life, and realizing that Jeff is interested in her, uses him to make her husband jealous and get him to quit rodeoing. Jeff knows that Louise tolerates him only because her husband needs him, so he encourages Merritt, hoping to lure Louise away from him.

This three-way relationship, based on mutual and conflicting interests, is a reflection of rodeo life itself: a struggle to win an elusive prize.

Finally, the two men have a big fight. Wes dissolves his partnership with Jeff, but, despite his decision to continue his rodeo career, Louise stays with him instead of running off with Jeff.

Jeff has been seriously hurt in the rodeo arena and Louise brings some consolation (left to right: Sam Flint, Susan Hayward, Arthur Hunnicut, Carol Nugent, and Robert Mitchum)

Wes does his best to convince Louise that he knows what is good for both of them, but she seems adamant (Arthur Kennedy and Susan Hayward)

Jeff finds Louise in a defiant mood — she has just had a
fight with a girl who was flirting with her husband
(Robert Mitchum and Susan Hayward)

Alone again, Jeff returns to rodeo, competing against Merritt, though out of practice and out of shape. Thrown by a bronco, his foot catches in the stirrup and he is dragged by the animal. One of his broken ribs punctures his lung and, dying, he achieves the significance that he could never attain in life.

Wes responds to Jeff's heroic gesture by making the courageous decision to return to the ranch, where he and Louise really belong.

REVIEWS

NEWSWEEK

"*The Lusty Men* is a bang-up impression of the rodeo as shown business, including raw life behind the scenes. Mixed with this is a personal drama of somewhat more than the average Hollywood impact. . . .

"In between the dazzling feats of horse and bullmanship, there is the trailer camp life around the circuit, the boozing, crap shooting, shop talk, and wrangling over women (Miss Hayward has a wonderful hen fight with a menacing little dish played by Eleanor Todd)."

QUICK

"This RKO drama is a good example of what an exciting background can do for a triangle love story. The background is the exciting spectacle and authentic inner workings of the rodeo.

"The triangle consists of a broken-down ex–rodeo champ (Robert Mitchum), a cowpoke learning the rodeo ropes (Arthur Kennedy) and Kennedy's wife (Susan Hayward). This combination is explosive, but rodeo thrills steal the film."

NOTES

Actual shots of rodeos were filmed in Tucson, Arizona; Livermore, California; Spokane, Washington; and Pendleton, Oregon; with some of America's most famed rodeo stars: Carroll Henry, Gerald Roberts, Les Sanborn, and Jerry Ambler. Ranch locations were also shot at five other spots in Arizona and California.

This is Nicholas Ray's most respected film and today it is regarded as a classic.

It was Susan's fourth picture for RKO Radio Pictures, and the last in which she had a good film brawl with another actress, in this case starlet Eleanor Todd. (In *Valley of the Dolls,* at the end of her career, she had another fight, but it wasn't the kind of spicy brawl where she was ahead all the way and never a victim.)

Lee Garmes, who had the record of filming a movie scene in the largest set (the burning of Atlanta in *Gone With the Wind*), came close to another record, filming a scene in the smallest one: the set for the scene in which Hayward takes a shower in a house trailer was only 28 by 32 inches.

Susan's hair was shorter than usual at the beginning because it had been cut for *With a Song in My Heart,* but it grew during the filming and the hairdressers had a hard time making it look the same length for scenes shot at opposite ends of the schedule. She would not let them cut it again!

Robert Mitchum's performance was a memorable one.

(Left) An intimate moment between Wes and Louise
(Arthur Kennedy and Susan Hayward)

The President's Lady
20th CENTURY-FOX, 1953

Rachel Donelson Robards, slandered wife of Andrew Jackson, elected the seventh President of the United States in 1829 (Susan Hayward)

CAST

Rachel Donelson Robards, Susan Hayward; *Andrew Jackson,* Charlton Heston; *John Overton,* John McIntire; *Mrs. Donelson,* Fay Bainter; *Lewis Robards,* Whitfield Connor; *Charles Dickinson,* Carl Betz; *Mrs. Phariss,* Gladys Hurlbut; *Moll,* Ruth Attaway; *Captain Irwin,* Charles Dingle; *Mrs. Stark,* Nina Varela; *Mrs. Robards,* Margaret Wycherly; *William,* Robert B. Williams; *Colonel Stark,* Ralph Dumke; *Jane,* Trudy Marshall; *Cruthers,* Howard Negley; *Dr. May,* Dayton Lummis; *Clark,* Harris Brown; *Jacob,* Zon Murray; *Samuel,* James Best; *Colonel Green,* Selmer Jackson; *Mrs. Green,* Juanita Evers; *Minister,* George Melford; *House Servant,* George Hamilton; *Slave Girl,* Vera Francis; *Jason,* Jim Davis; *Innkeeper,* Leo Curley; *Mary,* Ann Morrison; *Uncle Alfred,* William Walker; *Square Dance Caller,* Sherman Sanders; *Lincoya—Age 8,* Ronald Numkena; *Colored Boy,* Rene Beard; *Henry, Phariss' Driver,* Sam McDaniel; *Chief Justice Marshall,* George Spaulding; *Judge McNairy,* Willis B. Bouchey.

CREDITS

Directed by Henry Levin. *Produced by* Sol C. Siegel. *Screenplay by* John Patrick. *Based on the novel by* Irving Stone. *Director of Photography,* Leo Tover, A.S.C. *Art Direction,* Lyle Wheeler *and* Leland Fuller. *Film Editor,* William B. Murphy, A.C.E. *Sound,* Eugene Grossman *and* Roger Heman. *Set Decorations,* Paul S. Fox. *Wardrobe Direction,* Charles LeMaire. *Costumes designed by* Renie. *Makeup,* Ben Nye. *Assistant Director,* Joseph E. Rickards. *Special Photographic Effects,* Ray Kellogg. *Music,* Alfred Newman. *Orchestration,* Edward Powell. *Running time, 96 minutes.*

THE STORY

Although Rachel Donelson (Susan Hayward) is married when Andrew Jackson (Charlton Heston) meets her in a log cabin at Nashville in 1791, he knows that she will be his wife some day. And it is he who accompanies her when her mother, Mrs. Donelson (Fay Bainter), sends her to Natchez to get her away from Lewis Robards (Whitfield Connor), her husband, who is making her miserable.

In a riverboat, on their way to Natchez, they are attacked by Creek Indians and the danger brings them close to each other. When they reach Natchez, Rachel stays at the home of a relative and Andrew tells her that they can get her marriage annulled and be wed. Before they can do anything, however, Andrew receives a letter from his law partner in Nashville, John Overton (John McIntire), saying that Robards has been granted a petition for divorce on the grounds of adultery, naming Jackson as corespondent.

Andrew is humiliated by this injustice, but he feels proud of his love for Rachel and tells her so. They get married and go back to Nashville where Andrew becomes interested in pol-

Her husband is coming home from the war and Rachel wants to look her best but, in her excitement, makes a mess of everything (Susan Hayward)

The news that John Overton brings Andrew and Rachel is disturbing, but Andrew suffers more for Rachel's sake (John McIntire, Charlton Heston, and Susan Hayward)

Lewis and Rachel cannot make their marriage work (Whitfield Connor and Susan Hayward)

Andrew is delighted to see Rachel dressed like a real lady and in the proper surroundings (Charlton Heston and Susan Hayward)

itics. Soon, however, they find out from John Overton that although Robards had been granted a petition for divorce, it had not been consummated until now; therefore, Rachel and Andrew have been living together for two years without really being married. At Rachel's insistence, they are wed again at her mother's home.

The news spreads, however, and at a party Charles Dickinson (Carl Betz) makes a remark about Andrew "stealing another man's wife." Andrew challenges him to a duel and kills Dickinson. Andrew, wounded, makes a solemn vow to Rachel: he will lift her so high that no one will ever again dare say a word against her.

Their romance, in spite of all the slander, is tender and their marriage is lasting. No man that ever dared to insult Rachel escaped a thrashing by Andrew.

Years later, when Andrew Jackson is nominated for President, John warns him that the campaign may be hard and bitter, but Andrew accepts the nomination.

Toward the end of the campaign Andrew is making a speech, and Rachel, who had been ill, slips unnoticed into the crowd to hear her husband. Ugly shouts interrupt his speech, accusing him of being a gambler and a murderer, a man who stole another man's wife, and the crowd yells that "no one wants a woman of ill repute as a first lady." Rachel collapses.

Her illness gets worse and, when Andrew gets word that he has been elected President, Rachel is near the end. He calls her "the first lady" as she dies in his arms. Andrew's promise to his beloved Rachel is fulfilled, but she died three months before his inauguration as President of the United States in 1829.

REVIEWS

PHOTOPLAY

"History provides a batch of sure-fire elements—Indian-fighting, a tender love story, drama that aims straight for the heart—to make a satisfying vehicle for Susan Hayward and Charlton Heston.

"As the maligned wife of the future president Susan is beautiful and deeply sympathetic while Heston—showing a striking resemblance to Old Hickory—gives his best performance so far."

TIME

"Based on Irving Stone's bestselling 1951 biographical novel, the picture hews fairly closely to historical fact; and, unlike most movie biographies of famous men, it has more than its share of legitimate adventure. But in its writing, direction and acting, it comes out as a too-slick biography film. Susan Hayward makes a glamorous Mrs. Jackson even when she is smoking a pipe (as she did in real life), and she grows old becomingly."

NEW YORK TIMES *H.H.T.*

"History plays a curious second fiddle to love's old sweet song in *The President's Lady,* 20th Century-Fox's reverent and highly sentimental tribute to Andrew and Rachel Jackson. In this spaciously picturesque offering the equally picturesque Susan Hayward and Charlton Heston are allowed an emotional gamut perfectly befitting one of the most compelling and poignant romances of the early American scene."

NOTES

It is a pity that this well directed and well acted movie was not filmed in technicolor as Susan Hayward looked truly beautiful. It was a favorite of Hayward's fans. One scene is particularly remembered. She's deliriously happy at the news that her husband is on his way home. Then she realizes that, having worked in the fields all day, she's messy and dirty. In desperation, she grabs a pitcher of water to wash her face and drops it on the floor. Her husband walks in as she is picking up the pieces and her expression, a mixture of wild elation and acute embarrassment, is a masterpiece.

Her characterization of Rachel in old age was also unforgettable and the makeup artists did a wonderful job—she aged from eighteen to sixty-one.

Margaret Wycherly, the character actress, played Whitfield Connor's (Hayward's first husband) mother. Poor Connors didn't have much luck in his roles with Susan: in *Tap Roots* he was her treacherous fiancé who runs away with her sister; and here he is not only a cruel husband but has her branded as an adulteress when she leaves him.

This was the second time that Hayward's voice was used in parts of the narration.

She had two important visitors on the set: Irving Stone, author of the book on which the movie was based, and India's leading feminine star, Naris.

The movie was nominated for Art and Set Direction and for Costume Design, and it contributed to the rise of Susan's name to the list of the ten top money makers of 1953.

White Witch Doctor

20th CENTURY-FOX, 1953

CAST

Ellen Burton, Susan Hayward; *Lonni Douglas*, Robert Mitchum; *Huysman*, Walter Slezak; *Jacques*, Mashood Ajala; *Utembo*, Joseph C. Narcisse; *Kapuka*, Elzie Emanuel; *Jarrett*, Timothy Carey; *Bakuba Boy*, Otis Green; *Gorilla*, Charles Gemora; *Witch Doctors*, Paul Thompson, Naaman Brown; *Aganza*, Myrtle Anderson; *Bakuba King*, Everett Brown; *Chief's Wife*, Dorothy Harris; *De Gama*, Michael Ansara; *Paal*, Michael Granger; *Council Member*, Leo C. Aldridge-Milas; *Councilman*, Louis Polliman Brown; *Chief*, Floyd Shackleford.

CREDITS

Directed by Henry Hathaway. *Produced by* Otto Lang. *Screenplay by* Ivan Goff *and* Ben Roberts. *Based on the novel by* Louise A. Stinetorf. *Technicolor Color Consultant*, Leonard Doss. *Director of Photography*, Leon Shamroy, A.S.C. *Art Direction*, Lyle Wheeler *and* Mark-Lee Kirk. *Film Editor*, James B. Clark, A.C.E. *Sound*, Eugene Grossman *and* Harry M. Leonard. *Set Decorations*, Stuart Reiss. *Wardrobe Direction*, Charles LeMaire. *Costumes designed by* Dorothy Jeakins. *Makeup*, Ben Nye. *Assistant Director*, Gerd Oswald. *Special Photographic Effects*, Ray Kellogg. *Music*, Bernard Herrmann. *Running time, 96 minutes.*

THE STORY

Lonnie Douglas (Robert Mitchum) and his partner, Huysman (Walter Slezak), guide registered nurse Ellen Burton (Susan Hayward) to the distant jungle outpost where she, as a volunteer, has been sent to give medical aid to the natives. But Huysman and Lonni also have plans of their own: it is said that there is hidden gold in the Bakuba country, and they are determined to find it.

They penetrate the remote interior of the Congo by means of a primitive canoe propelled by a native crew. At one of their portages Ellen cures a wife (Dorothy Harris) of the native chief, and the witch doctor, seeking revenge for her interference, tries to kill her with a tarantula, but she manages to escape its poisonous bite.

Later, Lonni saves a boy who has been severely injured fighting a lion. The lad is the son of the Bakuba king and wears a necklace made of gold nuggets—the treasure Lonni and Huysman are seeking. Perhaps this is the opportunity they've been waiting for, Lonni thinks, and devises a plan for using the Bakuba boy to get the gold. He waits until the boy recovers from his wounds to send a message to his father, the Bakuba king, but the plan never materializes because six Bakuba warriors carry the boy off. However, when the lad does not recover, the king sends a message to Ellen by the talking drums, to come to their village and take care of his son.

Susan Hayward and Robert Mitchum

As soon as she arrives, Ellen has a taste of the perils that lie ahead in the Congo (Walter Slezak and Susan Hayward)

Ellen wants to know the situation as they head toward the interior regions of the Congo (Robert Mitchum and Susan Hayward)

Ellen and Lonni have fallen in love and Ellen explains that she has come to Africa in atonement for an injustice she did to her husband before he died. They go to the king's camp, but when Bakuba sentries discover Huysman and his cohorts in the vicinity, they accuse Lonni of leading them to their camp. Lonni confesses to Ellen that he has used her as a blind to get to the treasure and persuades the Bakuba king to let him go out and get Huysman to leave. But when Lonni tells Huyman that there is no gold in the Bakuba country, Huysman doesn't believe him, and, pointing a gun at his head, gives Lonni thirty seconds to reveal the location of the gold. Lonni wrestles with Huysman for control of the gun and kills him.

Lonni returns to the village. The boy is on his way to full recovery and they are free to go. He and Ellen decide to stay, however, to help the natives.

REVIEWS

NEWSWEEK

"This Technicolor film, a sentimental adventure story largely taken in Hollywood, is interlaced with striking sequences obtained in the Belgian Congo area occupied by the Bakuba tribe 1,200 miles inland from Africa's West Coast. With Leon Shamroy, three times an Oscar winner, as chief cameraman, the luxuriant Congo is richly suggested, the Bakubas are caught in their fantastic dances, and there are other African specialties. . . .

"Miss Hayward is a piquant missionary, Mitchum sidles through the clearings with wholly masculine aplomb, but it is the genuine Bakubas, in mask and paint, who have the best of things here."

PHOTOPLAY

"Full-blooded action in the depths of Africa teams Robert Mitchum, well-cast as a jungle-born hunter, and Susan Hayward, lovely and convincing as a brave nurse who tries to bring healing to the natives. Theatrical as it is, the plot is worked out neatly."

SILVER SCREEN

"Single-handed, the plucky Susan takes on the job of doctoring the local natives while Mitchum looks on admiringly and makes a mental note to cast out all further thought of doing the natives out of their gold. Enjoyable hokey adventure. 20th Century-Fox."

NOTES

This was her second movie "in Africa," and again Hayward never left the studio. She never saw the Dark Continent!

The role of nurse Ellen Burton didn't give Susan much chance at dramatic acting. There were too many savages beating drums, dancing and throwing spears, not to mention the tarantulas and gorillas, plus a malevolent witch doctor. (The

"What's next?" This seems to be the question in Ellen's mind (Robert Mitchum and Susan Hayward)

tarantula scene caused Hayward to tear a ligament in her left shoulder as she tried to move away from it as fast as possible.)

The hairdresser had a problem with how Susan should wear her abundant red hair. They ended up piling it on top of her head with a few curls on her forehead, to help her cope with the heat of "equatorial Africa."

This was Hayward's second movie with director Hathaway and with leading man Robert Mitchum. For *The Lusty Men*, their first, Susan had been loaned to RKO, and now Mitchum was loaned to Fox in return.

The movie was undistinguished African adventure nonsense, and not even Walter Slezak, playing his usual villain, got good reviews. In retrospect, it was a black spot in Susan's career.

Demetrius and the Gladiators

20th CENTURY-FOX, 1954

CAST

Demetrius, Victor Mature; *Messalina,* Susan Hayward; *Peter,* Michael Rennie; *Lucia,* Debra Paget; *Paula,* Anne Bancroft; *Caligula,* Jay Robinson; *Claudius,* Barry Jones; *Glydon,* William Marshall; *Dardanius,* Richard Egan; *Strabo,* Ernest Borgnine; *Cassius Chaerea,* Charles Evans; *Kaeso,* Everett Glass; *Macro,* Karl Davis; *Albus,* Jeff York; *Slave Girl,* Carmen de Lavallade; *Varus,* John Cliff; *Specialty Dancers,* Barbara James, Willetta Smith; *Senator,* Selmer Jackson; *Cousin,* Douglas Brooks; *Decurion,* Fred Graham; *Magistrate,* Dayton Lummis; *Chamberlain,* George Eldredge; *Prisoner,* Paul Richards.

CREDITS

Directed by Delmer Daves. *Produced by* Frank Ross. *Screenplay by* Philip Dunne. *Based on the Novel* The Robe *by* Lloyd C. Douglas. *Cinematographer,* Milton Krasner. *Art Directors,* Lyle Wheeler *and* George W. Davis. *Editors,* Dorothy Spencer *and* Robert Fritch. *Costumes by* Charles LeMaire. *Assistant Director,* William Eckhardt. *Special Photographic Effects,* Ray Kellogg. *Music Director,* Alfred Newman. *Music,* Franz Waxman. *Choreography,* Stephen Papick. *In CinemaScope, Technicolor, Stereophonic Sound. Running time, 101 minutes.*

THE STORY

Demetrius (Victor Mature), a freed slave and a Christian, is apprehended by Roman soldiers while trying to hide Christ's robe. Condemned to train as a gladiator, Demetrius refuses to kill his adversaries when he defeats them so he is greatly admired by the other gladiators.

His beautiful physique and powerful strength attract the attention of Messalina (Susan Hayward), a beautiful Roman, married to Claudius (Barry Jones), the future Caesar. She is fascinated by him and wants to find out if he will kill his opponent when his only alternative is being killed himself. The designing Messalina arranges for Demetrius to fight a gigantic and fierce Nubian warrior. But Demetrius defeats him and refuses to kill him when the big man slips and falls to the ground. Demetrius also refuses to yield to Messalina's passionate advances, so he is ordered to go back to his training.

Demetrius hears that Lucia (Debra Paget), a Christian girl whom he loves, is dead after having been attacked by Dardanius (Richard Egan) and other gladiators. His faith shaken, he makes a kill at the arena and succumbs to Messalina's charms. Favored by the passionate Messalina, he is set free after swearing his allegiance to the Emperor Caligula (Jay Robinson). But the latter, to prove Demetrius' loyalty, sends him to fetch the robe that Christ wore to his crucifixion.

At Lucia's shop, where the robe is hidden, Demetrius meets Peter the Apostle (Michael Rennie) again, and learns that

Messalina tries to stop Demetrius from entering the arena, but he is determined (Susan Hayward, Victor Mature, and John Cliff)

Susan Hayward as Messalina

Lucia is not dead. Peter persuades him to pray for her. When he touches the robe the scene at the Golgotha comes vividly to his mind and he repents of his sins. Lucia recovers and Demetrius, having returned to his Christian faith, is again condemned to the gladiator's arena. This time, however, he puts down his sword. Caligula, refusing to hear Messalina's pleas for the young man's life, orders the Praetorian Guard to kill him. But Caligula is slain by the Praetorian Guard, and Claudius becomes the new emperor.

Messalina, realizing that her love for Demetrius is impossible, stands by her husband when he pardons Demetrius and sets him free, ordering that there shall be no more slaughtering of Christians as long as they are not disloyal. Demetrius, accompanied by Peter, returns to his friends.

REVIEWS

NEW YORK TIMES   *Bosley Crowther*

"The matter of Christian devotion versus pagan tyranny, which became quite a subject for conversation through most of the two hours of *The Robe*, underlies the dramatic action in this sequel to be sure, but the conflict between the two forces is expressed in more direct and muscular terms."

MOTION PICTURE

"The millions who enjoyed the spectacular movie *The Robe*, have a chance to continue their pleasure at this truly exciting

and worthy sequel. Costing almost as much as its predecessor, $3,500,000 as compared with $4,500,000 for the first film, it's as handsome a CinemaScope production in every way."

TIME

"*Demetrius and the Gladiators* (20th Century-Fox), a sequel to *The Robe*, is an energetic attempt to fling the mantle of sanctity over several more millions of the entertainment dollar. It offers a number of *The Robe*'s sets, at least two of the same scenes, and three of the same stars—Jay Robinson, who plays the Emperor Caligula with a heavy sneer; Michael Rennie, who portrays Peter as a sort of apostolic Anthony Eden; and Victor Mature, a bulky fellow who helps in filling the huge CinemaScope screen."

NOTES

This sequel to *The Robe* was successful at the box office, one of the top grossers for 1954. From the critics' standpoint, however, it wasn't so good.

Two clips from *The Robe* were used: the Crucifixion and the last scene with Richard Burton and Jean Simmons, only, for *Demetrius*, Susan was seen watching them.

Hayward looked gorgeous as the wicked Messalina. The part, however, was not developed. It might have been an ideal role for Susan. *Demetrius'* Messalina repented at the end while the real Messalina went on to more promiscuity until she paid with her own life. (When *Demetrius* and *The Robe* were re-released in 1959, they were shown together with the two casts intermingled, and Susan Hayward, having just won an Academy Award, got top billing over everyone else, including Mature, Richard Burton, and Jean Simmons.)

This was Susan's second movie with Debra Paget, who was still considered a promising starlet, but, again, they were never together in a scene.

Future Academy Award winners Ernest Borgnine and Anne Bancroft had small parts.

Julie Newmeyer was one of the dancing girls, long before she became Julie Newmar and played Hayward's rival in *The Marriage-Go-Round*.

Messalina realizes that her life may depend on her choice of words as she confronts the insane Caligula (Susan Hayward and Jay Robinson)

With Victor Mature

Garden of Evil

20TH CENTURY-FOX, 1954

CAST

Hooker, Gary Cooper; *Leah Fuller,* Susan Hayward; *Fiske,* Richard Widmark; *John Fuller,* Hugh Marlowe; *Luke Daly,* Cameron Mitchell; *Singer,* Rita Moreno; *Vicente Madariaga,* Victor Manuel Mendoza; *Captain,* Fernando Wagner; *Priest,* Arturo Soto Rangel; *Waiter,* Manuel Donde; *Bartender,* Antonio Bribiesca; *Victim,* Salvado Terroba.

CREDITS

Directed by Henry Hathaway. *Produced by* Charles Brackett. *Screenplay by* Frank Fenton. *Based on a story by* Fred Freiberger *and* William Tunberg. *Directors of Photography,* Milton Krasner, A.S.C., *and* Jorge Stahl, Jr. *Art Direction,* Lyle Wheeler *and* Edward Fitzgerald. *Film Editor,* James B. Clark, A.C.E. *Sound,* Nicolas de la Rosa, Jr., *and* Roger Heman. *Set Decorations,* Pablo Galvan. *Wardrobe Direction,* Charles LeMaire. *Constumes designed by* Travilla. *Makeup,* Ben Nye. *Hair Styling by* Helen Turpin. *Associate Producer,* Saul Wurtzel. *Assistant Director,* Stanley Hough. *Special Photographic Effects,* Ray Kellogg. *Music,* Bernard Herrmann. *Songs:* "La Negra Noche," *by* Emilio D. Uranga, "Aqui" *by* Kent Darby *and* Lionel Newman. *CinemaScope lenses by* Bausch & Lomb. *Color by Technicolor. Running time, 100 minutes.*

Gary Cooper and Susan Hayward

THE STORY

Hooker (Gary Cooper), Fiske (Richard Widmark), and Daly (Cameron Mitchell) are stranded in a Mexican village after the ship that's taking them to California is put out of commission. Soldiers of fortune, the three were headed for the gold mines in California. Instead, they are now approached by a Spanish-speaking American woman, Leah Fuller (Susan Hayward), who offers to pay them good money if they lead her through dangerous Indian territory to rescue her husband, trapped in a gold mine cave-in. The mention of gold makes them accept.

They hire a Mexican guide, Vicente (Victor Manuel Mendoza), and start the long, hazardous journey. They are all experienced riders and there are no mishaps on the dangerous road running along the edge of a deep cliff, but Leah is alarmed when she discovers that Vicente is marking their trail. However, she manages to remove the traces without anyone knowing.

Leah faces another problem: Daly, who follows her to an isolated place off the road, tries to force his crude advances on her. Fortunately, Hooker sees them and saves Leah from Daly's clutches.

They finally arrive at the place the Indians call "The Garden of Evil," where the mine is located. Fuller (Hugh Marlowe) is still alive, but embittered and with a broken leg. That Leah risks her life to rescue him means nothing to him. Their troubles grow when they discover they are practically surrounded by Indians.

Leah offers to stay behind with a big bonfire and pretend they are still there, so that the men can leave unseen, but Hooker won't have it. At the last minute he knocks her out and they all start on their way back.

Fuller asks Daly to help him get on a horse by himself so as not to hold them back, but as soon as Daly does it, he runs off. They start after him and find him in a clearing: he has been killed by Indian arrows, tied upside down to a cross.

The rest of the group run for their lives, with the Indians after them. Daly is killed, then Vicente. Hooker, Fiske, and Leah hide behind the rocks to defend themselves, but the odds are against them.

Hooker and Fiske draw cards to see who stays behind to try to hold the Indians back, and who takes Leah to safety. Hooker is the one who takes Leah out of Indian territory, but he returns to help Fiske. It's too late. Fiske is dying, though he has almost wiped out the Indians.

Hooker returns to Leah who is waiting anxiously. "If all the world were gold," Hooker comments, "men would die for a handful of it."

REVIEWS

MOTION PICTURE HERALD   *James D. Ivers*

"It is a big production in every way, from the meticulous direction to the outstanding performances and the magnificent photography."

"Not the least of the stronger points in the Charles Brackett production is the CinemaScope treatment of the location-lensing in Mexico. The new anamorphic lens greatly increases the visual impact of the outdoor scenes and becomes such an important part of the story-telling it almost overpowers the plot drama at times."

NEW YORK HERALD TRIBUNE *Otis L. Guernsey, Jr.*

"Gary Cooper's hair is gray under his broad-brimmed hat, and he preserves a level, fatherly demeanor through most of the story. Miss Hayward keeps her thoughts and her affections pretty much of a secret, and Richard Widmark toys with his pack of cards and adds fuel to each flareup with his cynical comments. These trespassers in this 'Garden of Evil' are a puny presence in the great, remote outdoors, and they are dwarfed by its primeval splendor."

NOTES

Susan wasn't happy about going on location. It was the wrong time to leave home, just when she was having trouble with her husband, Jess Barker. She only had to go south of the border, but it was another country. Besides, the deserted Mexican landscapes, whose grandiosity all the critics praised as the best thing in the movie, were not ideal for soothing anybody's nerves. Susan's nervousness showed through her performance: she seemed perhaps a little more jumpy and uneasy than her role demanded.

The filming in Mexico was full of hazardous situations, and Susan risked her life once to save a little boy from falling into the crater of a volcano.

Horseback riding eased her jitters, and she did a lot of it in this movie. She had loved riding since childhood and was quite an experienced rider. (She had done some riding in *Canyon Passage* and *Tap Roots* and would ride in many films in the future.)

This was her second movie with taciturn Gary Cooper since *Beau Geste,* and her third with director Hathaway.

During the filming, Hayward learned that she had been voted the second top feminine ticket seller for the year 1953.

With nothing more serious than a broken leg, Fuller is carried out of the mine (Victor Manuel Mendoza, Hugh Marlowe, Susan Hayward, and Richard Widmark)

Untamed

20th CENTURY-FOX, 1955

Kurt releases her child, but points his gun at Paul as Katie watches in terror (Susan Hayward, Kevin Corcoran, and Tyrone Power)

CAST

Paul Van Riebeck, Tyrone Power; *Katie O'Neill,* Susan Hayward; *Kurt Hout,* Richard Egan; *Shawn Kildare,* John Justin; *Aggie,* Agnes Moorehead; *Julia,* Rita Moreno; *Maria De Groot,* Hope Emerson; *Christian,* Brad Dexter; *Squire O'Neill,* Henry O'Neill; *Tschaka,* Paul Thompson; *Jan,* Alexander D. Havemann; *Joubert,* Louis Mercier; *Jantsie,* Emmett Smith; *Simon,* Jack Macy; *Mme. Joubert,* Trude Wyler; *Bani,* Louis Pollimon Brown; *Maria's Children,* Brian Corcoran, Linda Lowell, Tina Thompson, Gary Diamond, Bobby Diamond; *Grandfather Joubert,* Edward Mundy; *Miss Joubert,* Catherine Pasques; *Young Joubert,* Christian Pasques; *York,* Robert Adler; *Captain Richard Eaton,* John Dodsworth; *Driver—Bree Street,* Alberto Morin; *Schuman,* Philip Van Zandt; *Young Paul,* Kevin Corcoran; *Sir George Gray,* Charles Evans; *Cornelius,* John Carlyle; *Lady Vernon,* Eleanor Audley.

CREDITS

Directed by Henry King. *Produced by* Bert E. Friedlob *and* William A. Bacher. *Screenplay by* Talbot Jennings, Frank Fenton, *and* Michael Blankfort. *Adaptation by* Talbot Jennings *and* William A. Bacher. *Based on the novel by* Helga Moray. *Color Consultant,* Leonard Doss. *CinemaScope Lenses by* Bausch & Lomb. *Director of Photography,* Leo Tover, A.S.C. *Art Direction,* Lyle Wheeler *and* Addison Hehr. *Film Editor,* Barbara McLean, A.C.E. *Sound,* Bernard Freericks *and* Harry M. Leonard. *Set Decorations,* Walter M. Scott *and* Chet Bayhi. *Wardrobe Direction,* Charles LeMaire. *Costumes designed by* Renie. *Makeup,* Ben Nye. *Hair Styling by* Helen Turpin. *Assistant Director,* Stanley Hough. *Special Photographic Effects,* Ray Kellogg. *Music,* Franz Waxman. *Orchestration,* Edward B. Powell. *Choreography by* Stephen Papich. *Color by* De Luxe. *Running time, 111 minutes.*

THE STORY

When Paul Van Riebeck (Tyrone Power), a leader of the South African Boers who goes to County Limerick to buy horses, and Katie O'Neill (Susan Hayward) meet, she falls in love with him. He likes this headstrong Irish girl who does not hide her uncontrollable passion for him, but realizes that no good can come of it and leaves to continue his campaign to establish Boer as a Free State in the land guarded by the Zulus —the hinterland of Africa.

The following year, when he does not return, Katie marries Shawn Kildare (John Justin) and is soon expecting his child, but when the potato famine strikes, she persuades him to go to South Africa. The child is born en route. Tante Maria (Hope Emerson) welcomes them in Capetown and takes them under her wing. Katie hears that the great trek for the Hoffen Valley is about to start and that the Commandos are led by Paul Van

Katie O'Neill, Irish spitfire (Susan Hayward)

The Zulus pose a threat to all of them, but Katie finds Kurt's presence just as threatening, even with Shawn at her side (Richard Egan, Susan Hayward, and John Justin)

Riebeck. She urges Shawn to join them and turns to Aggie (Agnes Moorehead), the servant she brought from home, for agreement, but Aggie mutters, "Isn't seeing him what you started out to do?"

They are on their way again before long and, en route, Katie's flamboyant beauty impresses Kurt Hout (Richard Egan), the handsome leader of the outriders. His interest enrages his mistress, Julia (Rita Moreno), and stirs up her hatred for Katie. The gentle Shawn suffers all of this. But the crisis comes later when the Zulu tribes attack the small band of settlers, before Paul arrives, and Shawn is killed.

Kurt and Paul, who are old friends, arrive together. Paul, surprised to see her, greets Katie warmly, but Kurt makes it known that he intends to have her.

The settlers reach the Hoffen Valley safely under the protection of Paul's Commando, and celebrate their arrival with a ball. Katie, her passion for Paul rekindled, offers herself to him quite openly. Kurt goes for Paul with his long bullwhip. They fight savagely, but Paul wins and he and Kate stake out a homesite. But Paul is soon compelled to return to the Commando and Katie is enraged and frustrated by his departure.

Carrying Paul's baby, Katie has a hard time keeping up the homestead and fighting off Kurt, who, impassioned, keeps after her. She sells some gold and raw diamonds which the natives have found in the Valley and, when her son is born, she goes to Capetown and buys Paul's ancestral home. At a ball Paul and Katie are reunited, but soon they are at odds again when he discovers that the little boy is his son and she had kept this from him.

When Katie's money runs out she goes back to the valley. Kurt, now the leader of the outlaws, meets her again in the town of Kalesberg, but Paul and his Commando are on their way to restore order. Kurt tires to ambush Paul's troops and is killed.

Now that the Zulus and the outlaws are under control, the Free State can become a reality. Paul asks Katie to go back to Hoffen Valley with him to reestablish their old homestead. She accepts, happily.

REVIEWS

NEW YORK TIMES   *Bosley Crowther*

"The performances of Susan Hayward as the lady, John Justin as her Irish spouse, Tyrone Power as the commando leader and Richard Egan as the fellow who works the farm are mechanical and unrevealing."

MOVIE TIME

"A magnificent outdoors drama laid in Ireland and South Africa more than 100 years ago, this CinemaScope production is one of the outstanding films of the year, both from a pictorial and an acting standpoint."

TIME

"Director Henry King (*The Snows of Kilimanjaro*) and a

crew of 40 were sent to South Africa. There, harassed by 'snakes, ticks and other insects' and 'in the presence of lions,' they shot the backgrounds for the picture. For one scene the studio hired 3,000 Zulu warriors, shipped them by plane and oxcart to the Valley of the Thousand Hills in Natal province, and there built a small city named 'Zanuck-ville' to house them.

"Fox did not go to all this trouble for nothing. *Untamed* is a Zulu lulu—the sort of costume adventure that may, in a generation or two, produce a race of moviegoers with their eyes popped out on stalks."

NOTES

In this South Africa saga, the heroine Katie O'Neill went through her adventures on a seesaw: from riches to rags, to riches to rags, à la Scarlett O'Hara.

She had to go to "Africa," again, on a Hollywood set. A lot of colorful footage had been filmed in Africa by a location crew, blended skillfully to show her in many places she knew only from the script. But the techniques in mounting of scenes, special effects, and rear screen projections were almost perfect and one could not tell that Hayward's Africa was not the real thing—this at a time when most pictures were filmed on location.

This was Hayward's fourth and last big spectacle with director Henry King, and the third in which her voice was used in part of the narration. It was her second movie with Power, Egan, Moreno, and Moorehead.

Katie and Paul are reunited and it seems to be for keeps; they ride with their children and a smiling Aggie (left to right: Kevin Corcoran, Tyrone Power, Christian Pasques, Susan Hayward, and Agnes Moorehead)

Katie removes a spear that has pierced Shawn's body, as they fight against the Zulus (John Justin and Susan Hayward)

Soldier of Fortune

20th CENTURY-FOX, 1955

CAST

Hank Lee, Clark Gable; *Jane Hoyt,* Susan Hayward; *Inspector Merryweather,* Michael Rennie; *Louis Hoyt,* Gene Barry; *Rene Chevalier,* Alex D'Arcy; *Tweedie,* Tom Tully; *Mme. Dupree,* Anna Sten; *Icky,* Russell Collins; *Big Matt,* Leo Gordon; *Poilin,* Richard Loo; *Daklai,* Soo Yong; *Ying Fai,* Frank Tang; *Austin Stoker,* Jack Kruschen; *Fernand Rocha,* Mel Welles; *Major Leith Phipps,* Jack Raine; *Gunner,* George Wallace; *Australian Airman,* Alex Finlayson; *Luan,* Noel Toy; *Chinese Clerk,* Beal Wong; *Father Xavier,* Robert Burton; *Frank Stewart,* Robert Quarry; *Hotel Desk Clerk,* Charles Davis; *Goldie,* Victor Sen Young; *Maxine Chan,* Frances Fong; *Billy Lee,* Danny Chang.

CREDITS

Directed by Edward Dmytryk. *Produced by* Buddy Adler. *Screenplay by* Ernest K. Gann. *Based on the novel by* Ernest K. Gann. *Color Consultant,* Leonard Doss. *Director of Photography,* Leo Tover, A.S.C. *Art Directors,* Lyle Wheeler *and* Jack Martin Smith. *Film Editor,* Dorothy Spencer, A.C.E. *Sound,* Eugene Grossman *and* Harry M. Leonard. *Set Decorations,* Walter M. Scott *and* Stuart A. Reiss. *Wardrobe Direction,* Charles LeMaire. *Makeup,* Ben Nye. *Hair Styling by* Helen Turpin. *Assistant Director,* Hal Herman. *Special Photographic Effects,* Ray Kellogg. *Music,* Hugo Friedhofer. *Conducted by* Lionel Newman. *Orchestration,* Edward B. Powell. *Vocal Supervision,* Ken Darby. *CinemaScope Lenses by* Bausch & Lomb. *Color by* De Luxe. *Running time, 96 minutes.*

THE STORY

In search of her missing photographer husband, Jane Hoyt (Susan Hayward) arrives in Hong Kong and learns at the U.S. Consulate that her mission is futile, that neither the United States nor the British government can help her. She must try, nevertheless, and registers at a hotel that services a conglomeration of businessmen, servicemen, entertainers, and ne'er-do-wells from all over the world.

Jane gets in touch with Inspector Merryweather (Michael Rennie), of the local marine police, who, although unable to help her officially, promises to do all he can for her on his own. He asks her to identify two cameras that the police had picked up from a junk captain at the harbor. She confirms that they belonged to her husband. Merryweather then suggests that she inquire at a place called "Tweedie's."

Jane is about to be thrown out of Tweedie's when Rene Chevalier (Alex D'Arcy) joins her at the table as if she were waiting for him. He tells her that he knew her husband and had seen him one night with Fernand Rocha (Mel Welles) and a girl named Maxine Chan (Frances Fong). With nothing more than this information she contacts Maxine, who leads her to Hank Lee (Clark Gable), of whom Merryweather had warned her.

Hank and Jane, a tough pair to deal with, anywhere in the world (Susan Hayward and Clark Gable)

Although their original plan was to return home, they
end up going their separate ways (Gene Barry and Susan
Hayward)

Rene is always charming although his motives are mostly
mercenary (Alex D'Arcy and Susan Hayward)

Although Hank and Jane seem delighted with each other, soon the situation will be different (Clark Gable and Susan Hayward)

REVIEWS

NEW YORK POST *Archer Winsten*

"What's really good about this picture is its before-credits shots of Hong Kong. As shown in De Luxe color and CinemaScope, they're better than a drawn-out travelogue. Thereafter, the background shots of the feverish Crown Colony remain impressively real.

"Director Edward Dmytryk permits the picture to drop from Grand Hotel vignettes to rough-and-tumbles verging on slapstick, but it keeps on rolling despite its quality flaws."

NEW YORK HERALD TRIBUNE *William K. Zinsser*

"Clark Gable fans will find their hero as suave, handsome and competent as ever. Miss Hayward conveys her usual modicum of emotion, and there is a good supporting cast of raffish black marketeers and hangers-on, headed by Tom Tully as a venal bar owner and Alex D'Arcy as a bibulous Frenchman."

NEW YORK TIMES *Bosley Crowther*

"Even if Susan Hayward, who plays the uxorial role, were ten times as beautiful and exciting as she inadequately is, it still wouldn't stand to reason that Mr. Gable would act as he does.

"Mr. Gann has tried to justify the nonsense by suggesting that his hero has a heart as well as a pocketbook of gold."

NOTES

Practically all the reviewers gave the movie a battering. All agreed that the real star of the film was the city of Hong Kong itself.

Susan never saw the real Hong Kong, only the one created at the studio. The mixing of Hayward's Hong Kong with the real one was very smoothly done.

Hayward looked different without her famous long tresses. This was her second movie with Michael Rennie; she had one scene with him in *Demetrius and the Gladiators*.

Anna Sten, Samuel Goldwyn's protégée of yesteryear, had little more than a bit part as Mme. Dupree.

Some reviewers complained that at the end, it is implied that Hayward will get a divorce from her movie husband, but she stays with Gable in Hong Kong in the meantime. Morals have changed!

Ironically, this anticommunist adventure film was directed by Edward Dmytryk, one of the "Hollywood Ten."

Hank is a drink-hard, fight-hard American soldier of fortune who, after deserting from the navy during the war, set up a profitable smuggling business with the Chinese Reds. Hank is attracted to Jane's sultry red-haired beauty. He realizes that if he wants to get anywhere with her he's going to have to bring her husband out from behind the bamboo curtain, but she resents his insinuations and decides to seek help elsewhere.

Still without a clue after making the rounds of all of her husband's likely haunts, Jane is forced to go back to Hank. He agrees to help: He goes to Tweedie's, which is in a shambles after a wild celebration. Hank threatens Tweedie (Tom Tully) if he doesn't find out the photographer's whereabouts. He is told that Louis Hoyt (Gene Barry) is being held in Canton.

Hank prepares to rescue Hoyt in his powered junk, *Chicago*, and is annoyed to find Inspector Merryweather aboard. Since the inspector knows the nature of Hank's merchandise, he is held prisoner aboard the junk. Later, however, when Hank's crewmen desert rather than enter Red China, Merryweather, realizing that this is a rescue mission, offers his help and Hoyt is successfully hustled onto the junk. An enemy patrol, however, has discovered them and the *Chicago* is providentially saved by hundreds of fishing junks that surround them, cutting them off from the Red ship.

They reach Hong Kong safely and Louis and Jane are reunited. But when they are ready to leave together, Hoyt admits, at the last minute, that he will soon be off on other trips. Jane then goes to Hank, this time for keeps.

V CHALKLEY AND FULFILLMENT
True Love, Blessed Awards and a Few Potholes

In December 1955, at a Christmas party in the home of columnist Vincent X. Flaherty, Susan Hayward met the man who would change her life. He was Floyd Eaton Chalkley, a wealthy attorney from Carrollton, Georgia. Chalkley was an ex-FBI man, divorced, with a son and two daughters who lived with their mother. He and Susan started seeing each other right after their first meeting.

At the general release of *I'll Cry Tomorrow* in New York, in early January, Hayward was seen escorted by millionaire builder Hal Hayes and Mike Connolly, who had co-authored the book. Lillian Roth's career as a nightclub singer took an upward turn after the movie. Hayward's role in *I'll Cry Tomorrow* was considered the best part she had ever played. (It was her personal favorite too.) She got top reviews everywhere and, again, *Look* magazine praised her in their *Look* movie review: "Lillian Roth's famous confession, 'I'll Cry Tomorrow,' cast Susan Hayward in a shattering, terrifying role. . . . Susan Hayward bids for an Academy Award. . . . The story's emotional power is vividly communicated by Susan Hayward in a shattering, intense performance that may win her an Academy Award." *Life* magazine also dedicated a few pages to the film. "Susan Hayward does a superb portrayal of Lillian from spotlight to blackout—including some unexpectedly fine, throaty singing." *Redbook* magazine chose the film as "Picture of the Month." And none other than Greta Garbo declared that Hayward was one of her favorite actresses.

It was the first time she ever really sang in a movie. Johnny Green, music supervisor at Metro, convinced her to do it. To her own surprise, her voice turned out to be much better than she expected. She sang four songs: "Sing, You Sinners," "Happiness Is a Thing Called Joe" (her drunken rendition of this song is haunting), "When the Red, Red Robin Comes Bob, Bob, Bobbin' Along," and "The Vagabond King Waltz." They were released in a 45-rpm record with another song that wasn't used in the final print of the film, "I'm Sittin' on Top of the World." (Inexplicably, Metro chose for the record cover a photograph of Susan from the earlier Fox movie *I Can Get It for You Wholesale*.) She made another MGM recording, which included "I'll Cry Tomorrow," the theme song, and the oldie "Just One of Those Things." *Cosmopolitan* had her on the cover, as seen by artist Jon Whitcomb, her old friend, who authored an article in the same issue entitled "Songbird Susan." He wrote: "Being queen of her own soundtrack in 'I'll Cry Tomorrow' is the biggest thing that has happened to Susan Hayward since she came to Hollywood thirty-eight pictures ago!" She was besieged by offers from nightclubs and cabarets, including Las Vegas hotels and places like Cuba's internationally famous Montmartre. But she refused, saying, "I'm not ready to face a live audience."

Honors for her role continued to pile up: she was on a *Look* magazine cover, together with James Cagney, as recipients of the "Best Actress" and "Best Actor" awards for 1955, the 15th anniversary of the "*Look* Movie Awards." The magazine gathered as many former winners as they could to sit with the

Susan Hayward and Lillian Roth at the New York première of *I'll Cry Tomorrow*

new winners for a special photographic display, and wrote: "A Hollywood-trained player since 1939, she gives a performance that does the industry great credit—a many-sided and poignant study of the dissolution of a human being and her fight to be rehabilitated." *Redbook* magazine, *Motion Picture Exhibitor*, and England's *Picturegoer* magazine also named her "Best Actress."

Hayward finally consented to appear on television, as a guest star in the hour-long "Climax," a drama based on *The Gay Illiterate*, autobiography of Hayward's old friend Louella Parsons, played by Teresa Wright. This tribute to Parsons was crowded with half of Hollywood's greats (Joan Fontaine, Gene Autry, Rock Hudson, Ida Lupino, Jeannette MacDonald, Kim Novak, Jack Benny, George Burns, Ginger Rogers, John Wayne, Joan Bennett, Charles Boyer, Jack Lemmon, Merle Oberon, Robert Wagner, and many others. But, after this, Susan continued to scorn television for the next fifteen years, just making guest appearances on a few programs. (When offered a special of her own in the late fifties she said, "Sure, for $100,000," and that ended that.)

Meanwhile, *The Conqueror* was released in CinemaScope and technicolor, to cash in on the publicity for *I'll Cry Tomorrow*. The ads read: "Two years in the making" (it was really more than a year shelved). The presenter was Howard Hughes who, after selling RKO, bought the picture back along with another John Wayne film, *Jet Pilot*, both for $12 million. (The latter had been filmed even earlier and was yet to be released.) The reviews for *The Conqueror* were unmerciful. Not one critic found anything good about the movie. Nevertheless, Wayne made a world tour promoting it, and it was a box office hit. Hayward played a Tartar princess and did a belly dance barefooted and with two swords.

This was the last picture in which her long beautiful hair was shown to best advantage. From then on she wore shorter hairdos, more becoming to her age.

She got her fourth Oscar nomination for *I'll Cry Tomorrow* and the night of the Oscars she was flanked by Chalkley and her eleven-year-old twins. The competition was really rough that year. The other nominees had all given excellent performances: Katharine Hepburn (*Summertime*), Jennifer Jones (*Love is a Many-Splendored Thing*), Eleanor Parker (*Interrupted Melody*), and Anna Magnani (*The Rose Tattoo*). Nevertheless, her chance of getting the award was greater than ever, in spite of the scandalous headlines of the past year. But Hollywood people, still morally oriented then, voted for Anna Magnani of *The Rose Tattoo*. The audience was visibly disappointed and Hayward, who had organized a "win-or-lose" party, had to carry on and wait until it was over to have a good cry. For weeks and months, the newspapers and movie magazines had to deal with dozens of letters from irate Hayward fans, complaining about Susan losing the Oscar to Anna Magnani.

In May Susan was invited to attend the Cannes Festival in France, where *I'll Cry Tomorrow* was going to be presented. In Cannes, she shared the spotlight with Hollywood's and Europe's luminaries, among them Ginger Rogers, Richard Todd, Diana Dors, Yvonne Furneaux, her old friend Ingrid Bergman, and Kim Novak. But the festival turned out to be

Susan's triumph; she was named the best actress in the world. When she cabled home, she signed the wire: Susan Magnani. Later she was invited to attend the Cork Film Festival, in Ireland, where she also received top honors.

After her *Tomorrow* triumph, Susan traveled a little, and then decided to wait "for the right role to come." She dated a few friends, among them publisher Gordon White, disc jockey Bill Ballance, FBI agent Hugh French, Brazilian millionaire Jorge Guinly, Dr. Frederick Mayer, a philosophy professor at the University of Redlands, and Chalkley.

In August she cut a giant cake at New York International Airport—Idlewild (now Kennedy), during the ceremonies marking the first anniversary of Varig Airlines' Deluxe Service between New York and South America. Later, she boarded a Varig plane to Rio de Janeiro to attend the annual ball of the "Grande Premio do Brazil" sweepstakes (the equivalent of the Kentucky Derby).

Upon her return, Susan finally accepted a role in a comedy called *Melville Goodwin, U.S.A.* during shooting (released later as *Top Secret Affair*). The movie had been intended originally for Humphrey Bogart and Lauren Bacall, before Bogart's death. Hayward was back at Warners for this, her starting point, and they wanted her to dye her hair black (which made no sense, since the film was in black and white). Reportedly, she started wearing a black wig around town to prove that she didn't look good in it. Susan won her point.

She was seen more and more in Chalkley's company, although she didn't talk with the press about the affair. She refused three more films dealing with alcohol: *The Helen Morgan Story*, *The Wayward Bus* (Joan Collins's part), and *Les Girls* (Kay Kendall's part, which propelled her to stardom). But Susan did want the part of Nellie Forbush in *South Pacific*, and wrote director Joshua Logan in strong terms. He answered that he was willing to test her for the part. She replied, "I am more than a proven actress; either I get it without a test, or I don't." She didn't. She also turned down *The Three Faces of Eve*, which made a star and Oscar-winner of Joanne Woodward. Susan was also supposed to star in a run-of-the-mill adventure film called *Stopover Tokyo*, but the part went to Joan Collins instead.

If she had starred in all the films she had been slated for in 1956, she would have averaged almost a picture per month, but she wanted to spend as much time as she could with Chalkley.

She made a brief appearance on television to receive an award for Pearl S. Buck, the famous writer, presented by Dr. Frank Baxter.

Susan's name continued to be up for roles she never got: in *The Seventh Sin*, a second version of Garbo's *The Painted Veil* (Eleanor Parker), *Band of Angels* (Yvonne de Carlo), and *The Sun Also Rises*, based on the Hemingway book (Ava Gardner). Nevertheless, at the end of the year she was selected among the ten most popular movie stars for 1956, according to a poll conducted by the trade publication *Boxoffice* among critics, theatre owners and representatives of various groups. She was number five, and Marilyn number four. The only man listed over her was William Holden, number two. The top star? Kim Novak.

Arriving at the Cannes Festival in 1956

Susan Hayward on "Climax" TV show in 1956

Ernest Borgnine and Susan Hayward give each other a hug after they were nominated by the Motion Picture Academy in 1956, Susan for *I'll Cry Tomorrow* and Borgnine for *Marty*

Early next year *Top Secret Affair* was released, with Kirk Douglas as co-star. She was billed above Douglas, and continued to get top billing for the next ten years, no matter who her leading man was. The ads said, "I haven't laughed like this since *Mister Roberts*. Who said it? Just about everyone who saw this motion picture!" But it was not a big hit, unfortunately for her, because it was the first movie in which she had a percentage. She was much better than expected at this kind of "sophisticated comedy."

On February 9, 1957, Susan surprised everyone by tying the knot again. She eloped to Phoenix, Arizona, with Eaton Chalkley. He was forty-seven, nine years older than she was. They tried to avoid publicity, but the reporters caught up with them. She was afraid they would try to sensationalize her marriage by recalling earlier headlines. But, with Eaton grasping her hand firmly, she said, "I don't want to look back. From now on I'm going to look forward always." No, she did not care to relive any of her past. And, for a change, the headlines were happy. She sent a photograph to *Modern Screen* magazine showing the smiling pair in front of the judge; the inscription was "This is it. Love, Susan." Sidney Skolsky wrote of her wedding: "Susan Hayward, my tintype for today, is thoroughly feminine, thoroughly feminine in her unpredictable behavior and surprising contrasts. She said she's a person who refuses to look back—I don't want to look back. That's where I've been. I want to see where I'm going. I hope to profit by all the past experience and never repeat a mistake. I expect this marriage to be it, or I wouldn't have married." And he continued: "She attends all rushes during the making of a movie, unlike many actresses. . . . If I'm making any mistakes, I can nip them in the bud. . . . She selects the wardrobe in her movies with the same care she picks a script. . . . Women should stop copying masculine style, from trousers to hairdos. A woman has greater power over men by emphasizing her natural equipment. . . . She drinks liquor, and doesn't try to hide the fact as do many actresses. . . . I try not to be a phony. . . . She sleeps in frilly nightgowns. She has pure satin sheets on her bed so that she can feel glamorous at the end of a night and also when she gets up in the morning."

The Chalkleys moved to Carrollton, Georgia, where at first she wasn't too well received by neighbors. When Eaton's mother and sister gave a party most guests accepted and a reception given by the Business and Professional Women's Club was a success, but not everybody came and a minister advised his congregation not to meet her. However, her newly found happiness tamed her and she won the friendship of many who were reluctant to accept her. The new docile Hayward was a far cry from "Hollywood's Hellcat." She was invited to open the baseball season in Atlanta: she kicked off her shoes and, like a seasoned player, threw the ball to third base.

The Chalkleys started building a modern house for themselves in a 450-acre ranch where they already had a smaller house for guests and a private lake. While the larger house was being built, they lived at the guest house. Susan drove Chalkley's truck to town to do her shopping or stayed home and welcomed her new fans: the neighbors' children.

Had she been in Hollywood, Susan might have had an extremely strong part: the leading feminine role in Alfred Hitchcock's *Vertigo*. It was said that Hitchcock was undecided between her and Audrey Hepburn, but finally the role went as usual to a blonde, this time Kim Novak, because he wanted to prove that he "could make an actress out of that stupid cow." He got a great acting job from her.

For more than a year Susan kept turning down script after script until finally, in the fall of 1957, she accepted Walter Wanger's offer to do "The Barbara Graham Story," which proved her best dramatic role. The screenplay was based on letters written by Barbara Graham herself, and some articles written by newspaperman Ed Montgomery. (Barbara was one of the few women condemned to the gas chamber in California for a crime that she may not have committed. She was executed at thirty-two.) Susan did it not only for Wanger, but for Chalkley too, who didn't want her talent to be wasted.

Robert Wise was her director and he praised her: "Susan Hayward is to the movies what Sarah Bernhardt was to the stage. She has a chemical combination that can excite and hold audiences as surely as Garbo and few other greats of the screen. She is one of the few actresses who can hold up a movie all by herself."

Early in 1958 her mother's death dimmed Susan's happiness. Mrs. Marrener had been taken to the hospital with a coronary thrombosis. Her condition worsened and Susan was with her until she died. After making the funeral arrangements, she decided that it wasn't fair to cause Wanger another delay in the shooting (she had already been out with the flu and the measles) and, in the best showmanship tradition, promptly appeared on the set of "The Barbara Graham Story" at eight o'clock the next morning. She was "reunited" with her sister Florence, at their mother's funeral, but they didn't make up. Mrs. Marrener was cremated as she had wished.

Because she could have Chalkley with her, she made another concession to television in 1958 and appeared on Edward R. Murrows' show, "Person to Person."

Before the end of the year she was filming another picture, *Between the Thunder and the Sun*, which, it was said, she made to help her friend and co-star Jeff Chandler. In November, her *I Want to Live* (final title of the Graham story) was released. The part of Barbara Graham was different from anything she had played before, and it was difficult. She had many memorable scenes and lines. One scene lingers in the mind: She is caught by a policeman with a "customer" in a hotel room, and says she has paid for the room herself, to avoid troubles for him. The grateful man mutters, "Life is a funny thing," and Hayward sarcastically answers, "Compared to what?" (A few years later, she found an answer in *Back Street*: "The funny thing about life is that all the old clichés are true.") Albert Camus, French Nobel Prize winner, praised the movie: "The whole world should see and hear it. Here is the reality of our time, and we have no right to be ignorant of it. The day will come when such documents will seem to us to refer to pre-historic times, and we shall consider them as unbelievable as we find it unbelievable that in earlier centuries witches were burned or thieves had their right hands cut off."

Edward R. Murrow interviews Susan on "Person to Person" in 1958

Hayward and Wanger arrive in New York to promote *I Want to Live*

213

At 1958 New York Film Critics Award presentations in New York early in 1959: from left, Elia Kazan, Fredric March, David Niven, and Susan Hayward with her Best Actress plaque for *I Want to Live*, presented by New York Daily Mirror's Justin Gilbert

Eleanor Roosevelt praised the film at a preview: "It holds one's attention every minute, and it is skillfully acted by Susan Hayward and the supporting cast. I think everyone of us will carry away from it the reminder that human justice is fallible." Susan drew Bosley Crowther's best review in her whole career in the *New York Times,* and great reviews came from every corner of the United States, and from abroad. *Life* dedicated an article to the movie titled "The Outcry of a Woman Condemned": "A new movie called 'I want to Live' is almost too stark and frightening to be true. But it is the faithful story of Barbara Graham, a woman who was convicted of murder and executed in the gas chamber at San Quentin on June 3, 1955. As Barbara, Susan Hayward gives a magnificent performance, and the final hours of her life are portrayed in harrowing detail."

Hayward went on tour to promote the movie, around the States and abroad—to France, Germany and Italy. On the way back she paid a visit to her ancestors' Ireland. In some countries they were reluctant to show a film that depicted human justice the way this film did. Such was the case in England. They didn't allow the movie to open there for years. (When they did, British censors cut most of the gas chamber sequences.) United Artists had been reluctant to allow any cutting: "This is the greatest plea for the abolition of capital punishment ever made, and must be shown in its entirety." The *London News Chronicle* urged the British censors to grant a certificate to the film: "It is about time that British adults were treated in an adult way." (All this notwithstanding, what the British finally saw was an edited version of *I Want to Live.*)

Back in the States, Susan and Eaton were driving home from Santa Anita after a not-so-lucky day at the races, when they heard on the radio that Susan had been nominated for the Oscar. Eaton hugged and kissed her and she said huskily, "I want to win! I want to win! I want this Oscar for you and my boys."

Only two months after its release, *I Want to Live* was one of the biggest grossers for the year, and made Susan number ten among the Top Ten Box Office Favorites selected by a trade magazine in 1959.

In February 1959, she flew to New York, from her Colorado location, where she was filming *Woman Obsessed* (called "The Snow Birch" during production), to receive the New York Film Critics' Award as best actress of 1958, together with David Niven as best actor for *Separate Tables.* The presentation was made by Justin Gilbert, chairman of the New York Film Critics' twenty-fourth annual poll. They met at Sardi's restaurant with Fredric March (accepting award for best picture, *The Defiant Ones*) and director Elia Kazan (accepting a plaque on behalf of director-producer Stanley Kramer, also for *The Defiant Ones*), and Hayward said, "I never dreamed this could happen to a girl from Brooklyn." Upon her return to Colorado for *Woman Obsessed,* she declared, "Hollywood has been very good to me, but I'm anxious to wind up my commitments. . . . I love my life in Carrollton and I don't want to go on doddering around until I'm playing grandmother parts."

Finally it was Academy Award night and Susan and Chalkley attended the ceremonies for the thirty-first year of the Oscar at the Pantages Theatre. This time—at long last—Susan won the coveted statuette. The roar of applause was deafening. She thanked Walter Wanger and ended her short speech saying, "Thank you, for making me so happy." Her rivals that year had been Rosalind Russell (*Auntie Mame*), Deborah Kerr (*Separate Tables*), Elizabeth Taylor (*Cat on a Hot Tin Roof*), and Shirley MacLaine (*Some Came Running*). When they announced the winner, Rosalind Russell turned to her husband and said, "Well, I have to admit that nobody deserved it more than Hayward. If it had to be somebody else, I'm glad it was Susie." Hayward was photographed, proudly holding her Oscar, with winners David Niven, best actor for *Separate Tables,* and Burl Ives, best supporting male role for

The Big Country. "I did it for my three men," Susan said, referring to Chalkley and her two sons. When photographers asked her to kiss the statuette she said, "I only kiss my husband." (This Oscar telecast obtained the highest ratings in the history of televised Academy Award ceremonies. It got a 46.1 rating and an 80 share was logged.)

This time Susan had not planned a party, so at the last minute she hired a ballroom. After the festivities were over, she declared, "I'm still in shock. After being up for it so, so many times, I didn't expect to win this time. This industry has been so good to me I don't know what to do in return."

Walter Wanger had given her a religious medal the night of the awards, with the image of a saint and the words "Please Guide My Destiny" on one side, and the engraving "To Susan —Best Actress and Best Friend" on the other side. Wanger commented later, "Finally we can relax: Susie's got what she's been chasing for twenty years."

On their return to Carrollton, there was a two-mile-long parade in her honor as several thousand fans cheered. (Quite a difference from the cold reception she got when she first came to town.)

Columnists kidded Susan about the way she overworshipped the Oscar. And maybe she did—but it was a goal she had set for herself, the culmination of her career. Winning the Oscar meant paying back the film industry, which had been so good to her. It represented the greatest achievement in the business.

Hours after the Oscars, her film with Chandler was released with the title *Thunder in the Sun.* They had been waiting for the good publicity she would get after winning the Oscar, but nothing could help this picture—her shortest one since *Among the Living* (1941)—which looked like a programmer of the late thirties or early forties. She must have loved Jeff Chandler dearly to sink herself into this messy western about French Basques crossing the plains and fighting Indians. Her French accent had to be heard to be believed. She even had the guts to pair up with a real flamenco dancer. For this period piece she had to wear a hairpiece attached to her own hair to make it look longer, since her own hair was shorter than ever. The movie was a Paramount release in Technicolor, but worse than any she had ever filmed at the studio when she was a contract player.

Gossip columnists hinted that maybe everything wasn't rosy between her and Chalkley because she was making movie after movie. The truth was that Chalkley wanted her to make movies—he was proud of his actress wife's talent. But after she finished *Woman Obsessed*, Susan said, "No more movies in 1959," and retreated to Carrollton to enjoy a self-imposed semiretirement.

To promote *Woman Obsessed,* and as a tribute to her, 20th Century-Fox offered a "Susan Hayward Dramatic Scholarship" at the summer session of the American Academy of Dramatic Arts, in the metropolitan area of New York. The contestants had to write a hundred-word account of why they wished to

During the Oscar ceremonies in 1959, left to right: Arthur Freed, Burl Ives, Susan Hayward, David Niven, Ingrid Bergman and Maurice Chevalier

The Chalkleys admire Susan's trophies: on the wall, three nominations; on the table, the 1952 Golden Globe for *With a Song in My Heart* (others are ready to be displayed)

embark on an acting career. (A Riverdale girl, Susan Trutsman, won the contest.)

Woman Obsessed was a disappointment. As one critic put it, "There was nothing to obsess anybody, least of all the remarkable Miss Hayward." It was one of two movies she owed to Fox, and was filmed in CinemaScope and De Luxe Color. Her co-star was Stephen Boyd. Hathaway praised Hayward during the filming: "Susie is a dynamo—she'll give you twenty-seven takes if you ask for them and never complain. She's always trying to improve."

Hayward was one of many guests present at the Coconut Grove for the 1959 Hollywood Foreign Press Association's Golden Globe dinner. They were honoring Samuel Goldwyn for his many years as producer of some of Hollywood's most admired movies. The list of guests included Sophie Tucker, Danny Kaye, Red Skelton, Ed Sullivan, Maurice Chevalier, Rosalind Russell, and others.

While in Hollywood, Hayward's name came up for a most improbable role: the part of Simone Pistache, the lead in *Can Can*. She decided against it.

Her *I Want to Live* was still accumulating honors at the end of the year. The movie was a top grosser for 1959, according to *Motion Picture Daily*, which made Hayward richer—she got 33 percent of the profits, and the earnings were expected to be over the $3 million mark.

She took another vacation from films and went with her husband to Greece and Italy. They visited the Vatican, where Chalkley introduced Susan to his old friend Reverent Daniel J. McGuire, who would play an important part in Susan's religious life later. Chalkley was a fervent Roman Catholic, and Susan became deeply interested in Catholicism.

While in Italy, it was rumored that Susan would substitute for Gina Lollobrigida in the film *Jovanka et le altre*, a Dino De Laurentiis production, but the part was finally played by Silvana Mangano. The movie, released under the English title *Five Branded Women*, was the story of five women accused of being Nazi collaborators who ended up with shaved heads. Would she have accepted the part—a bald Hayward?

After her vacation Susan was supposed to go to India to start filming a movie called "Elephant Hill," with Rock Hudson, but the project was never realized. And upon her return from Europe, she refused the role of Sheila Graham in *Beloved Infidel*, the story of the columnist's affair with F. Scott Fitzgerald. Instead, she spent most of her time at her ranch in Georgia, where she was happy as never before, and commuted to Hollywood only when it was necessary.

By the end of the year she was still collecting awards from all over the world for her Barbara Graham role: from Italy, the "David di Donatello" award; from Argentina, "The Golden Gaucho" award; from Germany, "The Silver Bear" award; and yet another from the South American Film Festival of Mar del Plata.

Once more Hayward was considered for a role she never played: Cleopatra. Unlikely as it may seem, she had been Walter Wanger's original choice for the role, but although Susan looked remarkably young at forty, it is difficult to imagine her as the eighteen-year-old queen at the beginning of the picture—and Cleopatra lived only to the ripe age of thirty-eight. (Joan Collins was also considered for this role, but they wanted a bigger name.) Elizabeth you-know-who was the producer's final choice.

As early as 1960 or 1961, there was talk about filming *The Way West* with Susan Hayward and Deborah Kerr in the leading roles, but when the film was finally released in 1967, the feminine roles were no longer important and gave way to the male characters, played by Kirk Douglas and Robert Mitchum.

Also early in 1960, Susan was one of the presenters at the Academy Awards ceremonies, and it was she who handed Charlton Heston his Oscar for *Ben Hur.*

At that time she started filming two pictures to be released the following year: *The Marriage-Go-Round* and Ross Hunter's *Back Street,* which was being filmed for the third time. (This Fannie Hurst novel had first been adapted for the screen in 1932, with Irene Dunne and John Boles, and again in 1941 with Margaret Sullavan and Charles Boyer.)

The Marriage-Go-Round, Susan's second try at sophisticated comedy, didn't fare too well. It opened with the year and had mixed reviews, although Susan was good in her role and Bosley Crowther treated it amazingly well in his *New York Times* review. James Mason was her co-star, and Julie Newmar, from the original Broadway play (starring Claudette Colbert and Charles Boyer), was also in the movie. This was Hayward's last CinemaScope movie and her last film under her old Fox contract.

Meanwhile, she started filming another movie for MGM: *Ada,* directed by Daniel Mann, her director in *I'll Cry Tomorrow.* Again Hayward played the "rags to riches" story which had so many different versions along her career: *Tulsa, I Can Get It for You Wholesale,* and a milder one in her next vehicle *Back Street.* (Just before the filming, Hayward had thrown a temper tantrum, which was unusual for her. She wanted Sidney Guilaroff to do her hair and, informed that he was in London with Taylor, said, "Well, get him back." But they didn't.)

Her husband, who came often when Susan was working, visited her on the set and the studio photographers recorded their smiling faces.

Their smiles didn't last long. An article appeared in *Confidential,* authored by her sister Florence, under the title: "My Sister Susan Hayward Has Millions, But I'm on Relief." A picture of Florence, along with one of Susan (separate), stared from the magazine cover. Susan did not comment on the painful article.

Ada, a perfect story for Hayward, opened in midsummer with the ads claiming, "From sharecropper's shack to Governor's mansion, Ada climbed the ladder of success." Familiar? It was a hit at the box office and so was *Back Street,* although this women's picture didn't find many appreciative reviewers.

At the turn of the sixties, Hollywood had started going slowly up the ladder on sex, violence, and gore. Nevertheless, *Back Street* was still good box office, and Susan managed to look younger than her age (about forty-two) even with her much younger partner, John Gavin.

Among the best qualities of the movie was the musical background (score by Frank Skinner), which was released by Decca. *Back Street* was considered Hayward's most synthetic movie.

Hayward was voted "worst actress of 1961" by the *Harvard*

Between takes of *Stolen Hours* in England

Lampoon, for *Ada* and *Back Street,* joining such past "winners" as Norma Shearer, Lana Turner, Jennifer Jones, Rita Hayworth, Eva Marie Saint, Jane Fonda, Barbra Streisand, Julie Andrews, and Diana Ross (quite a list of "untalented" Hollywood actresses). On the other hand, *Motion Picture Daily* listed *Back Street* among the top money makers of the year. Susan had a share of the profits.

She was so happy living in Carrollton with her husband, that she missed another good role: the part of Geraldine Page in *Sweet Bird of Youth,* which would have teamed her with another dynamic figure, Paul Newman.

Susan's first Anglo-American production *I Thank a Fool* took her to England. The film (originally planned for Ingrid Bergman and Cary Grant), with Peter Finch as her co-star, was released by MGM in the fall of 1962 to poor reviews. The director was Robert Stevens, with whom, reportedly, she didn't get along at all.

In an article at this time she was quoted as having said, before marrying Chalkley, "Marriage should be made much more difficult and divorce easier." Commenting at a later date Hayward said, "Now I like marriage. I am no longer so ambitious. I no longer take myself so seriously. My career is still important but now it is in proper perspective. I suppose one takes one's work too seriously when little else in life seems worthwhile."

She was putting less emphasis on her career, accepting fewer roles. Her position as Chalkley's wife was the one she really cared about. They spent most of their time together: fishing (they owned three yachts: the *Oh Susannah,* the *Little Susannah,* and the *Big Susannah*), riding, and traveling. They loved fishing and often sailed in one of their yachts. They would go

Bette Davis and Susan Hayward meet for the first time at Paramount Studios during a press luncheon to officially launch their picture *Where Love Has Gone*

to Florida, the Bahamas, Cape Cod. Susan even sold all her properties in California to make her anchors still more secure in the South (it was reported she made over $2 million on the sale).

Susan had been considered for one of the feminine leads in *Night of the Iguana*, but they went to Ava Gardner and Deborah Kerr. This was the second time she almost played opposite Richard Burton.

Only one Hayward film was released in 1963, *Stolen Hours*, a remake of Bette Davis's *Dark Victory*. Susan was costumed by Fabiani and surrounded with all the opulence the rich heiress role demanded. It was her second British picture, and it was enhanced by the location shots in the Cornwall Coast and a beautiful musical theme by Mort Lindsay. The movie, released by United Artists in De Luxe Color, was popular.

Discussing sex appeal, Hayward said, "It is not so much what you take off, what determines sex-appeal, but what you leave on. Sex-appeal is a state of mind, not a bold statement of fact. Simplicity in dress, with a minimum of undress, leaving much to the imagination of the beholder, is the key to glam-

our." This Hayward statement was at the beginning of the "undressing" era of the screen, long before "R" or "X" rated seventies films took the "appeal" out of "sex."

At the end of the year she signed to star in what could have been one of her best early sixties roles, with Bette Davis, who played her mother. The movie was Paramount's Technicolored *Where Love Has Gone*. Based on Harold Robbins's novel the movie seemed to be a left-handed account of the Lana Turner–Johnny Stompanato case of 1958. Davis and Hayward didn't clash seriously on the sets, as some avid newsmen were expecting, but their relationship was not exactly "ideal" either. The main problem was Davis wanting to do everything her way and Hayward appealing to the front office, complaining about sudden changes in the script. The ending was changed, too; Davis was supposed to die, but complained that she couldn't kill herself in two pages of dialogue—so Hayward had to commit suicide. The film was released in November 1964 and the reviewers were divided as to the merit of the actresses' performances. No one was the victor, because the movie was roasted by all of them.

I'll Cry Tomorrow

METRO-GOLDWYN-MAYER, 1955

Lillian Roth, as portrayed by Susan Hayward

David and Lillian make plans for their marriage, but fate intervenes (Ray Danton and Susan Hayward)

CAST

Lillian Roth, Susan Hayward; *Tony Bardeman*, Richard Conte; *Burt McGuire*, Eddie Albert; *Katie Roth*, Jo Van Fleet; *Wallie*, Don Taylor; *David Tredman*, Ray Danton; *Selma*, Margo; *Ellen*, Virginia Gregg; *Jerry*, Don Barry; *David (as a child)*, David Kasday; *Lillian (as a child)*, Carole Ann Campbell; *Richard*, Peter Leeds; *Fat Man*, Tol Avery.

CREDITS

Directed by Daniel Mann. *Produced by* Lawrence Weingarten. *Screenplay by* Helen Deutsch *and* Jay Richard Kennedy. *Based on the book by* Lillian Roth, Mike Connolly, *and* Gerold Frank. *Director of Photography*, Arthur E. Arling, A.S.C. *Art Directors*, Cedric Gibbons *and* Malcolm Brown. *Film Editor*, Harold F. Kress. *Recording Supervisor*, Dr. Wesley C. Miller. *Set Decoration*, Edwin B. Willis *and* Hugh Hunt. *Costumes by* Helen Rose. *Makeup created by* William Tuttle. *Hair Styles by* Sydney Guilaroff. *Assistant Director*, Al Jennings. *Special Effects*, Warren Newcombe. *Background Music Score by* Alex North. *Miss Hayward sings:* "Sing You Sinners," "When the Red, Red Robin Comes Bob, Bob, Bobbin' Along," "Happiness Is a Thing Called Joe," "The Vagabond King Waltz," *arranged and conducted by* Charles Henderson. *Running time, 117 minutes.*

THE STORY

Katie Roth (Jo Van Fleet) is a typical "stage mother," dragging her little Lillian (Carole Ann Campbell) from audition to audition. In fact, Katie pushes her daughter so hard that she often makes Lillian cry, and then she comforts her: "Cry tomorrow," she says, "you'll have the whole day to cry tomorrow."

Lillie, who has talent, finally lands on Broadway and keeps going on to fame. But Katie is still pushing—there is no time in Lillian's life for playmates or, later on, boyfriends. Even when grown-up Lillian (Susan Hayward) is a full-fledged star and a Hollywood actress, Katie continues to rule her life.

One day Lillian finds out that David Tredman (Ray Danton), one of her few childhood friends, is in a hospital near Hollywood. Mrs. Roth does not like the idea, but Lillian goes to see him. After his release from the hospital, they start going out together. They fall in love and want to get married. Katie, always dreaming of greater glories for her daughter, is devastated, even though David is an artist's agent who can get the best deals for Lillian.

But David returns to the hospital and Lillian resumes her theatre engagement. After talking to David one night, she starts her number. Meanwhile, her mother answers a telephone call backstage: it's the hospital and David has just died. When Lillian finishes her number and hears the news she desperately rushes to the hospital, but all she finds is an empty bed.

Lillian's world has collapsed. She performs on stage like a mechanical toy. She feels resentment toward her mother because she never liked David. Finally, she confronts her and tells her off. Katie decides to go away. But Lillian cannot sleep. Her friend Ellen (Virginia Gregg), trying to help her get some sleep, offers her a drink. Lillian starts to have a drink every night before going to bed, then before going onstage, and then she starts drinking every time she needs confidence.

She goes out with a young aviation cadet, Wallie (Don Taylor), and they have a wild night on the town, waking up in a hotel room, married. They do not love each other, so their marriage is doomed from the beginning. They go from one wild party to the next trying to drink off the foolish marriage, until they get divorced.

The parties go on, and at one Lillian meets Tony Bardeman (Richard Conte), a scheming, sadistic crook. In the meantime, Mrs. Roth has returned and is sick with worry over Lillian's constant drinking. Lillian tells her that she can stop any time, but then realizes that she has become an alcoholic. She *has* to drink to stop the pain.

Lillian is easy prey for Tony, who plays his cards carefully, getting closer to her, becoming indispensable, until they marry. Soon she learns that Tony doesn't care about her. She goes on

The parties and the drinking are only an escape for Wallie and Lillian: they want to forget that they don't love each other (Don Taylor and Susan Hayward)

drinking and runs away from him. Her money is gone and she has no place to go.

This time Lillian ends up in the Los Angeles Skid Row. She tries to go back to her mother, but both are impoverished and she is totally dependent on alcohol. She tries to jump from a hotel window, but is so weak that she faints. Then she goes to Alcoholics Anonymous. There she meets Burt McGuire (Eddie Albert), Selma (Margo), and Jerry (Don Barry), who offer to help her.

She suffers delirium tremens, but, with the help of her new friends, pulls through and slowly recovers. She realizes that she is more than grateful to Burt, who tells her she must make her own decision when she gets an offer to tell the story of her life on TV. She accepts and valiantly faces the cameras as the host announces: "This is your life, Lillian Roth."

REVIEWS

REDBOOK

"Already one of Hollywood's greatest box-office attractions by virtue of her beauty and acting ability, Susan Hayward has started a new career for herself—she is a very fine singer. As Jane Froman in *With a Song in My Heart,* Susan only mouthed the words to Jane's singing. But as Lillian Roth in *I'll Cry Tomorrow,* she puts across the tunes as well as Lillian or almost anyone else ever did."

MOTION PICTURE HERALD

"Miss Roth is played by Susan Hayward, who will no doubt please her fans but who will surprise and delight everyone with what is unquestionably her best performance to date."

NEW YORK TIMES   *Bosley Crowther*

"Lillian Roth's unrelenting story of her sixteen-year bout with booze, told straight, without water or sugar, in her auto-biographical *I'll Cry Tomorrow,* comes forth on the screen a poignant picture of a top vaudeville singer's decline into the valley of alcoholism and her tough but triumphant return."

LOOK

"Singer-actress Lillian Roth's autobiography, *I'll Cry Tomorrow,* is the real-life testament of a talented woman who falls prey to alcoholism but escapes, eventually, through her courage and will-to-live. It provides the theme for one of the year's most remarkable films, told with an unsparing truth that will leave audiences shaken. The story's emotional power is vividly communicated by Susan Hayward in a shattering, intense performance that may win her an Academy Award. Daniel Mann, who directed for MGM, also becomes an Oscar candidate for his sensitive, almost documentary handling of the tragic story."

Burt has been a big help to Lillian who by now is completely recovered (Eddie Albert and Susan Hayward)

Katie and Ellen are really worried about Lillian's grieving for David (Susan Hayward, Virginia Gregg, and Jo Van Fleet)

Richard Conte and Susan Hayward

"In *I'll Cry Tomorrow* Miss Hayward is not projecting that silly feminine wilfulness which has been her stock-in-trade, but something much subtler and of much more psychological interest—the dreadful paralysis of the will that besets an outwardly successful but inwardly frustrated woman. Again parenthetically, Miss Hayward can belt out a popular song as well as Miss Roth herself."

NOTES

June Allyson, Ann Blyth, Jane Russell, and Jan Sterling were among the Hollywood actresses who wanted to play Lillian Roth. (Ann Blyth played another torch singer the following year in *The Helen Morgan Story,* a role which Hayward had rejected.)

The film made Hayward an international star. She won the Cannes Festival Award in 1956; she also won an Oscar nomination and *Cue* magazine's award for the best performance by an actress.

This was the second time that Richard Conte was her leading man. Eddie Albert was around too for what seemed an encore of his role in *Smash-Up.*

Susan as a child (for the third and last time) was represented by Carole Ann Campbell. It was the fourth and last movie in which her voice was heard narrating parts of the story, and her fourth and last one to open at Radio City Music Hall.

Susan had met Lillian Roth in Las Vegas in researching the role, and Lillian was pleased that she had been chosen to do her story. Roth had one complaint after the movie was released. Susan had used her own singing voice, for the first time, and in her engagements Roth had to adapt her style to Susan's so as not to let down those who had seen the movie.

Jo Van Fleet was superb as Lillian's mother, and should have been nominated as best supporting actress. Instead, she won the award for her role as James Dean's mother in *East of Eden.* (Both were 1955 films.)

The movie won three Academy Award nominations besides Hayward's: Cinematography, Art and Set Direction, and Costume Design, which brought an Oscar to Helen Rose as designer. Some of the dresses, however, looked suspiciously like camouflaged versions of those worn by Elizabeth Taylor in *Rhapsody,* also designed by Miss Rose.

I'll Cry Tomorrow turned out to be the top money grosser for MGM after *Gone With the Wind* and *Quo Vadis.*

Although prereleased in 1955, in time to be an Oscar contender, the general release of this movie was in 1956.

Back home, Lillian tells Wallie off and he moves out after this quarrel (Don Taylor and Susan Hayward)

The Conqueror

RKO RADIO, 1956

CAST

Temujin, John Wayne; *Bortai,* Susan Hayward; *Jamuga,* Pedro Armendariz; *Hunlun,* Agnes Moorehead; *Wang Khan,* Thomas Gomez; *Shaman,* John Hoyt; *Kasar,* William Conrad; *Kumlek,* Ted de Corsia; *Targutai,* Leslie Bradley; *Chepei,* Lee Van Cleef; *Bogurchi,* Peter Mamakos; *Tartar Captain,* Leo Gordon; *Captain of Wang's Guard,* Richard Loo.

CREDITS

Directed by Dick Powell. *Produced by* Dick Powell. *Written by* Oscar Millard. *Photography,* Joseph LaShelle, A.S.C., Leo Tover, A.S.C., Harry J. Wild, A.S.C., *and* William Snyder, A.S.C. *Art Directors,* Albert D'Agostino *and* Carroll Clark. *Editors,* Robert Ford *and* Kenneth Marstella. *Photographic Effects,* Linwood Dunn *and* Albert Simpson. *Sound,* Bernard Freericks *and* Terry Kellum. *Associate Producer,* Richard Sokolove. *Editorial Supervision,* Stuart Gilmore. *Music,* Victor Young. *Presented by* Howard Hughes. *Color by Technicolor. Filmed in CinemaScope. Running time, 110 minutes.*

THE STORY

The Mongols, led by Temujin (John Wayne) and his blood brother Jamuga (Pedro Armendariz), attack a Merkit caravan, capturing the beautiful Bortai (Susan Hayward), daughter of Kumlek (Ted de Corsia), ruler of the Tartars and slayer of Temujin's father. Temujin's mother, Hunlun (Agnes Moorehead), fears Kumlek's wrath, and she and Jamuga beg Temujin to set Bortai free, but he refuses. Despite his vow to avenge his father's death, Temujin is fascinated by the girl's beauty and fire.

The Merkits attack in an attempt to rescue Bortai but are defeated. Bortai escapes but is soon recaptured by Temujin, who declares he will make her his wife. But she lets Temujin know how much she despises him. Temujin waits.

The Mongols then go on to Urga, ruled by the powerful Wang Khan (Thomas Gomez). The Chinese ruler welcomes his guests and entertains them at a banquet. Bortai attends and is seated next to him. She suddenly decides to dance for the Khan and, taking two swords, starts her elaborate dance. At the end, having discarded one of the swords, she aims the other one at Temujin, but misses.

Temujin enlists the aid of the Khan's treacherous Shaman (John Hoyt) to get the mighty Chinese ruler to join forces with them and wipe out the Tartars. The Khan agrees, but before they can put their plan into effect, Bortai is rescued and Temujin is wounded. Jamuga, trying to aid his brother, unknowingly leads the Tartars to his hiding place. Kumlek sentences Temujin to death, but Bortai, realizing that she loves him in spite of everything, sets him free. In her heart she knows, however, that Temujin and her father will not rest until one of them is dead.

Temujin's ardor does not impress Bortai, who is colder than ice to him (John Wayne and Susan Hayward)

Bortai caresses the sword as she dances towards Temujin — her target (Susan Hayward)

Princess Bortai is Genghis Khan's prisoner, but he has just informed her and his mother Hunlun that he plans to marry her (John Wayne, Susan Hayward, and Agnes Moorehead)

During shooting of *The Conqueror* (Susan Hayward, John Wayne, and Thomas Gomez)

The Shaman convinces Temujin that the Khan will double-cross him, so Temujin captures the Khan's city and becomes ruler of all the Mongols. In a bloody battle, Temujin defeats the Tartars killing Bortai's father. Bortai's grief is great, but her love for Temujin is greater; she becomes his bride, and she and Temujin prepare to play their role in history.

Temujin, now the mighty Genghis Khan, would lay the riches of all Asia at the feet of his queen, and their children for a hundred years would rule the world.

REVIEWS

SLIVER SCREEN

"As Genghis Khan, the 12th Century Mongol warrior who conquered half the world, John Wayne won't disappoint his ardent followers.

"A highlight in the film is the sensational veil and sword dance Susan does. Directed by Dick Powell, this Technicolor spectacle set the studio back a fast $6,000,000 and believe me, it's worth every last cent."

TIME

"This picture, which purports to be based on the life of the young Genghis Khan, carries a strong suggestion that, to Hollywood's way of thinking, Mongolia is in the western U.S. The part of the 'Perfect Warrior'—a man who became a supreme statesman and lawgiver as well as the most formidable military genius in Asiatic history—is played by Hollywood's best-known cowboy, John Wayne."

FILMS IN REVIEW

"John Wayne, Susan Hayward and Agnes Moorehead, didn't bother even to dissimulate their disinterest."

NOTES

Susan wore the skimpiest of costumes for this epic, said to be RKO's most ambitious film in a while. She was the only red-haired, hazel-eyed Tartar princess ever. Her only "orientalized" features were her eyebrows, which were curved slightly upward.

Had the movie not taken itself so seriously, it might have been more successful. Nobody took it lightly, least of all the critics.

This was Hayward's third and last movie with both John Wayne and Agnes Moorehead, and her second with Pedro Armendariz.

Two of Wayne's sons (Patrick and Michael) had bit parts as warriors.

The outdoor scenes were shot on location around St. George, Utah, where the mercury climbed to 120 degrees at times. Three hundred Indians from the Shivwit reservations were used as Mongols and Tartars.

But animals created the most trouble. There was supposed to be a black panther in a scene and Hayward had to kick it in the rear, but black panthers can be very nasty, so they used black paint to make a puma look like one, and the animal kept licking the paint off its body.

The movie was panned unanimously by the critics.

Top Secret Affair
WARNER BROS., 1957

CREDITS

Directed by H. C. Potter. *Produced by* Martin Rackin. *Supervising Producer,* Milton Sperling. *Written by* Roland Kibbee *and* Allan Scott. *Based on characters from* Melville Goodwin, U.S.A. *by* John P. Marquand. *Director of Photography,* Stanley Cortez, A.S.C. *Art Director,* Malcolm Bert. *Film Editor,* Folmar Blangsted. *Sound,* Stanley Jones. *Set Decorations,* William Wallace. *Costumes designed by* Charles LeMaire. *Makeup Supervisor,* Gordon Bau, S.M.A. *Assistant Director,* Russell Saunders. *Music by* Roy Webb. *Orchestrations by* Gus Levene *and* Maurice de Packh. *Technical Adviser,* Lieutenant Colonel Frederick J. Bremerman. *Running time, 100 minutes.*

THE STORY

Dottie Peale (Susan Hayward), the glamorous but tough publisher of *New World* magazine (one of the Peale Enterprises), has given her strongest support to a civilian for a major diplomatic post when she learns that Major General Melville Goodwin (Kirk Douglas) has been named for that post, pending approval by the Senate. She is furious and plans a campaign to discredit the general.

Goodwin and Colonel Gooch (Jim Backus), an Army public information officer, accept Dottie's invitation to go to her home in Long Island for a weekend interview, and she puts her plan into action. A photographer secretly snaps photos while the general, egged on by Dottie, does a balancing act on a bongo board. Then on to the nightclubs. Her efforts to get Goodwin drunk prove unsuccessful, but, while doing the samba, she sends him crashing against a table. Later, she persuades him to sing with the orchestra at a jive joint. But Goodwin, aware that she's trying to make a fool of him, leaves Dottie and returns to the Peale house. Dottie comes back drunk and makes a scene, tossing rocks into the general's room until he agrees to meet her by the pool. She falls in the pool and he pulls her out and kisses her.

The next morning, a happy Dottie announces that her article will be favorable to Goodwin. Then he tells her that he's going back to Washington. He is practically married to the army, says he had fallen in love once, and the woman turned out to be a spy. They had only talked about military matters.

A woman scorned, Dottie is determined to go on with the original plan to discredit "Blabbermouth" Goodwin, as she calls him. Goodwin realizes that he has made a mistake and comes back to the Peale house to ask Dottie to marry him. But it's too late. The story has been released and the general will soon face an investigation. Dottie is distraught at the injustice she has done him and plans to leave the country, but she is served with a subpoena to appear before the Senate committee.

Although she admits that her article is a pack of lies and that she has resigned as editor of *New World* and all of the Peale Enterprises, Dottie cannot deny the truth about the spy affair, and this is precisely the most damaging evidence. But an official interrupts the proceedings to turn over an important secret document that has been declassified: Goodwin had been ordered to continue his relationship with Ivette de Fresney, the spy to whom he had allegedly talked about military matters in Korea, so that he could feed her false information. This, together with Dottie's confession, clears Goodwin's name.

Giving orders is Dottie's forte (Susan Hayward)

CAST

Dottie Peale, Susan Hayward; *Major General Melville Goodwin,* Kirk Douglas; *Phil Bentley,* Paul Stewart; *Colonel Gooch,* Jim Backus; *General Grimshaw,* John Cromwell; *Senator Burwick,* Roland Winters; *Butler,* A. E. Gould-Porter; *Lotzie,* Michael Fox; *Sergeant Kruger,* Frank Gerstle; *Bill Hadley,* Charles Lane.

Melville is upset to see that Dottie can get what he cannot: a special table at a nightclub (Kirk Douglas and Susan Hayward)

While awaiting the approval of the Senate to take over his diplomatic post, General Goodwin sets out to get a more personal approval from Dottie.

REVIEWS

NEW YORK TIMES *Bosley Crowther*

"We'd say the writers and director H. C. Potter have simply tried to blow up a light romantic pastime out of characters that don't hold air. And because they are constantly deflating, the whole thing tends to wheeze. Kirk Douglas and Susan Hayward play the top roles with bruising aggressiveness.

"But they can't get this operation soaring. *Melville Goodwin, U.S.A.*, is still a bore."

FILMS IN REVIEW

"Though Susan Hayward exhibits in *Top Secret Affair* less of her pouting petulance that was once her trademark (up to *I'll Cry Tomorrow*), she is still too stiff for comedy, even a comedy about an egocentric Jane who inherited a *Life*-like magazine and tries to act global. Kirk Douglas is also too stiff."

MOTION PICTURE

"Here's the surprise of the year—Kirk Douglas and Susan Hayward in a comedy. Based loosely on John P. Marquand's book, *Melville Goodwin, U.S.A.*, it's one of the funniest movies of the year."

NOTES

This type of sophisticated comedy was a first for both Hayward and Douglas, at least since they found stardom.

This movie, directed by H. C. Potter, had some memorable moments: Hayward, drunk, balancing herself on a diving board dressed in evening clothes while Douglas watches and starts undressing. He knows that he's going to have to pull her out of the swimming pool. Douglas, a master at jiujitsu, teaching Hayward, who flew through the air, disdaining a double. Hayward dreamily asking Douglas about his past love affairs and his confession that he once fell in love with a spy. She wants to know what he did when he learned that she was a spy —"I had her shot," he replies matter of factly.

Jim Backus was on hand to help with the comedy, but his character was too pushy.

Susan sported a shorter hairdo and although she hardly looked her age—almost forty—she didn't look much younger. It is said that shorter hair takes years off a woman's face, but in her case this didn't work. It was a handicap, not an improvement. (The same thing happened to Ann Sheridan and Joan Bennett.)

The picture was a loser at the box office.

I Want to Live

UNITED ARTISTS, 1958

CAST

Barbara Graham, Susan Hayward; *Ed Montgomery*, Simon Oakland; *Peg*, Virginia Vincent; *Carl Palmberg*, Theodore Bikel; *Henry Graham*, Wesley Lau; *Emmett Perkins*, Philip Coolidge; *Jack Santo*, Lou Krugman; *Bruce King*, James Philbrook; *District Attorney*, Bartlett Robinson; *Richard G. Tribow*, Gage Clark; *Al Matthews*, Joe De Santis; *Father Devers*, John Marley; *San Quentin Warden*, Raymond Bailey; *San Quentin Nurse*, Alice Backes; *San Quentin Matron*, Gertrude Flynn; *San Quentin Sergeant*, Russell Thorson; *San Quentin Captain*, Dabbs Greer; *Sergeant*, Stafford Repp; *Lieutenant*, Gavin MacLeod.

CREDITS

Directed by Robert Wise. *Produced by* Walter Wanger. *Screenplay by* Nelson Gidding *and* Don Mankiewicz. *From newspaper articles by* Ed Montgomery *and letters of* Barbara Graham. *Cinematographer*, Lionel Lindon, A.S.C. *Editor*, William Hornbeck, A.C.E. *Settings by* Edward Haworth. *Assistant Director*, George Vieira. *Production Manager*, Forrest E. Johnston. *Music composed and conducted by* John Mandel. *Jazz Combo:* Gerry Mulligan, Shelly Manne, Red Mitchell, Art Farmer, Frank Rosolino, Pete Jolly, *and* Bud Shank. *Running time, 120 minutes.*

THE STORY

Barbara (Susan Hayward) is beautiful but amoral. Having worked every racket from perjury to prostitution, she comes to San Francisco, but is soon sent to a women's prison for a year. Barbara has her own code of ethics and it is for helping a pal in trouble that she ends up in jail.

Upon her release she goes to work for two gamblers, Emmett Perkins (Philip Coolidge) and Jack Santo (Lou Krugman). For a change, her job—steering likely prospects into card games—is nonviolent most of the time and brings in good money. After some time Barbara decides to go straight; she can afford it now. But she makes her first mistake when she marries Henry Graham (Wesley Lau), a handsome bartender and one of Perkins' helpers.

Graham is on dope, and when their baby is born, the marriage is already disintegrating. Henry demands their last ten dollars for a fix and she throws the bill at his feet and tells him to get out. Barbara, desperate and broke, with debt collectors hounding her, goes into hiding with Santo and Perkins.

The police follow them, however, and they are surrounded one night, as they talk quietly in a dark room.

At police headquarters in San Francisco, they are ruthlessly questioned and Barbara discovers that they have been picked up on a murder rap. The police are convinced that the three, with Bruce King (James Philbrook), murdered an old widow in her home a few weeks earlier.

Barbara surrenders to the police, her child's toy tiger still in her hand (Susan Hayward)

Trouble has now been sealed into Barbara's future: Henry just introduced her to Perkins (left to right: Wesley Lau, Susan Hayward, and Phillip Coolidge)

Director Robert Wise gives Susan some tips for her next scene

Her answers to the D.A.'s harsh questions are equally harsh and bitter (Bartlett Robinson and Susan Hayward)

Barbara, not realizing the seriousness of her situation, goads the police and refuses to answer their questions. Meanwhile, Bruce King turns state's evidence and names Barbara as the actual killer. With no other alibi than being home with her six-month-old son and her drug-addict husband, she agrees to "buy" an alibi from a friend of her former cellmate. The "friend" insists that Barbara admit her guilt to him before accepting the deal. In despair, seeing no other way out, Barbara tells him that she went to the widow's house that night.

During the trial, Santo and Perkins remain silent while she eagerly awaits her "friend's" testimony. Suddenly he turns up as a witness for the prosecution. The "alibi" had been a trick and the "friend" was a police officer. He testifies that Barbara had admitted that she had been at the scene of the crime.

Barbara gets a chance to defend herself on the stand, but the prosecutor focuses on her sordid past and her story is ripped apart. The jury is out for five and a half hours deliberating and returns the verdict "Guilty as charged." There is no recommendation for clemency, and Barbara is sentenced to die in the gas chamber.

As she leaves the courtroom, Barbara is interviewed by Ed Montgomery (Simon Oakland), the reporter who has been writing about the "titian-haired murderess." He is stunned when Barbara blames him for the verdict.

Barbara starts her terrifying journey to the gas chamber at the women's prison in Corona, and, as time passes, more and more people believe that she's innocent. Even Ed Montgomery switches over to her side and joins the campaign to free Barbara Graham. A famous psychologist, Carl Palmberg (Theodore Bikel), after interviewing her in prison, reports that she is amoral and antisocial, but incapable of killing.

But appeals, campaigns, and legal maneuvers to prove her innocent fail. Barbara is taken to the death cell at San Quentin, and eventually to the gas chamber.

REVIEWS

NEW YORK TIMES *Bosley Crowther*

"Susan Hayward has done some vivid acting in a number of sordid roles that have called for professional simulation of personal ordeals of the most upsetting sort. But she's never done anything so vivid or so shattering to an audience's nerves as she does in Walter Wanger's sensational new drama, *I Want to Live.*

And Miss Hayward plays it superbly, under the consistently sharp direction of Robert Wise, who has shown here a stunning mastery of the staccato realistic style. From a loose and wisecracking B-girl she moves onto levels of cold disdain, and then plunges down to depths of terror and bleak surrender as she reaches the end. Except that the role does not present us a precisely pretty character, its performance merits for Miss Hayward the most respectful applause."

VARIETY *Powe*

"It is hard to think of any other star except Miss Hayward who could bring off this complex characterization. She gives a performance that undoubtedly will return her, after her recent hiatus, to the top of popular and critical lists."

CUE *Jesse Zunser*

"As the ill-fated Barbara, Susan Hayward gives one of the most penetrating performances of the year, comparable with her superb acting in *I'll Cry Tomorrow.*"

SATURDAY REVIEW

"Not that *I Want to Live* makes any attempt to whitewash Barbara Graham. On the contrary, as portrayed by Susan Hayward at her intense best, she was obviously a tough nut for any police department to crack."

MOTION PICTURE HERALD *Charles S. Aaronson*

"Susan Hayward, in the leading role, gives the finest performance of a career noted for brilliant work."

NOTES

Her role as Barbara Graham brought her acclaim and recognition around the world, even from her most stubborn detractors. But Hayward still found a sour apple in *Films in Review.* The critic, after praising her in the first part of her review, concluded: "In the post-trial and pre-execution scenes Miss Hayward's inadequacies are embarrassing to watch."

There were also complaints about the movie, particularly from the Police Department. They alleged that Graham had been proven guilty and that the movie distorted the truth.

In view of this protest, rumors started about a countermovie, one that would show Graham guilty as charged. Who would play Graham? Terry Moore, no less!

When in 1960 American International released *Why Must I Die?* with Terry Moore playing the lead, it was chaos. Said the *New York Times*: "*Why Must I Die?* is *I Want to Live* squared. Miss Moore's performance is only slightly more ridiculous than the one given by Debra Paget."

I Want to Live was Susan's last black-and-white film. Cheaper techniques made the use of color a general practice in the sixties, and by the seventies black and white was a thing of the past.

Besides Hayward's own nomination for the Academy Award, the movie received more nominations than any of her other films: Best Director (Robert Wise), Writing, Cinematography, Sound, and Film Editing.

Barbara's time is running out and the warden tries to offer some comfort (Raymond Bailey and Susan Hayward)

The nurse is reluctant to accept the toy for her children, but Barbara insists (Alice Backes and Susan Hayward)

Gabrielle is distrustful of her brother-in-law's intentions toward her (Susan Hayward and Jacques Bergerac)

Thunder in the Sun

PARAMOUNT, 1959

CAST

Gabrielle Dauphin, Susan Hayward; *Lon Bennett*, Jeff Chandler; *Pepe Dauphin*, Jacques Bergerac; *Louise Dauphin*, Blanche Yurka; *Andre Dauphin*, Carl Esmond; *Fernando*, Fortunio Bonanova; *Danielle*, Felix Locher; *Duquette*, Bertrand Castelli; *Marie*, Veda Ann Borg; *Gabrielle's Dance Partner*, Pedro de Cordoba.

CREDITS

Directed by Russell Rouse. *Produced by* Clarence Greene. *Written by* Russell Rouse. *Based on an Original Story by* Guy Trosper. *Adaptation*, Stewart Stern. *Photography*, Stanley Cortez. *Art Direction*, Boris Leven. *Editor*, Chester Schaeffer. *Miss Hayward's Costumes*, Charles LeMaire. *Second Unit Director*, Winston Jones. *Music*, Cyril Mockridge. *Song "Mon Petit":* Music by Cyril Mockridge, *lyrics by* Ned Washington, *sung by* Jacques Bergerac. *Choreography*, Pedro de Cordoba. *Running time, 81 minutes.*

THE STORY

Andre Dauphin (Carl Esmond) is the middle-aged leader of a group of Basques traveling to California in the year 1847. They still wear the traditional costume from the French Pyrenees. Dauphin, who is a visionary, has persuaded the group to try a new life in California where they plan to start a wine industry with vines they have brought with them. Young, vibrant Gabrielle (Susan Hayward) is married to Andre, not because she is in love with him, but because she had been betrothed to him as a young girl according to Basque custom. She respects her husband and is faithful to him even though his younger brother, virile and handsome Pepe (Jacques Bergerac), is secretly in love with her.

Lon Bennett (Jeff Chandler), who guides their wagon train, is attracted to beautiful Gabrielle, who wants nothing to do with him. One night he lures her away from the wagons and kisses her, but she fights him off and screams. Her husband rushes out and a nervous young sentry shoots in the darkness and kills him. Gabrielle warns Lon she'll kill him if he comes near her again.

Without their leader, the Basques want to turn back, but Gabrielle talks them into continuing. It is the Basque custom that when a young woman loses her husband she is betrothed to his brother, and so it is with Gabrielle and Pepe. Lon does not give up, however, and continues to pursue her until Pepe stops him at gunpoint.

Along with their vine plants, the Basques carry their own "hearths": iron pots containing burning embers which they have brought from home, and constantly feed, to start their first fire in the new world.

When they find that the last waterhole before crossing the desert is dry, Lon rations the water carefully, but is disgusted when the Basques share it with their plants. Later, they openly refuse to toss their "hearths" when Lon orders them to because of the danger of fire in this dry land.

Finally they reach the river, and the wagon train makes better progress. But Gabrielle's "hearth" had fallen from her wagon, unseen by any of them, and the dry grass catches fire. The fire spreads. Lon, unaware of the inferno behind them, directs the wagons toward the river, but Gabrielle rushes back to gather the vines and the flames are about to engulf her when Lon saves her. He is furious and Gabrielle realizes for the first time that he really loves her. Even Pepe sees the change and bows out, leaving her free to lead her own life.

In the mountain pass ahead Indians wait in ambush. Lon warns the group that they are badly outnumbered, but the Basques have a plan. While the women drive the wagons through the pass, the men spring a surprise attack on the Indians from the craggy cliffs. Gabrielle leads the women and the wagons and, just as the Indians are about to attack, the blood-curdling Basque battle cry echoes through the pass. The Basques attack and, using their own weapons, engage the Indians in an unusual battle. The Indians flee in disorder.

The Basques have suffered heavy losses, however, and Gabrielle blames herself. In her anguish she rips out a vine plant, but Lon replants it and guides her gently to the top of a nearby slope. From there they can see the land where they will make their home together—California.

REVIEWS

SCREEN STORIES

"Chandler views the disorganized wagon train with ill-concealed contempt until his roving eyes light on Susan; she's dancing a fiery Basque dance, celebrating the wagon train's departure. And as the wagon train pushes on, lust, peril and death are the main ingredients of this Western film fare."

NEW YORK HERALD TRIBUNE   *Paul V. Beckley*

"Miss Hayward's performance last year in *I Want to Live* makes the waste here more than usually obvious."

VARIETY   *"Powe"*

"Really good sequence at the end, largely staged by second unit director Winston Jones. . . . A rolling, tumbling, bloody battle-scene that is genuinely different and exciting."

NOTES

This was the second worst, if not *the* worst, movie Hayward made during her starring years. The other was *The Conqueror*.

Her role was undemanding, except for her Flamenco dance. This number was cleverly staged, with the other dancers pirouetting around her.

Blanche Yurka, of *A Tale of Two Cities* fame (with Ronald Colman), was wasted as the mother of Hayward's husband, in the last movie in which she acted.

Susan found a small part in the film for one of Chalkley's daughters.

The pressbook for the movie stated: "Susan Hayward displays again the amazing versatility which has characterized her upward climb to the top of filmdom's ladder."

Two brave men in love with a fiery Basque girl (Jeff Chandler, Susan Hayward, and Jacques Bergerac)

Woman Obsessed

20th CENTURY-FOX, 1959

CAST

Mary Sharron, Susan Hayward; *Fred Carter*, Stephen Boyd; *Mayme Radzevitch*, Barbara Nichols; *Robbie*, Dennis Holmes; *Dr. Gibbs*, Theodore Bikel; *Sergeant Le Moyne*, Ken Scott; *Tom Sharron*, Arthur Franz; *Henri*, James Philbrook; *Mrs. Gibbs*, Florence MacMichael; *Ian Campbell*, Jack Raine; *Mrs. Campbell*, Mary Carroll; *Officer Follette*, Fred Graham; *Ticket Taker*, Mike Lally.

CREDITS

Directed by Henry Hathaway. *Produced by* Sydney Boehm. *Screenplay by* Sydney Boehm. *From the novel by* John Mantley. *Director of Photography*, William C. Mellor, A.S.C. *Art Directors*, Lyle Wheeler *and* Jack Martin Smith. *Film Editor*, Robert Simpson, A.C.E. *Sound*, W. D. Flick *and* Harry M. Leonard. *Set Decorations*, Walter M. Scott *and* Stuart A. Reiss. *Executive Wardrobe Designer*, Charles LeMaire. *Makeup*, Ben Nye, S.M.A. *Hair Styles*, Helen Turpin, C.H.S. *Assistant Director*, David Hall. *Special Photographic Effects*, L. B. Abbott, A.S.C. *Music*, Hugo Friedhofer. *Conducted by* Lionel Newman. *Orchestration*, Earle Hagen. *Color Consultant*, Leonard Doss. *CinemaScope Lenses by* Bausch & Lomb. *Color by De Luxe. Running time, 103 minutes.*

THE STORY

In the backwoods of Canada, a hard-working farmer (Arthur Franz) dies in a forest fire leaving his widow, Mary Sharron (Susan Hayward), and son, Robbie (Dennis Holmes), alone to run the farm. Unable to handle the rough work by themselves, Mary hires Fred Carter (Stephen Boyd) to help them.

Fred is a harsh, serious man whose life has been filled with misfortune. Robbie, at first, is happy to have a man around again, but when Fred asks Mary to marry him—partly because of the pressure of being together at the farm, partly because of the talk that starts in a nearby town—Robbie is confused. Mary assures him that nothing will change.

But things do change, because they lead a rugged life with great pressures. Robbie is now jealous of Fred and Fred treats the boy harshly to prepare him for the future, but he resents it.

The situation does not improve when Mary finds out that she's going to have a baby, and it gets even worse when Fred and Robbie have a violent argument.

Fred goes to town, where he gets into a fight with the boyfriend of Mayme Radzevitch (Barbara Nichols). He is arrested and sent to jail for one month. When he returns, Fred finds his belongings in the barn.

That same night, Mary is caught in a violent storm and has a miscarriage. Fred carries her six miles through the storm to a

Mayme makes a sarcastic remark about the new hand at the Sharron farm (Barbara Nichols, Susan Hayward, and Dennis Holmes)

country doctor and goes back to look for Robbie who has run away.

Not knowing what Fred has done and thinking that he killed Mary, Robbie lures his stepfather into a quagmire. As Fred starts to sink in the quicksand, he screams for help, realizing for the first time that all men are capable of fear. Robbie hesitates, but finally has a change of heart and helps Fred out of the mire, breaking down the wall between them.

Meanwhile, Dr. Gibbs (Theodore Bikel) explains to Mary that Fred saved her life and that the problem with Robbie stems from an incident with Fred's younger brother. Fred's wife, hurt, had died in a fire because the boy couldn't stand the sight of blood and, paralyzed with fear, didn't do anything to save the unconscious woman.

Mary returns home with an understanding, forgiving heart. She finds Fred, packing to leave, but all is straightened out. They are ready to try again to become a whole family.

Susan Hayward and Stephen Boyd

Dr. Gibbs has not only taken care of Mary's physical problems, but her spiritual ones as well (Theodore Bikel and Susan Hayward)

REVIEWS

NEW YORK TIMES *Bosley Crowther*

"It is hard to say what goes with Miss Hayward when she gets into these rugged outdoor films. Her good sense and concern as a dramatic actress appear to go by the board. She rigs herself out in fancy garments, tosses her head and breathes hard. Fresh air seems to unhinge her. She behaves more reasonably in jail."

VARIETY *"Powe"*

"Miss Hayward, who seems to be the only actress around today whose eyes really blaze on occasion, has plenty of room to act in this kind of story and delivers convincingly."

MOTION PICTURE HERALD *V.C.*

"Miss Hayward is fine, as usual, and Boyd is particularly forceful and believable as the hired hand she marries."

NOTES

To shoot the outdoor scenes, director Hathaway chose the same spot where almost a quarter of a century before he had shot the classic *The Trail of the Lonesome Pine* with Sylvia Sydney, Fred MacMurray, and Henry Fonda. This time they didn't have all the problems they had then, shooting a natural setting in Technicolor at its beginnings. Many different techniques had been developed since then.

This was Susan's second movie with Simon Oakland and with Florence MacMichael, who was in *Young and Willing* with her sixteen years before.

A promising blonde newcomer, Barbara Nichols, had a few scenes with Hayward, who looked a bit on the plump side.

When cameraman William C. Mellor was replaced by Leo Shamroy during the filming, it was rumored that Hayward had him fired because of an argument. Susan denied this and explained that Mellor had been rushed to a hospital for an operation. Mellor got credit for his work, with Hayward apparently protecting his interests.

Right from the start, family meals seem to bring added tribulations to Mary and her new husband (Stephen Boyd and Susan Hayward)

Delivering a lecture on marriage, on which, supposedly, Content is an authority (Susan Hayward)

The Marriage-Go-Round

20th CENTURY-FOX, 1961

CAST

Content Delville, Susan Hayward; *Paul Delville,* James Mason; *Katrin Sveg,* Julie Newmar; *Dr. Ross,* Robert Paige; *Flo,* June Clayworth; *Henry,* Joe Kirkwood, Jr.; *Mamie,* Mary Patton; *Crew Cut,* Trax Colton; *Professor,* Everett Glass; *Sultan,* Ben Astar.

CREDITS

Directed by Walter Lang. *Produced by* Leslie Stevens. *Written by* Leslie Stevens. *Director of Photography,* Leo Tover, A.S.C. *Art Director,* Duncan Cramer *and* Maurice Ransford. *Film Editor,* Jack W. Holmes. *Sound,* E. Clayton Ward *and* Frank W. Moran. *Costumes designed by* Charles LeMaire. *Music by* Dominic Frontiere, *conducted by* Dominic Frontiere. *Assistant Director,* Eli Dunn. Tony Bennett *sings* "Marriage-Go-Round" *by* Alan Bergman, Marilyn Keith, *and* Lew Spence. *Color by* De Luxe. *Running time, 98 minutes.*

What kind of prize is this? Content seems to be asking her new guest from Sweden (Julie Newmar and Susan Hayward)

THE STORY

Content (Susan Hayward) and Paul Delville (James Mason) are a happily married couple. He is Professor of Cultural Anthropology at a university where she is Dean of Women, and both give lectures on marriage, each from his or her own viewpoint. Their talks are based on sixteen years of marital fidelity, mingled with a knowledge of marriage customs of other lands.

The daughter of an old friend from Sweden—a Nobel Prize winner—comes into their life. They expect Katrin Sveg (Julie Newmar) to be a lanky teenager, but in walks a statuesque Viking beauty. And her father is not with her. At dinner, alone with Paul, she announces, quite naturally, that she has come from Sweden to see Paul "because I want you to be the father of my baby."

Katrin goes on to explain that she had seen him in a newsreel and decided that, with his mind and her body, they could produce the ideal child. Of course, Katrin is willing to allow Paul to think about her proposition. When his wife comes home, he tells her of his dilemma.

Content tells her friend, Professor Ross Barnett (Robert Paige), about the situation and he offers to run away with her to Bermuda so they can really confuse everyone. Instead, she contacts the head of the Athletic Department, Henry Granger (Joe Kirkwood, Jr.), and his wife Flo (June Clayworth) and gets them to invite Katrin to a party they are throwing. There she can meet all the handsome All-American athletes, including the swimming team.

When Katrin appears at the party in a bathing suit, there

is chaos. She outdoes them all in their own fields: diving, swimming, wrestling.

Later, at the house, Katrin informs Content calmly that she doesn't want her husband, she just wants a child by him. Content tries to explain marriage customs in America.

Paul and Katrin leave together, supposedly to attend a lecture. Content thinks that Paul has betrayed her, and starts packing to leave him. Meanwhile, Paul tells Katrin off, in a fatherly fashion. Katrin decides to leave.

Paul and his wife trade accusations. He flunked his test with Katrin, she says. She was going to run away with Ross, he says. Finally, Paul begs her forgiveness and they make up.

Soon, Professor Delville and his wife are back on the lecture platform, nervously telling their students how to stay happily married.

REVIEWS

TIME

"The $3,000,000 Deluxe Colored screen version of the play lacks two of the Broadway principals and most of the bawdier jokes. Instead of Boyer and Colbert, the picture offers James Mason, an actor who could not crack a joke if it was a lichee nut, and Susan Hayward, a bargain-basement Bette Davis whose lightest touch as a comedienne would stun a horse."

VARIETY   *"Tube"*

"James Mason is competent, managing to stay reasonably appealing in a perpetual state of mild flabbergastedness. Susan Hayward does exceptionally well.

"Brisk direction by Walter Lang fails to enliven the general tedium by much. There is also some structural confusion; choppy flashback transitions that indicate something has been lost of the play's novel staging technique."

NEW YORK TIMES   *Bosley Crowther*

"Mr. Mason is excellent.

"Susan Hayward is likewise excellent. Being a dandy with poison-tipped sarcasm and plenty of a looker herself, she easily holds her own against the menace and makes the standard moral ending bearable."

NOTES

This comedy, Hayward's second movie with director Lang, had a lot of bright touches. But, like most of her comedy roles, it was bombarded by most of the critics.

During the filming Hayward received from Niels Larsen, the Spanish-American producer, a trophy from Spain as best actress in 1959 for *I Want to Live*.

Julie Newmar, only member of the Broadway cast retained for the movie, got much praise (she had won the Antoinette Perry Award as best supporting actress for the play) and for a while it seemed that she was going to be the next Judy Holliday.

Looking for advice, or a shoulder to cry on, Content meets Dr. Ross at a bar (Robert Paige and Susan Hayward)

The Viking beauty has become the "Swedish menace" to Paul and Content's happy marriage (James Mason and Susan Hayward)

Ada

METRO-GOLDWYN-MAYER, 1961

CAST

Ada, Susan Hayward; *Bo Gillis*, Dean Martin; *Sylvester Marin*, Wilfrid Hyde-White; *Colonel Yancey*, Ralph Meeker; *Steve Jackson*, Martin Balsam; *Ronnie Hallerton*, Frank Baxwell; *Alice Sweet*, Connie Sawyer; *Speaker*, Ford Rainey; *Al Winslow*, Charles Watts; *Joe Adams*, Larry Gates; *Warren Natfield*, Robert S. Simon; *Harry Davers*, William Zuckert; *Clubwoman*, Mary Treen.

CREDITS

Directed by Daniel Mann. *Produced by* Lawrence Weingarten. *Screenplay by* Arthur Sheekman *and* William Driskill. *Based on the novel* Ada Dallas *by* Wirt Williams. *Photography,* Joseph Ruttenberg. *Color Consultant,* Charles K. Hagedon. *Art Director,* George W. Davis *and* Edward Carfagno. *Editor,* Ralph E. Winters. *Set Decorations,* Harry Grace *and* Jack Mills. *Recording Supervisor,* Franklin Milton. *Costumes,* Helen Rose. *Makeup,* William Tuttle. *Hairstyles,* Mary Keats. *Assistant Director,* Al Jennings. *Special Visual Effects,* Lee LeBlanc. *Music composed by* Bronislau Kaper. *Conducted by* Robert Armbruster. *Song* "May the Lord Bless You Real Good" *by* Warren Roberts *and* Wally Fowler, *sung by* Dean Martin. *In CinemaScope and Metrocolor. Running time, 108 minutes.*

THE STORY

Bo Gillis (Dean Martin), a politician who loves to play the guitar and make folksy speeches, is in the midst of his campaign for governor of a southern state. He meets Ada (Susan Hayward), a reformed prostitute, and falls in love with her. Steve Jackson (Martin Balsam), Bo's press agent, and Sylvester Marin (Wilfrid Hyde-White), his political adviser, are alarmed at her dubious background, but Bo marries her.

Ada turns out to be quite an asset in Bo's campaign; her resourcefulness is instrumental in helping Bo win the election. After he is in office, Ada, never fooled by Marin's mild manners and alleged loyalty, tries to convince her husband that Marin is an opportunist who is supporting him only because it is convenient for him. But Gillis cannot believe this, not even after Marin blackmails Bo's loyal lieutenant governor, and forces him to resign.

Since her husband refuses to accept the truth about Marin, Ada decides to change her tactics and, playing up to Marin, gets herself appointed as the new lieutenant governor. Soon after that, the governor is almost killed in an automobile explosion. Marin has made the "accident" happen because the governor has failed to follow his suggestions. Unfortunately, Bo now believes that his wife has sided with Marin, so Ada starts on yet another course of action. She gets herself sworn in as acting governor while her husband is incapacitated. In office, she defies Marin openly and supports a series of reform bills originally introduced by Bo.

As Ada Dallas (Susan Hayward)

How does it feel to sit on the governor's lap? Simply wonderful! (Dean Martin and Susan Hayward)

Eyes flaring in anger, Ada confronts Bo's public relations adviser with a piece of news she has just read. (Martin Balsam and Susan Hayward)

Taking the oath as interim governor while her husband is in the hospital (left to right, in the middle: Gene Stutenroth, Wilfrid Hyde-White, Susan Hayward, and Ralph Meeker)

Marin is not about to let her get away with it, so he enlists the aid of the corrupt police chief, Colonel Yancy (Ralph Meeker), and sets out to destroy Ada's reputation by attempting to introduce an incriminating tape recording.

But Bo is released from the hospital in time to defend his wife from the state capitol spectators' gallery. After his eloquent speech, the reform legislation that Marin had fought so ruthlessly is passed.

Bo realizes that his wife is quite a woman, and he and Ada are reunited.

REVIEWS

VARIETY

"Miss Hayward, an exciting actress to watch, puts a high-voltage charge into her lines, best in the picture, but the character is almost monotonously cocksure and triumphant, and her portrayal makes it more of an inverted snob than a true woman —by far the sharpest prostitute ever to grace the screen."

NEW YORK HERALD TRIBUNE   *Joseph Morgenstern*

"*Ada* succeeds neither as the story of a woman or the chronicle of a rancid administration. Its characterizations are sketchy, its political setting routine and synthetic.

"Miss Hayward is always professional but never inventive, and Mr. Martin also fills the bill without any flair or distinction."

FILMS IN REVIEW   *Henry Hart*

"This Susan Hayward sudser asks us to believe that a machine-bossed, guitar-strumming gubernatorial candidate could be elected even though he marries a prostitute just before the election."

SATURDAY REVIEW   *Arthur Knight*

"Above all else, it is the lack of any semblance of truth that vitiates a picture like *Ada*."

NOTES

The title of the original Wirt Williams novel was *Ada Dallas,* but perhaps the "Dallas" was dropped from the movie title to avoid confusing it with the old Barbara Stanwyck tearjerker *Stella Dallas,* a completely different story of motherly love.

This was the second time Susan played a prostitute (first time in *I Want to Live*).

In one of her best scenes, she is talking with a group of snobbish society women. At first she tries to be pleasant, even humble, but finally she throws the truth at them: "I'm a sharecropper's kid from off the Delta Road." This was Hayward at her best.

This was Susan's second movie at MGM with both director Daniel Mann and producer Lawrence Weingarten, of *I'll Cry Tomorrow* fame, but this time the trio was not as successful with the critics. At the box office, the movie fared better.

Back Street

What a handsome soldier! And Rae can feel his eyes on her (John Gavin and Susan Hayward)

CAST

Rae Smith, Susan Hayward; *Paul Saxon*, John Gavin; *Liz Saxon*, Vera Miles; *Janie*, Virginia Grey; *Curt Stanton*, Charles Drake; *Dalian*, Reginald Gardiner; *Caroline Saxon*, Tammy Marihugh; *Paul Saxon, Jr.*, Robert Eyer; *Mrs. Evans*, Natalie Schafer; *Miss Hatfield*, Doreen McLean; *Mr. Venner*, Alex Gerry; *Mrs. Penworth*, Karen Norris; *Charley Claypole*, Hayden Rorke; *Marge Claypole*, Mary Lawrence; *Airport Clerk*, Joe Cronin; *Hotel Clerk*, Ted Thorpe; *Proprietor*, Joseph Mell; *Sailor*, Dick Kallman; *Showroom Model*, Joyce Meadows; *Paris Airport Employee*, Lilyan Chauvin; *Harper's Bazaar Models*, Joanne Betay, Vivianne Porte, Isabelle Felder, Melissa Weston, Bea Ammidown.

CREDITS

Directed by David Miller. *Produced by* Ross Hunter. *Screenplay by* Eleanor Griffin *and* William Ludwig. *Based on the novel by* Fannie Hurst. *Photography*, Stanley Cortez. *Art Direction*, Alexander Golitzen. *Editor*, Milton Carruth. *Sound*, Waldon O. Watson *and* Frank H. Wilkinson. *Set Decorations*, Howard Bristol. *Costumes*, Jean Louis. *Makeup*, Bud Westmore. *Hairstyles*, Larry Germain. *Assistant Director*, Phil Bowles. *Music*, Frank Skinner. *Music Supervision*, Joseph Gershenson. *Title Song: Music by* Frank Skinner, *Lyrics by* Ken Darby. *Eastman Color by Pathé. Running time, 107 minutes.*

THE STORY

Marine Corps Captain Paul Saxon (John Gavin), on his way home to Chicago at the end of World War II, is stranded in Lincoln, Nebraska. At the airport he casually meets Rae Smith (Susan Hayward), a USO hostess who's waiting for her fiancé Curt Stanton (Charles Drake).

At his hotel, Paul learns that Rae has a late appointment with Venner (Alex Gerry) to show him her fashion sketches. Since his room is next to Venner's, he overhears their conversation. Suddenly, he realizes that Venner is making a pass at Rae, so he intervenes. Paul and Rae are instantly attracted to each other. When Rae tells him of her ambition to be a fashion designer, he asks her to come to Chicago where he is heir to Saxon Department Stores. Still, when Paul tells her that he has problems, Rae, suspecting another woman, has misgivings about accompanying him. Her sister Janie (Virginia Grey) urges her to go and pursue her career, but she hesitates and, by the time she finally decides to go, Paul's plane has left.

Soon Rae learns that Paul is married, so she moves to New York where she gets a job with famous couturier Dalian (Reginald Gardiner), and becomes a successful designer.

Paul traces her to New York and visits her there, but she informs him that she has no desire to be just "the other woman" in his life. Meanwhile, Dalian opens an office in Rome with Rae as his partner. There she meets Curt, with whom she had broken up, and one night, at a café, they run into Paul and his drunken wife, Liz (Vera Miles). Rae, realizing the predicament he's in, lets Paul spend a few days with her at her beach home. He tells her that Liz has been a chronic drinker for a long time and refuses to give him a divorce. He has not left her because they have two children, Paul, Jr. (Robert Eyer), and Caroline (Tammy Marihugh).

Liz attempts to commit suicide and Paul takes her to their home in Paris, where he buys a house for Rae. But Liz hears about Rae. Paul, Jr., saw her at the airport on one of Paul's frequent trips to London and ordered her to stay away from his father. Liz, attending a fashion auction, publicly accuses Rae.

Paul and Liz have a violent dispute that evening, and Paul gets in the car with her. She drives insanely and loses control of the car, dying in the ensuing crash. Paul is taken to the hospital seriously injured. He asks his son to call Rae. Paul only has time to tell Rae how much he loves her, and dies.

After the funeral, Paul's children come to see Rae. "We came because there is nobody left," Paul, Jr., explains, "nobody close . . . so we thought you wouldn't mind if we visited you once in a while."

REVIEWS

PHOTOPLAY

"Off we go into a world where love remains all-important, no matter how fate plots against the lovers. Susan and John are as decorative as the colorful locales, the luxurious interiors and the expensive clothes. With enthusiasm, Vera makes the wife so nasty we forget Susan's a 'sinner.'"

Dressed at her best: as Rae Smith

Janie is worried about Rae's infatuation with Paul, but she assures her sister there's no cause for concern (Virginia Grey and Susan Hayward)

SATURDAY REVIEW *Hollis Alpert*

"Ross Hunter has updated this old faithful of a Fannie Hurst story, and has given it a contemporary lack of significance. Susan Hayward provides a dreadfully serious parody of herself as Rae Smith, fashion designer and mistress of John Gavin, department store tycoon.

"Wrong casting, by the way. Miss Hayward would have been a natural for the boozy, unfaithful wife, and Miss Miles would have made a lovely mistress."

TIME

"In this third film version of the book—Ross Hunter's full color, wide-screen, $2,500,000 overproduction in which the bathrooms look like the lobby of the Beverly Hilton—the fallen woman falls, not into the pit of shame, but into the lap of luxury."

NOTES

The movie, although Hayward's most popular film of the early sixties, and a top grosser for the year 1961, was considered the worst version of Fannie Hurst's novel, updated to World War II for the lovers' first meeting, and to current times for the rest of the story.

John Gavin, fresh from the popular remake of *Imitation of Life* with Lana Turner, went forward another step.

Hayward's wardrobe was a fashion show in itself: furs, velvets, chiffons, lamés, and even a bathing suit, all by Jean Louis. As expected, the movie was nominated for its costume design.

Produced by Ross Hunter, it was filmed in its entirety at Universal Studios, including the "visits" to Rome and Paris.

Director Miller, a believer in theatre techniques, put his cast through two weeks of rehearsals so they could understand the screenplay as a unit and grasp their relationship with the other players. Thus he maintained continuity of mood, sticking to the story line instead of putting the story together like segments of a jigsaw puzzle.

I Thank a Fool

METRO-GOLDWYN-MAYER, 1962

CAST

Christine Allison, Susan Hayward; *Stephen Dane*, Peter Finch; *Liane Dane*, Diane Cilento; *Captain Ferris*, Cyril Cusack; *Roscoe*, Kieron Moore; *Aunt Heather*, Athene Seyler; *Ebblington*, Richard Wattis; *Nurse Drew*, Brenda De Banzie; *Woman in the Black Maria*, Miriam Karlin; *O'Grady*, Laurence Naismith; *Judge*, Clive Morton; *Coroner*, J. G. Devlin; *Irish Doctor*, Richard Leech; *Polly*, Yolande Turner; *Junior Counsel*, Edwin Apps; *Irish Barmaid*, Marguerite Brennan; *Wardress*, Judith Furse; *2nd Wardress*, Grace Arnold; *Sleazy Doctor*, Peter Sallis; *Restaurant Manageress*, Joan Benham; *Landlady*, Joan Hickson.

CREDITS

Directed by Robert Stevens. *Produced by* Anatole De Grunwald. *Screenplay by* Karl Tunberg. *Based on the novel by* Audrey Erskine Lindop. *Photography*, Harry Waxman. *2nd Unit Photography*, Douglas Adamson. *Art Direction*, Sean Kenny. *Editor*, Frank Clarke. *Sound*, Gordon Daniel, A. W. Watkins, *and* Cyril Swern. *Dress Designer*, Elizabeth Haffenden. *Makeup*, Tony Sforzini. *Hairstyles*, Joan Johnstone. *Assistant Director*, Dave Tomblin. *Associate Producer*, Roy Parkinson. *Production Manager*, Basil Somner. *Special Effects*, Tom Howard. *Music*, Ron Goodwin. *Color Consultant*, Joan Bridge. *In Cinemascope and Metrocolor. Running time, 100 minutes.*

THE STORY

Christine Allison (Susan Hayward), a Canadian doctor, follows her married lover to England. He is incurably ill and requests that she give him an overdose of morphine to end his life. She complies, but is accused and arrested.

The prosecuting attorney, Stephen Dane (Peter Finch), shows no mercy; she's convicted of manslaughter and sentenced to two years in prison.

When she completes her jail term, Christine finds herself penniless and jobless, and she is not allowed to continue practicing medicine. Things look desperate until she gets a mysterious offer. She is told to go to a house in the country where she finds out that her employer is none other than Stephen Dane, the attorney who had helped to send her to jail.

Dane's beautiful Irish wife, Liane (Diane Cilento), has been mentally ill since the death of her father in a car accident. Christine's job is to look after her.

Soon Christine senses that there is something strange about the situation. When Liane's "dead" father, Captain Ferris (Cyril Cusack), suddenly reappears, she is sure that there is something wrong. Why has Dane hired her?

Determined to help Liane, Christine takes her to her alleged lush country home in Ireland, only to find that it is really a broken-down hovel. Liane is then forced to admit that her

Christine seems to have other things on her mind while Stephen shows her his plants (Susan Hayward and Peter Finch)

The investigation is almost ending, with Christine and Stephen accusing each other of causing Liane's death (Peter Finch, Susan Hayward, and Cyril Cusack)

father is a drunken schemer who is behind all of this. But the shock of facing the truth proves too much for the poor girl and she has a breakdown.

Christine, advised by a doctor, gives Liane a sedative. When later Liane is found dead, Christine suspects that Dane planned the whole thing to get rid of his wife and blame it on her.

At the inquest Dane seems to be defending her, but she still has doubts. Not until he forces Captain Ferris to admit complicity in the death of his mentally defective daughter, does she realize that Dane really is defending her. It turns out that Liane had taken an overdose of pills herself, but that her father had hidden the empty bottle.

Ferris, after being forced to confess, makes a desperate attempt to escape and falls to his death.

Christine is exonerated and Dane is no longer tied down to a sick wife. Both are free to start their lives anew. Together?

REVIEWS

WASHINGTON POST   *Richard L. Coe*

"Stevens' direction is of the let-'er-rip variety, and I suspect he loathes the human race. Miss Hayward manages to be fairly above the fray her character has elected to stay with, but Diane Cilento, as the befuddled wife, has been ill-advised to perform as though she's taking stage center in the temple theater at Baalbek."

THE NEW YORKER   *John McCarten*

"As the lady doctor who is the heroine of *I Thank a Fool*, Susan Hayward has a terrible time."

NEW YORK TIMES   *Bosley Crowther*

"Poor Susan Hayward. If she isn't playing a drunkard or a kook or something of the sort in films, it appears she has to be involved with characters who are dunkards or kooks or some sort of psychopaths."

NOTES

Finally Hayward, with husband Chalkley, joined the latest fashionable trend: filming abroad. This was her first movie to be filmed in Europe—England and Ireland, to be more specific. Most of the location scenes were filmed in the tiny fishing village of Crookhaven in County Cork, Ireland—the same part of the country where Susan's grandmother was born.

The cast had the most primitive quarters; they could be seen every morning standing in line to pump water. But Hayward, not being the primitive type, stayed at a Gothic mansion, forty-eight miles from Crookhaven, in modern comfort—and with plumbing facilities.

This was her second movie with Kieron Moore, and the first where they shared some scenes. (They never appeared together in *David and Bathsheba*, their first.)

Neither Hayward nor the fine cast of English performers, headed by Peter Finch, could save this movie. It failed to create the suspense proclaimed by the ads: "A story shrouded in the mist and mystery of these lonely moors, of a fear-haunted girl, a strange madness—and murder." Its controversial and up-to-date theme, euthanasia, failed to hold audiences; it was a poor grosser.

Susan Hayward and Peter Finch

Stolen Hours

UNITED ARTISTS, 1963

Michael Craig and Susan Hayward

While straightening up her husband's office she comes across her own medical file (Susan Hayward)

CAST

Laura Pember, Susan Hayward; *John Carmody,* Michael Craig; *Ellen Pember,* Diane Baker; *Mike Bannerman,* Edward Judd; *Eric McKenzie,* Paul Rogers; *Peter,* Robert Bacon; *Dalporto,* Paul Stassino; *The Colonel,* Jerry Desmonde; *Miss Kendall,* Ellen McIntosh; *Hospital Sister,* Gwen Nelson; *Reynolds,* Peter Madden; *Mrs. Hewitt,* Joan Newell; *Himself,* Chet Baker.

CREDITS

Directed by Daniel Petrie. *Produced by* Denis Holt. *Executive Producers,* Stuart Millar *and* Lawrence Turman. *Screenplay,* Jessamyn West. *Story Adaptation,* Joseph Hayes. *Based on the play* Dark Victory *by* George Brewer, Jr., *and* Bertram Block. *Photography,* Harry Waxman. *Art Direction,* Wilfred Shingleton. *Editor,* Geoffrey Foote. *Sound,* C. T. Mason *and* A. N. Other. *Set Decorations,* Joan Hoesli. *Titles,* Maurice Binder. *Miss Hayward's Costumes,* Fabiani. *Wardrobe,* Evelyn Gibbs. *Makeup,* George Partleton. *Hairstyles,* Joan Smallwood. *Assistant Director,* Colin Brewer. *Production Supervisor,* Teddy Joseph. *Unit Manager,* John Peverall. *Assistant to the Producers,* Rose Tobias Shaw. *Music,* Mort Lindsey. *Song Lyrics by* Marilyn Keith *and* Alan Bergman. *A Barbican Film for Mirisch Productions. In Eastman Colour. Running time, 100 minutes.*

THE STORY

Laura Pember (Susan Hayward), a wealthy American playgirl, leaves her guests to pick up her sister Ellen (Diane Baker) at the London airport. The party continues at her home in the English countryside, Ascot Place.

Laura stops her car for a while because she feels dizzy. After a short rest, she continues to the airport and meets Ellen, who is concerned by her sister's request for her to come.

Back at Ascot Place, Laura introduces her sister to racing driver Mike Bannerman (Edward Judd), her most recent lover, and excuses herself. In her room she suffers a fierce head pain and barely has time to take her pills before collapsing on her bed.

Ellen, meanwhile, learns from Bannerman that her sister is seriously ill, suffering headaches and loss of vision, but refuses to see a doctor. Mike has brought Dr. John Carmody (Michael Craig), a leading London physician, to see Laura.

Laura joins her guests and meets Dr. Carmody. Without her realizing it, he performs some simple tests that indicate the seriousness of her illness. When Laura understands what he has done, she feels insulted and furious, but the mutual attraction that exists between them from the beginning makes her listen to Dr. Carmody when he asks her to see a brain specialist.

Carmody's diagnosis is confirmed by the surgeon, Dr. McKenzie (Paul Rogers), and Laura enters the hospital for a brain operation. She tries to take the whole thing lightly, but Carmody, who is falling in love with her, knows that she is really terrified. Having completed the operation, Dr. McKenzie tells Mike and Ellen that it has been successful. And it's John Carmody who has to tell them the truth about Laura's condition. Bannerman and Ellen beg John not to let Laura know. He does not agree, but later, when a happy Laura thanks him for his part in her recovery, he doesn't have the heart to spoil her joy.

They start seeing each other, and soon she's as much in love

Michael Craig and Susan Hayward

The idea of wearing wigs is not appealing, but Laura knows she has no choice: her hair must be shaved off. (Edward Judd, Gwen Nelson, Susan Hayward, and Diane Baker)

with him as he has been with her. They make plans to marry; then she learns that the operation did not cure her, but gave her only a few more years, or months, to live. She is angry at John for not telling her the truth and accuses him of treating her as a patient, not as the woman he loves.

Laura runs away to Italy and joins Bannerman, who is driving in the Grand Prix. But when John comes after her, she realizes how much she needs him. Reconciled, they return to England.

They get married and settle down in the Cornish village of Polruan, where John takes up his practice. For the first time Laura knows the meaning of love. Her two prior marriages had been failures. Their life is rich and full. The tragic knowledge they share makes their love even more precious.

She meets a little boy named Peter (Robert Bacon), whose mother pays no attention to him, and they become close. She has at last found her real self in her little home, away from all the glitter of London.

When her sight begins to fail, as John leaves to deliver a patient's baby, she bids him farewell without revealing her anxiety. The boy Peter gives her the courage she needs at the end, and she faces her fate serenely.

REVIEWS

TIME

"On Hollywood's form sheet, a woman with a brain tumor can be practically certain that she will win the love of a handsome and successful doctor and live out her days in his tender loving care. It happened to Bette Davis in *Dark Victory* (1939), and now it has happened to Susan Hayward."

VARIETY *"Kali"*

"Female audiences haven't had a good cry for a while, which will be remedied by *Stolen Hours*.

"Miss Hayward's performance should arouse audience compassion via her deft handling of the role, which she essays with latterday restraint."

NEW YORK HERALD TRIBUNE   *Robert Salmaggi*

"The drama is a sentimental story that has the benefit of an intelligent screenplay, tight direction, and subdued, sensitive performances by Susan Hayward, Michael Craig, Edward Judd and Diane Baker. . . . There is no hand-wringing, martyred posturings, or playing to the grandstand."

NOTES

This movie, her second filmed in England, fared better than the first one, but it was not a success.

She was dressed like a clotheshorse and wore over a million dollars' worth of jewelry. It was a remake of the earlier Bette Davis sudser, and it is said that "seconds" are rarely any good. Some reviewers panned it, one accusing Hayward of "striking poses."

In this remake, Hayward had a goody-goody sister, Diane Baker, where Davis had a secretary (Geraldine Fitzgerald), and lots of boyfriends before her marriage to Michael Craig.

Susan had to learn the bossa nova and the twist (with dance instructor Chubby Checker) for this movie, but her twist was never seen by the audiences. It "died" on the cutting room floor.

This movie had a long shooting schedule—14 weeks—and Hayward appeared in 181 of the 188 scenes and had 32 wardrobe changes.

Mrs. Hayden is having her way while Valerie smiles condescendingly (Bette Davis and Susan Hayward)

Where Love Has Gone

PARAMOUNT, 1964

CAST

Valerie Hayden, Susan Hayward; *Mrs. Gerald Hayden,* Bette Davis; *Luke Miller,* Michael Connors; *Dani,* Joey Heatherton; *Marion Spicer,* Jane Greer; *Sam Corwin,* DeForest Kelley; *Gordon Harris,* George Macready; *Dr. Sally Jennings,* Anne Seymour; *Judge Murphy,* Willis Bouchey; *George Babson,* Walter Reed; *Mrs. Geraghty,* Ann Doran; *Mr. Coleman,* Bartlett Robinson; *Professor Bell,* Whit Bissell; *Rafael,* Anthony Caruso.

CREDITS

Directed by Edward Dmytryk. *Produced by* Joseph E. Levine. *Screenplay by* John Michael Hayes. *Based on the novel by* Harold Robbins. *Photography,* Joseph MacDonald. *Art Direction,* Hal Pereira *and* Walter Tyler. *Editor,* Frank Bracht. *Sound,* John Carter *and* Charles Grenzbach. *Set Direction,* Sam Comer *and* Arthur Krams. *Costumes,* Edith Head. *Makeup,* Wally Westmore *and* Gene Hibbs. *Assistant Director,* D. Michael Moore. *Special Photographic Effects,* Paul K. Lerpae. *Process Photography,* Farciot Edouart. *Production Manager,* Frank Caffey. *Dialogue Director,* Frank London. *Music,* Walter Scharf. *Title Song by* Sammy Cahn *and* James Van Heusen, *sung by* Jack Jones. *In Techniscope and Technicolor. Running time, 114 minutes.*

THE STORY

Luke Miller (Michael Connors) is in a conference at the construction company where he is one of the partners. There is an urgent phone call for him: his fifteen-year-old daughter Dani (Joey Heatherton) has been accused of murder.

Luke walks out of the conference and rushes to a daughter he hasn't seen in years. Gordon Harris (George Macready), the Hayden family lawyer—who handled his divorce from Valerie Hayden (Susan Hayward) and who deprived him of the right to visit Dani—has called him because he needs Luke to provide a favorable family setting for the coming hearing at Juvenile Court. Dani, Luke learns, has apparently killed her mother's lover. Luke tells Harris that, when the case is resolved, he wants custody of his daughter, but the attorney indicates this is impossible.

Nothing seems to have changed and the familiar setting revives Luke's memories of his unhappy life with Valerie and her mother (Bette Davis). The autocratic, domineering Mrs. Hayden would go to any extreme to have the family name protected, even Valerie's, in spite of her reckless infidelity and alcoholism.

Mrs. Hayden is still the same ruthless, scheming woman. Luke renews his acquaintance with her and Valerie, for Dani's sake.

There are endless days of preliminary hearings. Valerie visits Luke seeking a second chance for all of them together; when Luke refuses, she is despondent and hurt.

At the final custody hearing, Luke, trying to get the true story, accuses Valerie of committing the murder. Valerie, terrified that Mrs. Hayden might be given custody of Dani, reveals that she is more to blame for the murder than Dani, because of her failure as a mother.

She had been brought up with so many restrictions as a young girl that she had not imposed any at all on her daughter. Valerie then reveals the truth behind the murder. Yes, Dani had killed the man, but he had been the wrong victim. It was Valerie herself, her mother, whom the girl had tried to kill.

Dani had been in love with the dead man and could not bear the thought that her mother was taking him away from her.

Valerie, shattered by her confession, has at least one satisfaction: she has freed Dani from Mrs. Hayden's claws. She flees the courtroom, leaving her mother humiliated. Luke tries vainly to stop her.

At home, Valerie faces her mother's portrait and, in a frenzy, rips it down and tears it to shreds. Then she kills herself.

At Valerie's funeral, Luke and Dani are together, closer than ever. Mrs. Hayden is alone. She will not tyrannize anyone again.

REVIEWS

NEWSWEEK

"One watches *Where Love Has Gone* in disbelief, wondering how, in a movie from a major studio, there could be such

Valerie destroys her mother's portrait with all the hate that had been building up in her heart (Susan Hayward)

Every time Luke and Valerie meet, they end up blaming each other for what has happened (Mike Connors and Susan Hayward)

Another argument between mother and daughter (Bette Davis and Susan Hayward)

universal and serene ineptitude. Even the sets are ridiculous. Art directors Hal Pereira and Walter Tyler have all the flair and style of the interior desecraters who do the new motels.

". . . one must credit Miss Hayward at least for slashing a terrible portrait of Bette to shreds."

TIME

"Producer Joseph E. Levine has dressed it up as what used to be called 'a woman's picture.' Amidst sumptuous settings, supposedly inhabited by the 'haut monde' of San Francisco, heroine Susan Hayward plays a world-famous 'sculptor, pagan, alley-cat.' "

VARIETY   *"Whit"*

"Susan Hayward and Bette Davis share top honors in impressive performances. Picture is a brilliant showcase for both actresses and projects them in roles which will find much comment."

NOTES

At the press conference to sign the contracts for this movie, Davis and Hayward were photographed in friendly conversation, but it seems to have been just play-acting because they did not get along at all during the filming. Perhaps it was too much to ask. It is a difficult task for two women of such strong character to mesh and other circumstances did not improve the situation:

Susan had just completed the new version of *Dark Victory.*

At forty-six Hayward looked so young that when she appeared as a young bride (in a flashback) one could almost say she was twenty-six.

Davis, only ten years older, was playing the role of her mother (and grandmother to Joey Heatherton, Hayward's "teenage daughter").

The portrait of "Mama Davis" is torn to shreds by Susan just before she commits suicide at the end.

Michael Connors played the husband (prior to his "Mannix" TV fame).

Jane Greer, who had co-starred with Susan in *They Won't Believe Me,* back in 1947, had a small role. She was trying to make a comeback after a serious illness, but to no avail.

This was Hayward's second movie with director Dmytryk. The critics hated it, but the picture was successful at the box office.

The title song, rendered by Jack Jones, was nominated among the best songs.

Susan Hayward as young Valerie, in her wedding gown

Mame (1968)

In Italy in 1965, during filming of *The Honey Pot*

Where Love Has Gone was the last picture in which Susan reigned as a superstar of the first magnitude. Making movies had ceased to be her main ambition after her marriage, and after the Oscar. It has been said many times that an Oscar is a jinx, and in Susan's case, at least career-wise, it was, because after the award no major roles came her way. During her last ten years of life, she appeared in only three theatrical movies (in parts that amounted to "guest appearances" or "cameos"), one stage show, and two TV movies. But she had not planned it that way, not even her semiretirement after her marriage to Chalkley—this happened naturally when her new-found happiness filled her life to capacity. After that it was the turn of events that dictated her staying away from the cameras, and before long she found that it was becoming increasingly diffi-cut for an older actress to find appropriate vehicles for her talents.

She was in seventh heaven with Eaton, but their happiness was clouded that year when Eaton's only son died in a plane crash, and after that she was away from the screen for two con-secutive years.

At the end of 1965, she went to Italy to make a movie that had three different titles—"Mr. Fox of Venice," "Tale of the Fox," and "Anyone for Venice?"—before it was finally released as *The Honey Pot*. Finally? In some places the movie was known as "It comes Up Murder"—a fifth title. The movie was plagued with almost as many misfortunes as it had titles: cinematographer Gianni di Venanzo died suddenly during the shooting (his name appeared in the credits) and Chalkley was stricken with hepatitis.

He had developed hepatitis because of the contaminated blood he had been given in an earlier operation, and had to be flown to the United States. Susan flew back and forth from Italy to the States, to be with him as much as possible. But he got steadily worse, and on January 9, 1966, a few days after they released him from the hospital, he died, at the age of fifty-six. He was buried at Carrollton, and Susan, devastated as she was, flew to Italy only a few days after the funeral to com-plete the movie. She was a true professional. Ironically, the movie was a comedy, and she had one of the funniest parts: a sarcastic, hypochondriac Texas oil millionaire. *Variety* surveyed the Hollywood stars with the most appeal to the public, and Hayward was "lucky thirteen" among the top female box office stars of all time.

By mid-1966 she went to Pittsburgh, Pennsylvania, where she officially became a Catholic, her husband's faith, on her forty-eighth birthday. Eaton Chalkley had been a leading layman and a devout churchgoer and benefactor of the church of his community. She wanted to learn to love God the same way Eaton had. The ceremony was officiated over by the Rever-end McGuire, Susan's and Eaton's old friend from Rome, who had returned from Italy to take over the pastorate of St. Peter and Paul Roman Catholic Church in that city. He had been her spiritual support during Eaton's illness.

Later that year she was approached by a Broadway producer who offered her $5,000 a week to star in one of his shows, but he had chosen the wrong time to offer the wrong salary—Hayward's laconic answer was: "You are not even close." She went into seclusion for the rest of the year, and it was said that "she was grieving as a Spanish widow of the eighteenth century." It was also hinted, in some news columns, that she was drinking heavily.

The Honey Pot was released in May 1967 by United Artists, in color. The picture was considered a very good one by the reviewers, but it didn't click at the box office. Susan's part was scissored and, although she still had good scenes in what was left, she was murdered halfway through the film. She didn't look too good in the movie—the inner anguish and anxiety for Chalkley had to show. She took second billing to Rex Harrison, who was the main character. Her part was more like a cameo in the longest movie of her career: 131 minutes. The best reviews were for Maggie Smith, already on her way up to her "Miss Jean Brodie" peak days.

Susan, who had moved from Carrollton to an apartment in Fort Lauderdale (the memories in Georgia were too much for her to handle), came out of retirement to replace Judy Garland in 20th Century-Fox's film version of Jacqueline Susann's novel *Valley of the Dolls,* collecting a handsome $50,000 for only two weeks of work. She won the part over Bette Davis and Jane Wyman, both of whom had wanted it. She could have chosen instead the part of Mrs. Robinson in *The Graduate;* she had been considered for it before it went to Anne Bancroft. One can't help but wonder what she would have done in this role that won an Oscar nomination for Miss Bancroft. At 20th, her old studio, the musicians greeted her with a rendition of "If You Knew Susie" on her first day of shooting for *Valley of the Dolls.* Before the movie was released Fox made a short directed by Richard Fleischer, entitled *Think 20th,* to present a preview of the company's most important pictures for 1967 and 1968, including a clip from *Valley* with Hayward and Patty Duke. The feature was narrated by Richard D. Zanuck, son of Hayward's ex-boss Darryl, by then the executive vice president in charge of production at 20th.

In an interview, she made statements that she was going to disprove: "I won't be able to live in California any more" and "I'm not going into television, and I don't want to go on the stage. Why should I? I've always been a movie gal."

The movie came out in Panavision and De Luxe Color, by the end of 1967, and was treated terribly by all the reviewers, who spared only Susan a battering. This time she really had a cameo part (only four scenes) with two "stars" of the new wave, Barbara Parkins and Patty Duke. It was the only time she had any contact with "new breed" stars, since she had played all of her theatrical movies with "veteran" movie stars. Susan's dialogue in this movie was the spiciest she ever had, to say the least. It was sprinkled with the four-letter words that had become so popular by then—even though the script was "whitewashed" by Helen Deutsch and Dorothy Kingsley. Ill-fated Sharon Tate was another *Valley* star, but she and Susan didn't share any scenes. Susan got the special billing treatment: at the end of the cast, "Susan Hayward as Helen Lawson." She had one song to "sing"—"I'll Plant My Own Tree," dubbed by Margaret Whiting—and her best scene was

During filming of *Valley of the Dolls* for Fox, 1967

the ladies' room brawl with Patty Duke at the end, when Duke flushes Hayward's wig down the toilet.

Said Hayward in an interview: "I returned because I got itchy feet. . . . I didn't retire, but my days were so full of happiness and there were so many things to do at our home in Carrollton that work could wait. I got in the habit of saying I was happy to be away from the business. . . . Now, however, I don't think I'd want to do a full-length role again. . . . I'm glad I had the bulk of my career when you didn't have to take your clothes off. There's just too much nudity now."

When *Valley of the Dolls* was released to television, Judith Crist, long-time reviewer for *TV Guide,* wrote: "The movie lacks the smut but compensates by being badly acted, badly photographed and sleazily made, with a cheapjack production underlining the near-idiot literacy level of the script. Patty Duke, who scores high in the repulsive bracket, and Susan Hayward, who can count this as her horror movie (all-middle-aged stars have to do one, it seems) fortunately survived their appearances herein."

Ironically, this Hayward movie made the most money at the box office. (She had already appeared in six movies in the "all-time champions at the box office" list: *Reap the Wild Wind, David and Bathsheba, The Snows of Kilimanjaro, Demetrius and the Gladiators, I'll Cry Tomorrow,* and *The Conqueror.*

263

Publicity shot for *Mame*

The late sixties marked the start of "nostalgia" times. Publishers and film people realized that the movie multitudes were turning their eyes back to the old movie stars and their old movies—"when movies were really better than ever."

Hayward profited from this, too, since she was already considered one of the immortals of the screen. Magazines started to print articles about her again after a long dry spell. She even shared a few covers with other old and new movie stars. By this time, her son Tim had enlisted in the army.

Early in 1968 she was a guest on the Joey Bishop show, where she introduced an organist by the name of Jack Frost, for whom she was sponsoring a record album. Frost was a salesman from Fort Lauderdale who played the organ as a hobby and was coaching Susan, who also played the organ—her most prized possession was a Hammond organ she had owned for a long time. Susan also reviewed her entire career on this show, which she shared with singer Paul Anka and comedian Don Rickles.

Later, she appeared at the boat première of *Valley of the Dolls* in Miami, but then retreated to Fort Lauderdale, trying to overcome the deep sorrow that engulfed her after her husband's death, but the memory of her nine happy years with Chalkley was still alive. She did not want to work the year round—although friends had suggested this as a possible cure for her loneliness. Instead she went fishing, took long safaris in Africa, motorcycled.

Not until mid-1968 was she lured into action by producer Martin Rackin who called her and said: "Hey, Hooligan (his favorite name for her), how about coming to Las Vegas to do *Mame* for me?" The producer was surprised when Susan accepted. (Perhaps she was prompted by a hidden desire to do the role in the movie version.)

Susan rehearsed for a few months under the supervision of choreographer Onna White at Fort Lauderdale and New York, where she was to do *Mame* at a benefit matinee at the Winter Garden in December, just before the Las Vegas opening.

In November Susan had another heartbreaking loss: her friend Walter Wanger, who had always believed in her, died of a heart attack. Susan never backed out of a commitment, so rehearsals went on without interruption. Paradoxically, the Winter Garden show had to be canceled when Susan claimed she had a cold (was it acute "stage fright" brought on by the thought of facing a New York audience for one day?).

At the end of December, *Mame* did open at Caesars Palace in Las Vegas, with Susan doing two performances a day. (This would be her only incursion into the legitimate stage in front of live audiences.) Hayward, who had called herself "a genuine product of the movie industry," received good reviews for her Mame, although everyone seemed to agree that she was better in the dramatic parts than in the funny ones. One reviewer wrote that "she was best on lines like 'Oh, hell' and 'That word, darling, is bastard' and 'Who gives a damn about money, I've lost my child! Oh, Vera, what are we gonna do?' Hokey, sure, but just glutted with Susan Hayward's own very special brand of sexiness and suffering. I guarantee you will never see the likes of it again." She had detractors too. Stanley Eichelbaum wrote in the *San Francisco Examiner*: "The important thing about Susan Hayward's first appearance on any stage, last weekend at Caesars Palace, wasn't so much that she could do it well but that she'd have the guts to do it at all. She chose to make her debut in *Mame,* which is like volunteering to climb the Matterhorn for an actress who has no experience whatever in the theatre. . . . She learned to dance and wasn't half bad in the routines Onna White choreographed for her. She sang Jerry Herman's songs in surprisingly attractive fashion and a couple of them were quite good. . . . But the main trouble is that Miss Hayward simply isn't Auntie Mame! She is wrong for the part of a merry, madcap Bohemian, because it's nothing like those suffering, down-in-the-dumps movie heroines she's played so well (and so appealingly) through the years."

Only two months after the opening, a tearful Hayward announced she had to retire from the show on doctor's orders: she had developed a throat ailment.

Her understudy, Betty McGuire, took over, till Celeste Holm came to the rescue. The disappointment of the public could be appraised by the hundreds of cancellations Caesars Palace had to handle after her retirement. (A few years later she commented in an interview: "I could not wait for the run to finish. Talk about being bored! The same old lines, the same old songs every night. Not for me, baby, not for me.") She took to traveling again, and resting, and she globetrotted with son Tim, who was back from Vietnam (he wanted to become an actor but ended up as an actor's agent), during the balance of 1969 and part of 1970. But in June 1969 she took time to attend her son Gregg's graduation from Auburn University of Alabama; he got a degree in veterinary medicine. Gregg married soon after, and he and his wife Suzanne made Susan a grandmother in 1970 when they had a baby boy, Chris.

During the winter of 1970–71, Hayward made headlines again; her Fort Lauderdale apartment caught fire because of a neglected cigarette. Her neighbors, Mr. and Mrs. Russell Carson, heard her screams, called the Fire Department, and tried to help her get down to their floor through the balcony. Clad in nightgown and robe, Susan was trying to lower herself to the balcony below on two blankets tied together when firemen broke down the door of the apartment and came to her rescue.

In mid-1971, she went back to Hollywood "frankly, to look for work," and attended parties and celebrations, such as Frank Sinatra's "farewell" of that year, sometimes escorted by son Tim, who that year married actress Ilse Schenk. By the fall she had signed with Norman Brokaw of the William Morris Agency, and was making the rounds with her agent, Jay Bernstein. She took a cameo role, replacing Mary Ure in another Martin Rackin venture, *The Revengers*, a western to be filmed in Mexico. Her co-star, and the only one with whom she had about three or four scenes, was her old friend William Holden.

At about the time this film was completed, she was offered the chance to star in her first TV venture, "Fitzgerald and Pride," to replace the ailing Barbara Stanwyck, to whom she sent flowers with a card: "All love from another Brooklyn broad." The project was being filmed with hopes that it would become a weekly series, which she agreed to do if it clicked. *TV Guide* dedicated an article to Susan in her debut on television: "Just Like Paramount in 1945." They said: "Aside from a better-than-usual script, the only thing that distinguished it from a dozen other movies-for-television being filmed in Hollywood was the genuine excitement caused by what everyone called . . . 'The Return of the Redhead.'" In this TV movie, she was seen for the first time in almost five years, in any medium. It was aired via "The New CBS Friday Night Movies," on March 3, 1972, under the new title *Heat of Anger*.

The reviewers complained that the material was not up to what was expected, although it was an above-average TV movie. Her co-stars were Lee J. Cobb and James Stacy, with whom she never looked out of place—even when there was an underlying sex attraction between them that probably would not have been possible with any other star her age. (She was fifty-three and he was in his early thirties.) The movie had a 23.2 rating with a 37 share of the audience. Many actors and producers wanted her in their shows. One was Sonny Bono, who wanted her as a regular guest in his new show opening in the fall—without Cher: he wanted glamour and considered her perfect for the spot. But Susan declined.

In May 1972, she was a presenter on the Twenty-fourth Annual Emmy Awards show, introduced by Johnny Carson and escorted by George Peppard. Also in 1972, she was seen dining out occasionally with . . . Jess Barker! Time heals all wounds.

At about this time she started filming her second TV movie, ironically entitled *Say Goodbye, Maggie Cole*, which would

At the graduation of son Gregory in 1969

With Celeste Holm and understudy Betty McGuire bidding farewell to *Mame*

Mike Curb, Susan Hayward, Danyel Gerard, Carol Curb
at a recording industry party in Hollywood, April 1972,
shortly before she fell mortally ill

The *National Enquirer* was one of the first newspapers
to print an article about Susan's illness

indeed be her last movie ever.

The Revengers was released by Cinema Centers (before *Maggie Cole*). Most reviewers complained about the waste of Hayward's talent in this minimal role, special billing notwithstanding. This role proved to be a double sorrow since it was her last one for movie audiences, and not a proper farewell for a career that spanned about thirty-five years and fifty-five credited theatrical movies. Her role as Elizabeth had no redeeming qualities. Photographed in De Luxe Color, but in the most unflattering way, she looked every one of her fifty-three years, in sharp contrast with the way she really looked in person. (She had just lost the role of Steve McQueen's mother in *Junior Bonner,* because the producers found her "too young looking" for this part, which went to Ida Lupino.)

Hayward always had stubborn detractors. A middle-aged woman columnist wrote, at the end of Susan's career: "Without being able to act (she's no Bette Davis) Susan Hayward has been the epitome of actresses." In contrast, famous movie critic James Agee had once written that she "could do a paralyzing good job on any important kind of vicious American women."

In September 1972, shortly after the 1972–73 TV season opened, *Say Goodbye, Maggie Cole* was released. The reviewers again complained that the story was not suited to Hayward's talents, although the story seemed much like Hayward's recent autobiography. (The author's inspiration was Susan's life after Eaton's death.) The movie had a catchy title song (sung by Dusty Springfield) and paired her with Darren McGavin, Michael Constantine, Michele Nichols, and Jeanette Nolan (as Nichols' grandmother).

The irony of this being her last movie went even further: she played Dr. Cole, who saved Beverly Garland's husband by operating on a brain tumor.

In 1973 *Variety* published a "Familiarity of TV Performers (From 1972 'Performer Q' survey of Viewers 6 Yrs. & Older)," in which 577 TV performers were ranked in descending order of familiarity to the viewers. Highest score was 99, and that was Lucille Ball. Tied in second place, with 97, were Carol Burnett and Johnny Cash. Susan, who in no way could have been considered a popular TV performer, with only two TV movies to her credit and less than a year in the medium, scored a 75. (Others with 75 were Valerie Harper, Brandon Cruz, and Goldie Hawn, all very popular at the time.)

Hayward was the main subject of a Hollywood Star-O-Scope, by Jack Bradford: "In June and October of 1973, Susan will have still more opportunities to win some big roles. Also during this period, there is some caution for an accident prone possibility beginning in October and November 1972, which repeats itself again in March, August and September 1973. More important, in Susan Hayward's horoscope there is an extremely fortunate astrological influence of a most surprising type, which will get touched off briefly during the second week of July 1973. This favorable influence comes into play again beginning December 22, 1973 and carries on steadily through March 1974, at which time it gets doubly accented. This influence is so favorable and stretches the most perfect span of time to suggest that Susan will win her second Oscar! . . . However, beginning the latter part of April, 1974, and extending through mid August, there will be some strong pressures brought to bear, which could involve a great sum of money. Based upon this possibility, it would be most wise and judicious that Susan take proper precautions in the handling of her estate to make sure that any and all financial dealings, contracts of all kinds, are properly executed."

Depending on the viewpoint, this could either be a masterpiece of misforecasting or very close to the truth.

In a newspaper interview, Susan confided that she had the perfect character traits for an actress: "I'm very lazy . . . my idea of relaxing is just doing nothing. . . . As a child I was the world's biggest liar. . . . I guess that's when I began acting. . . . This I was born with: an imagination and a natural talent for lying. The perfect ingredients for an actor. I require very strong men in my life. . . . I like women but I like men much better. . . . I know loneliness very well. . . . All this sexual freedom the kids have today can hurt later on, especially the women, you've got to be able to respect yourself and if you just sleep around with anybody, how can you have any self respect. I'm in favor of capital punishment. If somebody hurt anyone who was close to me or whom I loved and they weren't put to death for it, I would kill them myself. I couldn't care less about the star's treatment, the star's dressing room, the limousine. That's all junk. I never cared if I had to dress in a broom closet as long as I had privacy."

While in Georgetown, D.C., during the Christmas season, she had a convulsive seizure, and for the first time in her life, this tough fighter started to procrastinate, to leave things "for tomorrow" instead of facing whatever was coming. Maybe she was afraid of facing a difficult truth.

Early in 1973, Fabergé, the cosmetic brand, spent around $10,000 and got together about two hundred stars to honor Henry Hathaway, Hayward's four-time director. She was present, naturally, along with John Wayne, Cary Grant, Rita Hayworth, Jean Peters, Carolyn Jones, David Janssen, Martin Landau, Barbara Bain, Cyd Charisse, Robert Mitchum, and others.

Shortly after this, Earl Wilson pointed out in his column that when Susan heard about Doug McClelland's book about her, which was just going to press, she was intrigued by the title, *The Divine Bitch*. But finding out that it referred only to her screen roles, she said, "Go ahead, publish it."

She attended the première of Ross Hunter's big fiasco *Lost Horizons* and was also seen at Hollywood parties. Then, suddenly, late in March 1973, the news broke: Susan Hayward was hospitalized in Los Angeles (Cedars of Lebanon Hospital) because of a serious illness of an unknown nature. Rona Barrett was the first movie columnist to break the news, via her syndicated television spot, and Susan's family was overwhelmed by the amount of letters and telegrams they received wishing her a speedy recovery. The reports started coming out, more confusing every time, but never conclusive, about the disease that had stricken her.

In April 1973, her son Tim was legally granted permission to take over her estate, since her condition made this necessary. She was having blackouts and persistent dizzy spells, and her fans and the public in general worried about how serious Susan's condition was, to make her son take such steps. Tim declared, "I hope that people understand that I am doing this in my mother's interest. I hope they realize that her welfare is my concern—not greed or opportunism. It just had to be

At the 1974 Academy Awards presentation, with Charlton Heston

done."

The first movie magazine to write about her illness was *Motion Picture,* which ran an article entitled: "Pray for Susan Hayward! Her Mystery Illness."

On July 1, 1973, the weekly newspaper *National Enquirer* printed a large, unflattering photograph of her on its front page; it had been taken at a recent party, and she looked wan and ill. They announced: "Susan Hayward Near Death." In the caption below the photograph they stated: "Actress Susan Hayward has been stricken with brain tumors and could die at any moment." The *Enquirer* went further. "You may have heard of her death before you read this story." The title of the article inside? "Good-bye, Susan Hayward!"

Son Tim made a series of sorrowful statements: "No one can hide this anymore. She has multiple brain tumors and they are inoperable. My mother could live another six months. No one can answer that question—not even the doctors, it is in the hands of God. She's got the best doctors in the Western United States. Sometimes she's in, sometimes she's out. She fluctuates. She forces herself to stay awake for long periods. She's in good spirits. She's a fighter."

Dorothy Manners, the *Modern Screen* columnist, dedicated a whole page to her in July 1973: "Salute to Susan." Miss Manners stated that Susan had called her son Tim's employer and told him "Don't let my boy worry. I'm going to be fine."

The news about Susan continued to be vague and contradictory. No one knew exactly what was happening. After leaving Cedars of Lebanon, she had apparently gone back to Georgia. A brief news bulletin in July stated, "Susan Hayward leaves hospital," referring to Emory University Hospital in Atlanta, where she had entered the week before for another series of tests. She was reported as saying that her ailment was "exaggerated."

In a movie magazine, there was an article entitled "The Miracle of Love That Kept Susan Hayward Alive," which suggested that the one thing that made her cling to life was her desire to see her next grandchild. Tim's wife was going to have a baby, and she was praying that God would help her live till the baby arrived. (She lived to see granddaughter, Nadia.)

But the news was still vague and confusing. Some said she was in seclusion and didn't want to see anybody. Others said she was in good spirits and willing to start working again. *Modern Screen* printed another article with an ominous title, "Her Faith Helps Her Face Dying." They wrote about how she reacted when confronted with the truth: "You are keeping something. I want to know my condition. Tell me the truth; I can take it," she said to the doctors. Only then did they let her know that she had multiple brain tumors that were inoperable, that they couldn't know for sure how long she had to live. Susan didn't weep; on the contrary, she had to cheer up her son Tim.

For the rest of the year Susan was in and out of hospitals having all kinds of brain tests and physical checkups, but she refused to stay in any hospital or nursing home. Instead, she went back to live in her newly decorated apartment, and got a trained nurse to attend her, and a housekeeper. She didn't want to be a burden to anybody. And when her brother Walter had a heart attack, Susan seemed more concerned about him than about herself. The first time she called the hospital, an excited nurse told the patient, "It's *Miss Susan Hayward*, the movie star, Mr. Marrener. She wants to talk to you." "I know, she's my sister," he answered, smiling. Susan called him daily and they talked about traveling when both were well again. "Just us—nobody else. We'll show 'em they can't keep a Marrener down," she said—just like a line from one of her movie roles.

The *Hollywood Reporter*'s Hank Grant wrote toward the end of November that she was "recovering miraculously at her Beverly Hills home." Old friends of hers, like actress Kathryn Grayson and fashion designer Nolan Miller, sent her yellow roses. She was feeling so much better that she told a reporter, "I'm going to lick this, and when I do, I'll go to Mexico or take a trip around the world with my brother."

Susan's hopes of overcoming her troubles were very real indeed, and early in 1974 she surprised everybody when she agreed to be a presenter for the next Academy Awards ceremonies to be held in April. That night people were more concerned about whether she was really going to show up, than about the awards themselves. Just before she came on stage, David Niven gave her a most unusual introduction: "Mr.

Heston [Charlton Heston was the co-presenter] has created many miracles—just illusions on the screen. But in presenting our next award he brings with him not an illusion but the real thing—Miss Susan Hayward!" She appeared to present the Best Actress Oscar clutching Heston's arm. She seemed to be leaning on him and not too steady, but she was welcomed with a warm ovation. Susan looked beautiful from afar. The camera kept a respectful distance and closeups were avoided.

What she did that night, her last appearance in front of a camera, was a bravura performance. Yet the extent of her bravery was not known until a few years later when Frank Westmore's book *The Westmores of Hollywood* came to light. He wrote: "The afternoon of the Oscar ceremony, I got a phone call from Susan Hayward. She was going to present the Oscar for Best Actress that night, and with 53 million televiewers looking on for her first public appearance in some time, she wanted only a Westmore to make her up. I said I'd be glad to do so, and I arrived at her house at about 2 p.m. I was distressed at what I saw. Susan had been undergoing radioactive cobalt treatments for a malignant brain tumor, and the damaging rays had destroyed her beautiful red hair, her eyebrows, even her eyelashes. The basic pert and beautiful face was still there, but I had to reconstruct her as she had been thirty years before. I worked feverishly for hours, until she had to leave for the Music Center presentation site at 6 p.m. I was never more proud of my craftsmanship than when I saw Susan walk out on that stage, leaning on Charlton Heston's arm, as she announced that the winner was Glenda Jackson. She looked not much different from the Susan Hayward of 1945, and that's how the world will remember her."*

After that, articles appeared in newspapers and magazines, praising the "miracle" of Susan's recovery. The reports said that Susan felt she had been misdiagnosed about those cancerous brain tumors she was supposed to have, that she was talking of a complete comeback. Another weekly tabloid, the *National Insider,* ran an article, "How Susan Hayward Overcame Death by Using Mental Powers." In the article, Tim Barker was quoted as saying, "It was the power of positive thinking that cured her. She refused to even believe she was ill; that determination cured her. She laughed off the diagnosis."

She was seen at the Governor's Ball, chatting with friends, and it was hard to tell she was ill. Friends continued to visit her regularly, among them Barbara Stanwyck and Loretta Swit. Katharine Hepburn brought flowers that she had picked herself. Even Greta Garbo flew in from Florida, where she spent her winters, to share some personal health secrets she hoped would pull Susan through. Stanley Cortez, her cinematographer in four movies, was a constant visitor. She told him, "Don't worry about me, Stan—I'll make it."

Soon, enthusiasm started to fade. During the rest of 1974, nothing much was published about her. The silence was ominous.

When, early in 1975, her son Tim was a guest on Merv Griffin's show, the fact that she was not mentioned was a hint that something was wrong indeed. Finally, on March 14, 1975,

* From *The Westmores of Hollywood* by Frank Westmore and Muriel Davidson. Copyrighted © 1976 by Muriel Davidson and Frank Westmore. Reprinted by permission of J. B. Lippincott Company.

the news was announced on the TV channels: "At 2.25 p.m., Los Angeles time, actress Susan Hayward died after a seizure at her home."

The news of her death made headlines. The New York *Daily News* carried a front-page headline: "Susan Hayward Dies at 56."

Her spirit had been invincible till the very end. She kept making plans and let no one know if she was depressed. Her doctor and friend, Lee Siegel, of Beverly Hills, attested to her courage: "She knew what she had, and she knew she was going to die. She dearly wanted to live—but at the same time, down deep, she knew the inevitable was coming."

Funeral arrangements were made by her sons, to be held in Carrollton the following Monday. Services would be private, conducted by the reverends Danny McGuire, her old friend, and Thomas Brew, of Carrollton. According to her wishes, she was going to have in her hands the onyx cross that belonged to her husband, Eaton Chalkley. She had given strict orders that the cross remain in her hands at all times during her illness. She was taken to rest in peace side by side with her beloved Eaton, on Monday, March 16, from the Catholic Chapel of Our Lady of Perpetual Help, which she had helped build in Carrollton, Georgia, just across a one-lane country road from the large estate where she and her husband had lived for nine years.

Susan Hayward will be remembered as long as there are movies. She belongs to a Hollywood past that will never die, and her legendary life story made a reality of the old saying, "Truth is stranger than fiction." If ever filmed, one of her own movie titles could be used, in true Hayward fashion, to sum up her life: "They Won't Believe It."

At the opening night of *Mame* in Las Vegas, 1968

The Honey Pot

UNITED ARTISTS, 1967

The dream sequence (Susan Hayward and Rex Harrison)

CAST

Cecil Fox, Rex Harrison; *Mrs. Lone-Star Crockett Sheridan,* Susan Hayward; *William McFly,* Cliff Robertson; *Princess Dominique,* Capucine; *Merle McGill,* Edie Adams; *Sarah Watkins,* Maggie Smith; *Inspector Rizzi,* Adolfo Celi; *Oscar Ludwig,* Herschel Bernardi; *Revenue Agent,* Cy Grant; *Revenue Agent,* Frank Latimore; *Massimo,* Luigi Scavran; *Cook,* Mimmo Poli; *Tailor,* Antonio Corevi; *Assistant Tailor,* Carlos Valles; *and in a performance of* Volpone: *Volpone,* Hugh Manning; *Mosca,* David Dodimead.

CREDITS

Directed by Joseph L. Mankiewicz. *Produced by* Charles K. Feldman *and* Joseph L. Mankiewicz. *Based on the play* Mr. Fox of Venice *by* Frederick Knott. *Written by* Joseph L. Mankiewicz. *Adapted from the novel* The Evil of the Day *by* Thomas Sterling. *Based on the play* Volpone *by* Ben Jonson. *Photography,* Gianni Di Venanzo. *Art Direction,* Boris Juraga. *Editor,* David Bretherton. *Sound,* David Hildyard. *Assistant Director,* Gus Agosti. *Production Designer,* John De Cuir. *Production Manager,* Attilio D'Onerio. *Music,* John Addison. *Choreography,* Lee Theodore. *In Technicolor. Running time, 131 minutes.*

THE STORY

It is the twentieth century, but millionaire Cecil Fox (Rex Harrison) lives in the splendor of a seventeenth-century *palazzo* in Venice. He attends a performance of the play *Volpone* and inspired by it devises a wild scheme to trick his three former mistresses. He hires an actor, William McFly (Cliff Robertson), to act as his secretary-servant, and invites all three women to the palace, making them believe he is about to die. Although the three of them are wealthy in their own right, they come. All seem to have a reason to covet his fortune.

First to arrive is Merle McGill (Edie Adams), a fading Hollywood sex symbol whose career was launched by Fox. Then comes Princess Dominique (Capucine), who had taken a cruise with Fox in his yacht—a "floating white bordello."

Last to come is Texas millionaire Lone-Star Crockett Sheridan (Susan Hayward), a hypochondriac who travels with her companion-nurse Sarah Watkins (Maggie Smith).

Lone-Star claims that she is the only one who is really entitled to Cecil's fortune because she was his common-law wife.

That night, Lone-Star is found dead from an overdose of sleeping pills.

Sarah Watkins suspects McFly and wastes no time in telling him, so he locks her in her room. But Sarah, escaping in a dumbwaiter, ends up in Fox's chambers. However, the "dying man" has suddenly found new energy and she sees him dancing about the room (one of Cecil's unfulfilled ambitions was to be a ballet dancer).

Despite all her sarcasm, McFly gets along well with Mrs. Sheridan (Cliff Robertson and Susan Hayward)

It is soon discovered that Fox was Lone-Star's murderer. He was flat broke and hoped to inherit her vast fortune. Realizing that his scheme backfired and he is facing a murder charge, he dances into a Venice canal to his death.

As it turns out, it is Sarah Watkins—and McFly—who inherit Lone-Star's wealth.

REVIEWS

SATURDAY REVIEW   *Hollis Alpert*

"Probably no American filmmaker has tried harder to bring a literate quality to the screen than Joseph L. Mankiewicz.

"Mr. Mankiewicz, throughout, appears to be trying to say something poetic and profound about time and living life to the full, for timepieces abound in the film, but something more exciting than this was needed."

NEW YORK TIMES   *Bosley Crowther*

"Joseph L. Mankiewicz is playing an elegant and intricate joke in *The Honey Pot.*

"With Cliff Robertson as an actor who is recruited for his

What's keeping her awake — memories or a new illness?

She is quite pleased with the way she is handling the situation (Susan Hayward, Maggie Smith, and Edie Adams)

cynical deceit, and with Susan Hayward, Edie Adams and the saturnine Capucine as the three disparate companions of the hero's apparently checkered past, Mr. Mankiewicz manages some delightful and hopeful introductory ploys, in which the agile Mr. Harrison is at his mischievous best.

". . . John Addison has contributed a dandy musical score. So, for all the slow and murky stretches, you should be adequately entertained by this film."

NOTES

This was the last Hayward movie filmed abroad, in Venice, and Mankiewicz did a good job of filming around her when Susan had to fly back to the United States several times because

of her husband's illness. There was talk that she would be replaced, but the director was understanding and she managed to complete the movie. This was their second association since *House of Strangers*.

Hayward was photographed in the most unflattering way for the movie, although the stills were not as bad.

The movie had too much dialogue, in spite of the cutting; it lacked action. Perhaps the problem was that some of the best parts were cut, like the much publicized dream sequence between Hayward and Harrison. It also dragged after Hayward's death in the film, since her character was one of the liveliest.

The movie, with a good cast and good reviews, was not appreciated by the public.

Valley of the Dolls

Helen Lawson, aging Broadway star (Susan Hayward) 20th Century-Fox, 1967

Mouthing "I'll Plant My Own Tree" (Susan Hayward)

CAST

Anne Wells, Barbara Parkins; *Neely O'Hara,* Patty Duke; *Lyon Burke,* Paul Burke; *Jennifer North,* Sharon Tate; *Tony Polar,* Tony Scotti; *Mel Anderson,* Martin Milner; *Kevin Gillmore,* Charles Drake; *Ted Casablanca,* Alex Davion; *Miriam,* Lee Grant; *Miss Steinberg,* Noami Stevens; *Henry Bellamy,* Robert H. Harris; *First Reporter,* Jacqueline Susann; *Director,* Robert Viharo; *Man in Hotel Room,* Mike Angel; *Man in Bar,* Barry Cahill; *Claude Chardot,* Richard Angarola; *MC at Telethon,* Joey Bishop; *MC at Grammy Awards,* George Jessel; *Helen Lawson,* Susan Hayward.

CREDITS

Directed by Mark Robson. *Produced by* David Weisbart. *Screenplay by* Helen Deutsch *and* Dorothy Kingsley. *Based on the Novel by* Jacqueline Susann. *Photography,* William H. Clothier. *Art Direction,* Jack Martin Smith *and* Richard Day. *Editor,* Dorothy Spencer. *Sound,* Don J. Bassman *and* David Dockendorf. *Set Decorations,* Walter M. Scott *and* Raphael G. Bretton. *Gowns,* Travilla. *Makeup,* Ben Nye. *Hairstyles,* Kay Pownall. *Hairstyles for Miss Parkins,* Mr. Kenneth. *Assistant Director,* Eli Dunn. *Production Manager,* Francisco Day. *Special Effects,* L. B. Abbott, Art Cruickshank, *and* Emil Kosa, Jr. *Music adapted and conducted by* Johnny Williams. *Music Editor,* Kenneth Wannberg. *Orchestration,* Herbert Spencer. *Choreography,* Robert Sidney. *Songs by* Andre *and* Dory Previn. Title Theme sung by Dionne Warwick; "Give a Little More" *and* "It's Impossible" sung by Patty Duke; "Come Live with Me" sung by Tony Scotti; "I'll Plant My Own Tree" dubbed for Miss Hayward by Margaret Whiting; *In Panavision. Color by De Luxe. Running time, 123 minutes.*

THE STORY

Anne Welles (Barbara Parkins) leaves her New England home to come to New York. She is filled with enthusiasm, and is thrilled when she gets a job as a secretary in a theatrical law firm. On her first day she attends a Broadway rehearsal with Lyon Burke (Paul Burke), an associate of the firm, and is disillusioned when she sees Helen Lawson (Susan Hayward), a hard-boiled musical comedy star, have a young newcomer, Neely O'Hara (Patty Duke), fired because she is trying to steal the show from her. But Anne stays with her job because of Lyon, whom she likes.

Lyon helps Neely find a spot on a TV show and she becomes a star almost instantly. Meanwhile, another Hollywood aspirant, Jennifer North (Sharon Tate), who is beautiful but untalented, falls in love with nightclub singer Tony Polar (Tony Scotti) and marries him despite the objections of Tony's overly protective sister, Miriam (Lee Grant).

Anne and Lyon have a quarrel because he refuses to get married, and while he quits the law firm to pursue his career as a writer, she is signed for a series of TV cosmetic commercials as "The Gilliam Girl."

Neely is having a hard time adjusting to fame, and after two unsuccessful marriages—to Mel Anderson (Martin Milner), the press agent, and Ted Casablanca (Alex Davion), the dress designer—turns to alcohol and drugs. Her career crashes around her and she is finally persuaded to enter a sanitarium. Tony Polar is at the same sanitarium where he is dying of an incurable disease. Jennifer has been in Europe making nudist films so she can pay Tony's bills, but, learning she has breast cancer, commits suicide by taking an overdose of sleeping pills.

Anne and Lyon have made up and broken up again, and she's also having a bout with pills. Meanwhile, Neely gets a chance to get back to Broadway, but she is still incapable of facing an audience, even after she gets her long-awaited revenge on Helen Lawson by tearing off her wig. She gets drunk and passes out in the theatre's alley while her understudy scores a triumph on opening night.

By now, having won out over pills, Anne is back home in New England. Lyon visits her and begs her to marry him, but Anne, having regained her sense of values, kisses him affectionately and rejects his offer.

REVIEWS

CHRISTIAN SCIENCE MONITOR   *Alan N. Bunce*

"*Valley of the Dolls* is careful, skillfully deceptive imitation of a real drama. A host of attractive players move agilely through a long episodic plot. They are recognizable social types. The feelings that impel them can be labeled easily—fear, jealousy, ambition. And their speech echoes the sound of unnumbered predecessors.

"But on closer look the characters turn out to be images that have almost nothing to do with people."

CUE   *William Wolf*

"Let's just say that director Mark Robson tried. He didn't endeavor to make a cheap sex exploitation film from the best-selling book. He tried to convey how young hopes are pulverized in the show-business mill. But what *can* one really do with such inferior material?"

SATURDAY REVIEW   *Arthur Knight*

"Susan Hayward, the only 'pro' of the lot, sports a makeup that makes her look more like Katisha than an aging Broadway queen."

Neely is amused to find Helen's hair is a wig (Patty Duke and Susan Hayward)

NEW YORK TIMES   *Bosley Crowther*

"Amid the cheap, shrill and maudlin histrionics of Patty Duke, Sharon Tate and Barbara Parkins, our old friend, Susan Hayward, stands out as if she were Katharine Cornell."

NOTES

This was Hayward's last movie for 20th Century-Fox, and the character she played was not unlike her own at the time: an aging movie star fighting for survival. Her fans liked to think that her big fight with Patty Duke in the film was not at all like her; Susan never took a beating like the one Patty gave her.

Mark Robson, who had directed her in *My Foolish Heart*, got the best out of her for this film too, but she didn't have much competition from the rest of the cast: Barbara Parkins, Sharon Tate, and Patty Duke gave uniformly poor performances.

It is said that Jacqueline Susann, author of the original novel (who also played a bit part), based all her characters on real show business people: Hayward's on Ethel Merman; Duke's on Judy Garland; Tate's on Marilyn Monroe combined with Mansfield and Carole Landis.

There was talk of a sequel with Hayward, Parkins, and Duke repeating their roles, but the film that was released a few years later with the title *Beyond the Valley of the Dolls* was not related to Hayward's movie. It was considered almost a porno movie.

The original *Valley of the Dolls* grossed over $20 million, becoming the biggest money maker for Fox up to then. It also got an Oscar nomination for the music score (Dionne Warwick sang the title song), but the reviews were terrible.

The case is going to be a tough one, but she is a tough lady (Susan Hayward)

A tense moment during the trial (James Stacy and Susan Hayward)

Heat of Anger (TV)

METROMEDIA PRODUCERS CORPORATION, 1972

Frank looks defiant, but Jessie is ready for the defense
(Susan Hayward and Lee J. Cobb)

CAST

Jessie Fitzgerld, Susan Hayward; *Gus Pride,* James Stacy;
Frank Galvin, Lee J. Cobb; *Vincent Kagel,* Fritz Weaver;
Stella Galvin, Bettye Ackerman; *Chris Galvin,* Jennifer Penny;
Obie, Mills Watson; *Ray Carson,* Ray Simms; *Jean Carson,*
Tyne Daly.

CREDITS

Directed by Don Taylor. *Produced by* Ron Roth. *Written by*
Fay Kanin. *Executive Producer,* Dick Berg. *Photography,*
Robert C. Moreno. *Editing,* John Link. *Executive Vice President in Charge of Production,* Charles W. Fries. First Television Feature Film for Metromedia Producers Corporation and
Stonehenge Productions (Color) 1971. *Running time, 74
minutes.*

THE STORY

Beautiful Jessie Fitzgerald (Susan Hayward) is a liberated
and feminine lawyer, currently defending a close friend, Frank
Galvin (Lee J. Cobb), who is facing a murder trial.

Frank has been charged with murdering one of his employees, Ray Carson (Ray Simms), a married construction worker
who was having an affair with Galvin's daughter.

Jessie's health is not up to the stress she's undergoing with
Frank's case, and her doctor advises her to hire an assistant.
She hires Gus Pride (James Stacy), a rash young attorney, who
after meeting with Frank feels that he is holding something
back. All they know is that Frank is a respected man, a civic
leader, with a fierce temper, that Frank's daughter, Chris (Jennifer Penny), is adopted, and that Carson has practically
forced Chris to tell her father about their affair, seeking a
direct confrontation.

After the trial begins, Jessie and Gus learn that Frank has
been holding something back—he had been convicted for
extortion years before. Fearful that this revelation is going to
affect the trial, Frank jumps bail and heads for his private
plane.

Gus finds out and calls Jessie. They rush to the airport to try
to stop Frank, but Jessie's desperate efforts to convince him
that he should stay for the trial fail. Frank gets in his plane
and takes off.

At court the next morning, Jessie and Gus are about to
inform the judge that their client has escaped when Frank
walks in. He had thought about it and decided to face the
ordeal.

Gus questions him and his old felony conviction is revealed.
However, Frank confesses something he had been holding
back: at the construction site, Ray Carson had swung at him on
the steel beams, and Frank had refused to hit back. Then
Carson had lost his balance and fallen to his death. It had
been hard for Frank, a proud man, to admit that he had not
fought back.

Frank Galvin is cleared and Jessie and Gus begin an unusual
partnership.

REVIEWS

"Miss Hayward, still very shapely and attractive, gave a very
solid performance. It wasn't an easy story to move along and
sustain a viewer's interest since there wasn't very much to it."

"*Heat of Anger* is the 90-minute pilot-movie starring Susan
Hayward. What a joy it is to see an intelligent, warm, vibrant
woman character as a series lead in a professional position,
played by such a wonderful actress as Miss Hayward. If this
doesn't become a series there is no justice."

NOTES

If ever a movie was jinxed, this was it. Within a few years
after its filming Hayward was gone; Stacy had an accident,
losing an arm and a leg; Lee J. Cobb died of a heart attack.
The only star spared was Fritz Weaver of TV's "Holocaust"
fame.

Susan was excited about this film, her first for TV (directed
by Don Taylor, who had played one of her husbands in *I'll
Cry Tomorrow*), although she had to learn more pages of dialogue a day, and the pace was different from that of theatrical
movies. Ironically, she declared, "Fortunately, my brain is in
good shape."

Upon its release, *Variety* wrote: "As CBS has been minus a
house law firm on the tube since the 'Storefront Lawyers'
closed up shop, 'Fitzgerald and Pride' has an outside chance to
fill that void, with Miss Hayward's star power the main asset."
It never happened.

The Revengers

NATIONAL GENERAL PICTURES, 1972

CAST

John Benedict, William Holden; *Hoop,* Ernest Borgnine; *Job,* Woody Strode; *Elizabeth Reilly,* Susan Hayward; *Quiberon,* Roger Hanin; *Zweig,* Rene Koldehoff; *Chamaco,* Jorge Luke; *Cholo,* Jorge Martinez de Hoyos; *Free State,* Arthur Hunnicutt; *Tarp,* Warren Vanders; *Arny,* Larry Pennell; *Whitcomb,* John Kelly; *Lieutenant Mercer,* Scott Holden; *Morgan,* James Daughton; *Mrs. Benedict,* Lorraine Chanel; *Warden,* Raul Prieto.

CREDITS

Directed by Daniel Mann. *Produced by* Martin Rackin. *2nd Unit Director,* Ray Kellogg. *Screenplay,* Wendell Mayes. *Based on a story by* Steven W. Carabatsos. *Photography,* Gabriel Torres. *Art Direction,* Jorge Fernandez. *Editors,* Walter Hannemann *and* Juan Jose Marino. *Sound,* Jesus Gonzalez Gancy *and* Angel Trejo. *Set Decorations,* Carlos Grandjean. *Wardrobe,* Carlos Chavez. *Makeup,* Felisa L. Guevara *and* Elvira Oropeza. *Hairstyles,* Maria de Jesus Lepe. *Music composed and conducted by* Pino Calvi. *Assistant Director,* Robert Goodstein. *Special Effects,* Frank Brendell, Jesus Doran, *and* Laurencio Bordero. *Executive Production Manager,* William C. Davidson. *Production Manager,* Armando Solis. *Co-Production of* Martin Rackin Productions (Hollywood) *and* Estudios Churubusco (Mexico City). *A Cinema Center Film* (U.S.-Mexican). *In Panavision. Color by De Luxe. Running time, 106 minutes.*

THE STORY

John Benedict (William Holden) enjoys the peace of his ranch in Colorado with his wife and children. Being a former Union captain, he is proud that his oldest boy has been accepted for West Point.

But their peaceful life comes to an abrupt end when, returning from a hunting expedition, Benedict finds his whole family slaughtered and a band of Indians riding off with his horses. One of his ranch hands, before he dies, tells him that the Comanches were led by a white man, a renegade named Tarp (Warren Vanders).

Benedict swears revenge. He learns that Tarp is hiding in Pueblo Plata, Mexico, a place full of thieves. Riding across the border, he poses as a mine owner looking for laborers, and manages to hire six inmates of a prison known as "El Hoyo" (The Hole): Cholo (Jorge Martinez de Hoyos), a Mexican; Quiberon (Roger Hanin), a Frenchman; Job (Woody Strode), who used be a slave; Zweig (Rene Koldehoff), a German; Chamaco (Jorge Luke), a young Mexican killer; and Hoop (Ernest Borgnine), a not-too-brave American who knows how to get to Pueblo Plata.

Susan Hayward as Elizabeth

They get there, disguised as trappers, and invade the outlaws' stronghold, but Tarp escapes. They continue their pursuit, but Benedict and his men grow increasingly hostile toward each other, until Chamaco shoots Benedict during a drunken quarrel. Believing him dead, the convicts disband.

A frontier woman, Elizabeth Reilly (Susan Hayward), finds the wounded Benedict and nurses him back to health. She falls in love with him and, when she learns the reason for his being there, she begs him to abandon his plans for vengeance. But he is determined to find Tarp. As soon as he regains his health, he leaves, but he is captured and imprisoned by the former warden of ''El Hoyo'' (Raul Prieto), who, tricked by Benedict, had lost his job for freeing the six men.

Chamaco hears what happened, rounds up his five companions, and they help Benedict escape. They ride to the post where Tarp, now captured, is kept under guard. The soldiers at the post, under the leadership of young Lieutenant Mercer (Scott Holden), are fighting off a horde of Comanches who want to rescue Tarp. Benedict and his men get to the post's dynamite supply and drive off the Indians after a bloody battle, but Chamaco is fatally wounded.

When they finally find Tarp in the shack where he's held captive, he is no longer the savage who used to lead the Comanches. He is insane and cowardly, cringing in the darkness. Benedict, realizing how brutalized he has become because of his vendetta, leaves Tarp to stand trial for his crimes. He rides back north, alone, to try to pick up the pieces of his life—and, perhaps, to find Elizabeth.

REVIEWS

LOS ANGELES TIMES   *Kevin Thomas*

''*The Revengers* is a solid, big-scale, traditional-style western with all the familiar larger-than-life qualities and durable virtues of the genre. . . .

''Holden has the stature and strength to play his tough, reflective character, and Susan Hayward, ever the sultry beauty, is just the lady to play a feisty Irishwoman who nurses him back to health and falls for him as well.''

SAN FRANCISCO CHRONICLE   *Dennis Hunt*

''The movie could have ended at six different spots, but, with the aid of various contrivances, it always bounced back after each false climax.''

NOTES

Susan didn't look good in any of her last theatrical movies, some because of the makeup to make her look older, some merely because of bad lighting and photography.

Oddly enough, she traveled to Mexico for the second time in 1972, for a film that did not require it. Her sequences, not showing Mexican landscapes or anything else in Mexico, could have been filmed anywhere in Southern California or at any studio lot.

Elizabeth helps nurse injured John back to health (William Holden and Susan Hayward)

John has to leave, but promises Elizabeth he will be back some day (Susan Hayward and William Holden)

It was a delayed reunion for Hayward and Holden, her leading man. They had been together in a film twenty-nine years earlier, before his son Scott was born. Now, Scott was playing a soldier in the movie.

Ernest Borgnine, a lot more important than when he did his first movie with Hayward, *Demetrius and the Gladiators*, was in this one, replacing Van Heflin, originally slated for the role. But they didn't share any scenes.

The film, although completed before her first TV film, was released later at showcase theatres instead of at first-run movie theatres.

Say Good-Bye, Maggie Cole (TV)

SPELLING/GOLDBERG PRODUCTION, 1972

As Maggie Cole

Maggie takes her stand with Dr. Grazzo (Susan Hayward and Darren McGavin)

CAST

Maggie Cole, Susan Hayward; *Dr. Lou Grazzo,* Darren McGavin; *Dr. Sweeney,* Michael Constantine; *Lisa Downey,* Michele Nichols; *Hank Cooper,* Dane Clark, *Mrs. Anderson,* Beverly Garland; *Mrs. Downey,* Jeannette Nolan; *Fergie,* Madie Norman; *Ben Cole,* Richard Anderson; *Mr. Alissandro,* Frank Puglia; *Isadore Glass,* Harry Basch; *Night Nurse,* Leigh Adams; *Ivan Dvorsky,* Jan Peters; *Brig,* Robert Cleavers.

CREDITS

Directed by Jud Taylor. *Produced by* Aaron Spelling *and* Leonard Goldberg. *Written by* Sandor Stern. *Photography,* Tim Southcott. *Art Director,* Tracy Bousman. *Film Editor,* Bill Mosher. *Sound,* Glen Anderson. *Music by* Hugo Montenegro. *Theme Song: "Learn to Say Goodbye," sung by* Dusty Springfield. *ABC Television. Running time, 74 minutes.*

THE STORY

Maggie Cole (Susan Hayward) helplessly watches as her husband Ben (Richard Anderson) has a heart attack while flying his private plane. In desperation, she tries to help him from the ground, but he falls unconscious, and the plane, completely out of control, crashes right before her eyes.

Stunned by Ben's sudden death, Maggie decides to give up her work as a research doctor. Her boss, Hank Cooper (Dane Clark), is not happy with her decision but has to accept it. She wants to get away from the people and the places that will keep memories alive and go back to general practice. This might be hard after fifteen years away from it, but she has to try.

Maggie goes to work for Dr. Lou Grazzo (Darren McGavin), a tough street doctor who runs a twenty-four-hour practice in the slums of Chicago. Luckily, she meets a pretty young girl, Lisa Downey (Michele Nichols), who befriends her and gets her a room in her grandmother's house.

Dr. Grazzo's rough manners and the long hours make demands on Maggie that she never met before; neighborhood emergencies come up day and night, but the hard work is helping her overcome her deep feeling of loss.

She's not ready to face another ordeal: Lisa has leukemia; tests confirm this. Maggie cannot get involved; she loves the girl too much and refuses to make her a personal patient.

She goes on with her work, curing people and performing operations; she saves Mr. Anderson's life by removing a brain tumor. Mrs. Anderson (Beverly Garland) is ever grateful.

Yet Maggie continues to avoid Lisa's case until Dr. Grazzo confronts her with the truth: she can't run away from sorrow and heartache; she has to face reality. Maggie realizes how wrong she has been. She is a doctor and she is Lisa's friend so she takes her place at her bedside.

Dr. Grazzo still has doubts about Maggie being able to cope with the work, but she convinces him by working long hours (Darren McGavin and Susan Hayward

The heartache is there and the wound opens wide again when the girl dies, but Maggie learns her lesson and goes back to the task of being a doctor without detaching herself from human nature.

REVIEWS

NEW YORK DAILY NEWS

"Redheaded Susan Hayward, who only last season returned to Hollywood film making, performs like she never left Lotus land.

"She looks as beautiful as she did years ago and she performs with the same strength and conviction."

HOLLYWOOD REPORTER   *Sue Cameron*

"This is Chapter Two in the 'Let's Get Susan Hayward a TV Series' saga that started with the CBS movie *Heat of Anger* last season. In *Heat of Anger* she played a lawyer very effectively and it was a quality movie.

"*Say Goodbye, Maggie Cole* was strictly a poorly written, below average soap opera that had her playing a widowed doctor trying to start anew in general practice in a Chicago slum."

VARIETY   *Bok*

"The production seemed to be suffering from mixed emotions as to which direction to follow, with the tearjerker aspects winning out over the reality values."

NOTES

In her farewell movie, her second for TV, Susan looked so full of life that the thought of her being stricken with a fatal disease could not enter anyone's mind.

Richard Anderson played Hayward's husband, but they never shared a scene. He appeared only in the first sequence, flying his plane while Susan is looking on from the ground.

Beverly Garland, a good actress who could not make it in Hollywood, was wasted in a short role.

Both of Hayward's TV movies had excellent ratings and both were reportedly considered for weekly series. About this one, the *Hollywood Reporter* wrote: "Susan Hayward would be a pleasant addition to television on a regular basis. She was a bit saccharine at times as Maggie Cole, but on the whole, a series developed from the concept of a doctor in the environment could work. If one just disregards the vehicle in which we first met her, there might be a future." There was none. *Say Goodbye, Maggie Cole* turned out to be "Say Goodbye, Susan Hayward."

Mame

1968

(Susan Hayward's only stage appearance)

A Final Word

The contradictory reports about Susan Hayward's illness were frustrating, but not even the most alarming ones prepared her admirers for the final news. Her death was a shock.

Many paid tribute:

• The day after she died, three major Hollywood figures talked about her in a radio interview: Robert Montgomery, Fred MacMurray (both of whom had played opposite Susan), and Rosalind Russell (who had twice battled her for the Oscar—in 1948, when both lost to Loretta Young, and in 1959, when Susan won the award). They expressed sorrow upon her passing, and Hollywood's deep loss.

• The people of Carrollton were touched. To them she had been "Mrs. Chalkley," and they loved her for her "un-Hollywood" behavior among them.

• Greta Garbo, one of her last visitors, took the news quite badly. Susan had been her favorite star.

• Alan King, another Brooklynite and personal friend, interrupted his show at a nightclub in Las Vegas to say a few words about Susan and offer a minute of silence in her memory.

• Several movie magazines ran articles about Susan, and Rona Barrett used a photo of Susan on the cover of one of hers with the caption: "A tribute to the redhead."

• McClelland's book was reprinted with a new, mellower title: *The Complete Life Story of Susan Hayward . . . Immortal Screen Star.*

• A few years later, a long-playing record of the series called *Legends* came out with the original soundtrack of *With a Song in My Heart* and *I'll Cry Tomorrow,* plus two songs from *Smash-Up* and two more she had recorded at the time of the Lillian Roth movie: "Just One of Those Things" and "I'll Cry Tomorrow."

The demise of Susan Hayward, however, did not receive the coverage that a star of her stature deserved. Ironically, she was mourned the most in foreign countries like Spain, France, Italy, and Germany. She had long been a favorite in Europe.

Fans, however, paid her tribute:

• In Brooklyn, Saul Kutner had a plaque made and installed at Susan's old high school (now "Erasmus"). It reads: "Actress Susan Hayward, Illustrious Graduate of Erasmus Hall High School, Nominated Five Times and Finally Won an Academy Award for 'I Want to Live' in 1959."

• Carmine Capp, also from Brooklyn, has been placing an ad in *Variety,* year after year, on the anniversary of Susan's death. It reads: "Academy Award Winning Actress Susan Hayward—June 30, 1918–March 14, 1975. A Star is a Star, is a Star. P.S. You were great in 'Smash-Up,' 'With a Song in My Heart,' 'I'll Cry Tomorrow' and 'I Want to Live.'"

Susan Hayward was a "hard luck" person who never knew defeat—fighting was a way of life with her, and she fought till the end. Her material fortune, over a million dollars, she left to her two sons and her brother Walter. But her spiritual legacy was greater. She left us the memory of her distinctive beauty and versatility in many films. New generations will enjoy the emotions portrayed by this individualistic actress. Her films will live, and she will live in the hearts of those who knew her.

Her last public appearance in front of any cameras: the Oscar ceremonies of 1974

Receiving the Oscar for her performance as Barbara Graham in *I Want to Live,* in 1959

(Left) Looking her best circa 1952, as the world and
her fans will always remember her